·杨 子编·

英语泛读与分析性阅读

EXTENSIVE AND ANALYTICAL READING IN ENGLISH

清华大学出版社
北京

内 容 简 介

本教材以训练阅读技巧为先导、开展主题阅读为渠道、形成自主阅读为核心、培养独立思考能力为目标，旨在潜移默化中提高学生自主学习的能力。尤其在教学理念上作了大胆创新，引入了探究式学习和"泛读—分析性阅读"相结合的理念。教材分为两大板块：阅读基础、实用泛读与分析性阅读，前者关注阅读技巧，后者围绕东西方文学、文化、经济、社会、科技等不同话题展开，注重阅读技巧的整合和阅读能力的综合培养。

图书在版编目（CIP）数据

英语泛读与分析性阅读 / 杨子编. —北京：清华大学出版社，2018（2023.8 重印）
（高校英语选修课系列教材）
ISBN 978-7-302-48430-1

Ⅰ. ①英… Ⅱ. ①杨… Ⅲ. ①英语–阅读教学–高等学校–教材
Ⅳ. ①H319.37

中国版本图书馆CIP数据核字（2017）第220849号

责任编辑：钱屹芝
封面设计：平 原
责任校对：王凤芝
责任印制：丛怀宇
出版发行：清华大学出版社
    网 址：http://www.tup.com.cn，http://www.wqbook.com
    地 址：北京清华大学学研大厦A座 **邮 编：**100084
    社 总 机：010-83470000 **邮 购：**010-62786544
    投稿与读者服务：010-62776969，c-service@tup.tsinghua.edu.cn
    质量反馈：010-62772015，zhiliang@tup.tsinghua.edu.cn
印 装 者：三河市龙大印装有限公司
经 销：全国新华书店
开 本：185mm×260mm **印 张：**16.25 **字 数：**395千字
版 次：2018年4月第1版 **印 次：**2023年8月第6次印刷
定 价：65.00元

产品编号：075001-02

前言

　　国内现有英语专业泛读教材多为遵循传统语言教学法的习题驱动型教材：选取不同题材、体裁的文章，按主题收录在不同单元，文章后附各类习题，如单项选择、选词填空、判断正误、英汉翻译、问答题、思考题等。与精读教材相比，只是增加了每单元的阅读篇幅，形式区别并不明显。一方面，大量时间花费在词汇练习、句法分析与细节理解上，失去了"泛"的意义，不利于弥补学生在精读课上阅读速度与阅读量的不足；另一方面，与精读选材相比，泛读文章虽篇幅加长，但难度缩水、深度不足，学生阅读流于表面，收获不大，形成对泛读的轻视。

　　为解决上述问题，本教材在编写理念上做出如下创新：

1) 教学理念上，引入探究式学习（Enquiry-based Learning）和"泛读—分析性阅读"相结合的理念，以提升泛读课程的意义和价值，激发学生的学习热情。前者通过提升课堂挑战性和参与度，迫使学生加大对泛读课的重视；后者通过在泛读中引入互补阅读方法，保证信息和主旨捕捉的准确性，提高泛读课程的实用性。

2) 选材标准上，在主题多样、文体丰富的普遍原则基础上，从两方面扩展了"泛"的内涵：一是在引介西方科学、文化、文学的同时，兼顾国际视野下的中国形象，促使学生积累与本国相关的言语表达，了解西方看法，促进跨文化沟通；二是在兼顾趣味性、知识性文章的同时，更多纳入有思想深度的文章，提高阅读深度和挑战性的同时，培养学生的分析和批判性思维，锻炼其独立思考、形成个人观点的能力。

3) 问题设计上，从提供标准化习题转变为设定灵活、开放的阅读任务，由学生形成学习小组，通过合作完成阅读任务，在团队的思想碰撞中自行发现、习得相关知识，突出探究式学习理念，培养自主学习的能力。

4) 内容结构上，将阅读技巧训练从主题阅读中抽离，先针对不同阅读技巧进行专门集中训练，提高学生对各种技巧的认知与使用意识；进而通过主题阅读，训练学生对这些技巧的综合灵活应用，并在此基础上形成从阅读中获取、分析和加工信息的能力。

　　概言之，本教材以训练阅读技巧为先导、开展主题阅读为渠道、形成自主阅读为核心、培养独立思考能力为目标，旨在潜移默化中提高学生自主学习的能力。

具体而言，整部教材分为两大板块：阅读基础和实用泛读与分析性阅读，前者五个单元，关注阅读（特别是泛读）的基本技巧，如词义猜测、预测式阅读、略读和查读等，后者七个单元，围绕东西方文学、文化、经济、社会、科技等不同话题展开，注重阅读技巧的整合和阅读能力的综合培养。这两个板块分别具有以下特征：

1) 第一板块放弃了以往对阅读技巧直接讲解的做法，没有知识灌输环节，通过有针对性的课堂任务，让学生基于团队任务，自行摸索领悟相关阅读技巧。

2) 第二板块摒弃了以语言学习为目的的内容设计，没有与词汇、语法相关的选择题或翻译练习，只有以理解文章、激发与主题相关思考为目的的阅读任务，让学生在任务驱动型阅读中附带习得词汇、提高阅读速度、增强语感，体现泛读的宗旨所在。此外，以往教材中同一单元内的文章仅话题相关，而本板块各单元中的多篇文章不但主题相关，且在其他不同方面也存在可比性，如体现对同一主题针锋相对的看法、截然不同的写作手法或隐匿的共性写作策略等，能够让学生在对比或比较阅读中培养分析性和批判性思维能力。

在该教材的使用过程中应注意以下问题：

1) 本教材的设计以学生为主体，学生需要在课前分别以个人和小组为单位做大量准备工作，课堂活动以课前自学为前提，包括对课前任务完成情况的汇报展示和在其基础上的任务拓展。同时，教材的使用对教师也提出了较高要求，学生在探究式学习过程中对知识的归纳总结会出现各种问题，如零散、不全面、不到位、思路偏差等，都需要教师通过适当的引导、提炼或补充，把握课堂学习的进度、准度与深度。

2) 本教材后半部分的阅读篇幅较一般泛读教材明显偏长，因为比起以往基于短文的专项限时阅读训练，长文的阅读量不但可以在无形中提高学生的阅读速度，还有助于培养学生时下欠缺的持续专注力和复杂长文的信息捕捉和分析能力，对泛读能力提高大有裨益。但习惯短文阅读的学生很可能对此存在抵触厌倦心理，对非故事性长文尤其如此。虽然教材在单元安排上已尽力考虑到篇幅的渐进性，使学生能有适应过程，但仍需教师结合学生的课堂反应，予以适当引导和干预，鼓励学生克服畏难心理，敦促其保质保量完成各类阅读任务。

3) 基于教材的指定阅读可以与学生课外自选阅读同时进行。一方面，教材受篇幅所限，阅读量不足以满足真正泛读的要求；另一方面，泛读又名"快乐阅读""轻松阅读"，其前提之一就是阅读者基于个人兴趣对阅读材料的自由选择权，而教材中的阅读内容难于迎合所有学生的口味，故学生课外自选阅读不失为调动学生阅读积极性、强化泛读训练的一个好办法。只是教师需要设计好学生自选阅读的检查方式，如阅读周记、读书报告、课堂陈述等，同时，还要明确指定阅读与自选阅读间联系和在课程中的比重关系等。

教材中内容在北京科技大学外国语学院英语专业一年级经历了四轮应用，期间对部分时效性较强的文章做过调整，但整体架构和文章长难度等基本保持不变，学生反馈较好，从最初读千字文章时的焦虑不安，到课程结束时读万字内容的从容淡定，英语泛读水平进步明显。本教材对于学生日后独立查阅外文文献、阅读外文专著有较大帮助。

本教材适用于英语专业低年级本科生或以英语为辅修专业的高年级本科生，可满足一学期的泛读课量，其中第一板块的各单元均应在两课时内完成，第二板块可视各单元阅读任务量大小、课堂活动类型和占时情况等，每单元安排在 2~4 个课时内完成。

本教材编写依托 2014 年北京科技大学研究型教学示范课《英语泛读与课外必读》建设项目，系北京科技大学"十二五"规划教材。本书的编写和出版得到了北京科技大学教材建设经费的资助。

编者
2017 年 7 月

Contents

Part I
Skills needed for extensive reading

Part II
Theme-based extensive and analytical reading

Part I
Skills needed for extensive reading

This part is intended to introduce to you some fundamental extensive reading skills, different from those used usually for close reading. Since enquiry-based learning (EBL) is advocated in this textbook, those reading skills will not be spoon-fed to you through lectures by your teacher. Instead, there will be reading tasks designed specially to guide you through an exploratory process on your own, with your teacher serving as an assistant or facilitator. In other words, when using this textbook, your teacher will only direct your way as to how to learn, and you are expected to shoulder more responsibilities for your own learning.

Preliminaries

You are required to work in groups when using this textbook. Make sure that you join a group (about 4 to 5 members per group) before the first class and your group members will sit close to each other in class.

Unit 1

How to deal with new words or phrases

Warm-up

- What do you usually do when encountering new words or phrases in English reading?

- List all the possible ways you can think of to deal with an unknown word or phrase.

- What are the respective strengths and weaknesses of those ways you have listed above?

In-class reading

To consult a dictionary whenever coming across an unfamiliar word is a bad habit which can result in slow and inefficient reading because it distracts your attention from the message conveyed. In extensive reading, which requires a large amount of reading to be done in a limited time, the best way to deal with an unknown word or phrase is to guess its meaning by taking full advantage of the context. Have you ever tried not looking up new words or phrases in a dictionary while reading? In this section, you are required to read the following two texts in class in 6 minutes without consulting dictionaries of any kind. Then finish tasks 1 to 5 in the next section.

✒ Text 1 What is autism?

Autism is a lifelong developmental disorder that affects the ways a person communicates and relates to other people. The range and intensity of disability vary widely, but all individuals affected by autism have difficulty in communication, learning and social skills. Autism usually manifests during the first three years of life. Impaired social interaction is the hallmark symptom. Many people affected by autism do not have even one friend. This is very stressful to them and to their families. Individuals affected by autism may also exhibit repeated body movements, unusual responses to people or attachments to objects, resistance to changes in routine and extreme sensory sensitivity. This commonly includes severe reactions to noise and touch, may contribute to increased levels of anxiety and often means that significant levels of supervision are required.

There is no definitive cause or cure, but specialized interventions can give individuals affected by autism the tools they need to lead full and productive lives.

There are many different myths surrounding autism in the world. Here are some of the truths about it. Autism is not rare. The latest statistics indicate 1 in 165 Canadians is affected by autism, an increase of over 600% in the past ten years. What was once viewed as a rare disorder is now recognized as the most common neurological disorder affecting children. It is not an emotional disturbance, but a neurodevelopmental disorder. Parents do not cause autism. It is not the fault of poor parenting. However, parents do need support to manage difficult behaviors with structure and consistency.

People do not "grow out" of autism. With early intervention and good educational programs, progress may be significantly larger. The autistic needs to be learning, living and working in settings where there is ample opportunity to communicate and interact with others who have the skills they need.

Although no specific cause of autism is known, current research links it to biological or neurological differences in the brain that may begin during pregnancy and shortly after birth. Research suggests there may be a genetic base to many cases of the disorder and is currently focused on several specific genes.

☑ Text 2 Lip-synching

Painfully awkward moment Chinese singer exposes her lip-synching sham by holding her microphone UPSIDE DOWN

By Gabriel Samuels

A well-known Chinese popstar accidentally revealed she was lip-synching instead of singing during a televised concert by brandishing her microphone the wrong way around.

A 32-year-old folk singer-songwriter from Inner Mongolia was performing yesterday at the Lantern Festival Gala broadcast on channel CCTV 15 when the embarrassing faux-pas occurred, according to a report by People's Daily Online.

In 2009, China introduced a national ban on lip-synching by its pop stars following the controversy over the opening ceremony of the Beijing Olympic Games, along with the promise of a hefty fine.

Opening the song with a section of interpretive dance, the star only realized she was holding her microphone upside down when she began singing.

The video shows the singer smiling sheepishly as she quickly reverses her mistake before carrying on with her performance like a true professional as if nothing had happened.

After the broadcast ended, she reportedly took to Sina Weibo to tell her 1.6 million followers: "Next time I'll sharpen up my acting skills."

However, the post does not exist on her account this morning. It's unclear whether or not she has taken it down.

Some internet commenters were not surprised, believing lip-synching is not uncommon in China.

One user Chen Jianqiang wrote: "How many singers don't lip sync in China? It would be news if she doesn't lip sync."

Others on Weibo argued the singer made her error on purpose to expose that she was asked to lip-sync by the director of the show.

"Tu'er Joker" said the whole thing was a setup: "It was definitely deliberate. She could have felt the microphone in her hand."

Performing on the star-studded show alongside the singer were a veritable whos-who of Chinese pop talent, including the popular TFBOYS boyband who unveiled their highly-anticipated new single.

The singer, who released her sixth LP "The Butterfly Dream" in November last year, is known to sing in languages including Mandarin, Sanskrit, Tibetan, as well as an imaginary language of her own creation.

In 2008 she won a World Music award from BBC Radio 3, being voted as the best singer in Asia and the Pacific.

Two famous Chinese starlets were handed a total fine of 80,000 yuan (£8,700) in January 2010 for miming during a staged concert in Sichuan, central China.

One of the pair, Fang Ziyuan, made an almost identical mistake by holding her mic the wrong way up for half of her performance.

Group discussion

In this section, you are required to discuss with your group members on how to make an effective meaning guess. You need to carry out the following tasks within groups and then exchange findings across groups.

Task 1

Identify the words and phrases new to your group in the above two texts. Underline them and present your best guess at their meanings through group discussion. Then fill in the blanks in the following table.

For example, "lip-synching" in the title of Text 2 may be new to you. You should underline the word and try to guess its meaning by putting it in the context. After gathering relevant information like "lip-synching instead of singing" and "holding the microphone upside down", along with analyzing the formation of the word "lip-synching", which suggests that the action involves the use of mouth, we can infer that "lip-synching" means pretended singing by moving your lips at the same time as a recording is being played.

Word	Meaning in context
lip-synching	Pretended singing by moving your lips at the same time as a recording is being played.

Summarize and classify the variety of context clues you employed in making the above guesses. Note down your findings in the following table.

For example, we can infer the meaning of the word "autism" in Text 1 by noticing the sentence pattern of the beginning sentence "Autism is a lifelong developmental disorder that affects the ways a person communicates and relates to other people". And the context clue that helps our guess here can be called DEFINITION.

Type of context clue	Example
Definition	Autism is a lifelong developmental disorder that affects the ways a person communicates and relates to other people.

Is there a possibility for several types of context clues to be available at the same time? Are all types of context clues equally effective or do they produce the same degree of precision in meaning-guess? Illustrate your points with examples from the assigned texts. Which type of context clue do you like best? Can you arrange those context clues in an optimality scale?

> **Hint:** Since the definition shows the precise meaning of a word in a straightforward way and thus make the guess easy and reliable, it is the type of context clue that readers like most. Doubtlessly, it heads the optimality scale of context clues.

Optimality scale:
Definition > _____ > _____ > _____ > _____ > _____ > _____

Task 4

Is it always possible to obtain the exact meaning of an unknown word or phrase by guessing in context? And is it necessary to find the precise meaning of an unknown word all the time? Is it feasible to ignore the meaning of certain unknown words completely? In what cases will a broad meaning guess suffice? And on what occasions will a new word be too important to be overlooked or downplayed and thus justify the use of dictionary?

> **Hint:** You may pay special attention to the difference of "lip-synching" "faux-pas" and "veritable" (all from Text 2) in terms of meaning-guess.

When finishing the above four tasks, you can reconsider the following questions in a more detailed way:

- What will you do when coming upon new words or phrases while doing extensive reading?

- What will you do if the available context clues are too weak to render a good meaning guess?

Further practice

⌐ Text 3 Uniform appeal: Entertainment in South Korea

PRETTY actors, a labyrinthine plot and high jinks are the stock-in-trade of South Korean dramas. "Descendants of the Sun", a 16-part television series that recently came to an end, is no exception. But its runaway success may be the result of a new winning combination. Gone is the typical rotten-rich boy who woos a plain Jane and is a better soul for it. In its place, a love story between a special-forces captain and a headstrong female surgeon, an evenly matched duo, unfolds not at workstations but in a war zone.

That setting, in a fictional war-torn Mediterranean land, has struck a chord in the country which requires all able-bodied men to complete at least 21 months of military service. One in three South Koreans tuned in to watch the series. In a first, it was aired simultaneously in China. At the time of its finale, in mid-April, its title was the third most-searched term on Weibo, a Chinese version of Twitter. The series was praised for its positive portrayal of soldiers and urged Chinese producers to follow suit to help boost recruitment (A Chinese remake is now in the works).

Like "Real Men", a hit South Korean reality show that thrust celebrities into the armed forces, "Descendants of the Sun" may help the image of a conscript army in which a culture of abuse has festered. The role of special-forces captain was the first for the male lead, Song Joong-ki, after returning from his own military service, and the special-warfare command says it has seen an uptick in inquiries. Singers and actors keen to show a common touch now make much of reporting for their national service. In January, Lee Seung-gi, a pop star, released "I'm Joining the Army" to tell fans of his upcoming conscription (Hundreds gathered to see him off). In a further blurring of celebrity and the real world, three Miss Koreas have been made the new faces of the forces.

The series is patriotic, up to a point—the captain keeps ditching his date in order to go off on yet another mission. That may appeal to those who feel South Korea now punches above its weight in its international obligations. But most, says Kim Kyo-seok, a columnist and social commentator, seem to be charmed by a new concept for South Koreans: the soldier as romantic hero. The human touch that transcends duty appealed, as did the refreshingly strong female lead.

Earlier this year, as part of reform efforts, the defense ministry recommended that officers drop a respectful form of speech, used only among soldiers, and use a less formal register with superiors. In a twist, since the show, young South Koreans have adopted that honorific form of address as a badge of coolness.

Try out the meaning-guess skills summarized in the above section on this text.

Identify all words that are unfamiliar to you. Circle those that are essential to text comprehension and need narrow guess. Underline those that will not cause serious troubles for text comprehension and need not much effort in guessing.

Underline all the context clues for the meaning guess of each new word. Check whether the available clues will suffice for the required degree of specificity in each case of meaning guess. Decide for which words consulting a dictionary is a necessity.

Fill in the blanks in the table below (You may follow the examples given in the table). The use of a dictionary is only allowed when you can fully justify it.

Negligible new words	Words requiring broad guess		Words requiring narrow guess	
	Word	Broad meaning	Word	Narrow meaning
labyrinthine	stock-in-trade	features	conscript	force someone by law to serve in one of the armed forces

Skill acquisition check

At the end of this unit, check whether you have acquired the following skills as expected:

1. To spot context clues for word meaning guess;

2. To tell different types of context clues and their respective advantages;

3. To apply various types of context clues either individually or in combination;

4. To decide the degree of specificity in meaning guess according to the context;

5. To use a dictionary sparingly in extensive reading.

Unit 2

How to make predictions

Warm-up

Reading is an active process in which you often raise questions and guess the answers before the author presents them. This is called making predictions. Predictions are made on the basis of a pre-existing schema and they are (dis)confirmed as the text unfolds during your reading.

- Can you recall from your past reading experiences some notable occasions of making predictions?

- What kinds of predictions do you usually make in reading? Do you guess the subject matter, the line of development or the structure of the reading?

- At which stage(s) of reading are predictions usually made?

In-class reading

In Unit 1, we have learned to guess the word meaning. To make predictions is actually another kind of guess—guessing at the level of larger units (e.g. what a title suggests, what a sentence is about and what will be illustrated in the next paragraph). Predictions can be made from various aspects with different degrees of specificity, involving the exploitation of background knowledge. For example, predictions can be made for the genre, subject matter, main idea, forthcoming topics, a certain detail, etc. As another tip to read efficiently, making proper predictions can ensure better understanding with less reading effort, and thus improve your reading speed. In extensive reading, where speed is a key factor, it is especially important to master the predicting skill. In this section, you are required to read the following texts in class with special attention to all possible predictions to be made in the reading process. Then prepare yourselves for tasks 1 to 6 in the next section. Be aware that some predictions may be made subconsciously and thus likely to escape your notice.

Note: Although the focus of this unit is not to guess the word meaning anymore, it is still highly suggested that you keep the use of dictionary to a minimum. Meaning guess, as a rudiment of extensive reading, should be practiced throughout the study of this textbook.

Text 1 Four kinds of reading

Everywhere one meets the idea that reading is an activity desirable in itself. It is understandable that publishers and librarians—and even writers—should promote this assumption, but it is strange that the idea should have general currency. People surround the idea of reading or the value of what is being read. Teachers and parents praise the child who reads, and praise themselves, whether the text be *The Reader's Digest* or *Moby Dick*. The advent of TV has increased the false values ascribed to reading, since TV provides a vulgar alternative. But this piety is silly; and most reading is no more cultural nor intellectual nor imaginative than shooting pool or watching *What's My Line*.

It is worth asking how the act of reading became something to value in itself, as opposed for instance to the act of conversation or the act of taking a walk. Mass literacy is a recent phenomenon, and I suggest that the aura which decorates reading is a relic of the importance of reading to our great-great-grandparents. Literacy used to be a mark of social distinction, separating a small portion of humanity from the rest. The farm laborer who was ambitious for his children did not daydream that they would become schoolteachers or doctors; he daydreamed that they would learn to read, and that a world would therefore open up to them in which they did not have to labor in the fields fourteen hours a day for six days a week in order to buy salt and cotton. On the next rank of society, ample time for reading meant that the reader was free from the necessity to spend most of his waking hours making a living. This sort of attitude shades into the contemporary man's boast of his wife's cultural activities. When he says that his wife is interested in books and music and pictures, he is not only enclosing the arts in a female world, he is saying that he is rich enough to provide her with the leisure to do nothing. Reading is an inactivity, and therefore a badge of social class. Of course, these reasons for the piety attached to reading are never acknowledged. They show themselves in the shape of our attitudes toward books; reading gives off an air of gentility.

It seems to me possible to name four kinds of reading, each with a characteristic manner and purpose. The first is reading for information—reading to learn about a trade, or politics, or how to accomplish something. We read a newspaper this way, or most textbooks, or directions on how to assemble a bicycle. With most of this material, the reader can learn to scan the page quickly, coming up with what he needs and ignoring what is irrelevant to him, like the rhythm of the sentence, or the play of metaphor. Courses in speed reading can help us read for this purpose, training the eye to jump quickly across the page. If we read *The New York Times* with the attention we should give a novel or a poem, we will have time for nothing else, and our mind will be cluttered with clichés and dead metaphor. Quick eye-reading is a necessary to anyone who wants to keep up with what's happening, or learn much of what has happened in the past. The amount of reflection, which interrupts and slows down the reading, depends on the material.

But it is not the same activity as reading literature. There ought to be another word. If we read a work of literature properly, we read slowly, and we hear all the words. If our lips do not actually move, it's only laziness. The muscles in our throat move, and come together when we see the word "squeeze". We hear the sounds so accurately that if a syllable is missing in a line of poetry we hear the lack, though we may not know what we are lacking. In prose we accept the rhythms, and hear the adjacent sounds. We also register a track of feeling through the metaphors and associations of words. Careless writing prevents this sort of attention, and becomes offensive. But the great writers reward it. Only by the full exercise of our powers to receive language can we absorb their intelligence and their imagination. This kind of reading goes through the ear—though the eye takes in the print, and it can never be quick. It is slow and sensual, a deep pleasure that begins with touch and ends with the sort of comprehension that we associate with dream.

Too many intellectuals read in order to reduce images to abstractions. One reads philosophy slowly, as if it were literature, but much time must be spent with the eyes turned away from the page, reflecting on the text. To read literature this way is to turn it into something it is not—to concepts clothed in character, or philosophy sugar-coated. I think that most literary intellectuals read this way, including brighter professors of English, with the result that they miss literature completely, and concern themselves with a minor discipline called the history of ideas. I remember a course in Chaucer at my university in which the final exam required the identification of a hundred or more fragments of Chaucer, none as long as a line. If you like poetry, and read Chaucer through a couple of times slowly, you found yourself knowing them all. If you were a literary intellectual, well-informed about the great chain of being, chances are you had a difficult time. To read literature is to be intimately involved with the words on the page, and never to think of them as the embodiments of ideas which can be expressed in other terms. On the other hand, intellectual writing—closer to mathematics on a continuum that has at its opposite pole lyric poetry—requires intellectual reading, which is slow because it is reflective and because the reader must pause to evaluate concepts.

But most of the reading which is praised for itself is neither literary nor intellectual. It is narcotic. Novels, stories and biographies—historical sagas, monthly regurgitations of book clubs, four- and five-thousand word daydreams of the magazines—these are the opium of the suburbs. The drug is not harmful except to the addict himself, and is no more injurious to him than Johnny Carson or a bridge club, but it is nothing to be proud of. This reading is the automated daydream, the mild trip of the housewife and the tired businessman, interested not in experience and feeling but in turning off the possibilities of experience and feeling. Great literature, if we read it well, opens us up to the world, and makes us more sensitive to it, as if we acquired eyes that could see through walls and ears that could hear the smallest sounds. But by narcotic reading, one can reduce great literature to the novel of *The Valley of the Dolls*. One can read *Anna Karenina* passively and inattentively, and float down the rivers of lethargy as if one were reading a confession magazine: "I Spurned My Husband for a Count".

I think that everyone reads for narcosis occasionally, and perhaps most consistently in late adolescence, when great readers are born. I remember reading to shut the world out, away at a school where I did not want to be; I invented a word for my disease: "bibliolepsy", on the analogy of narcolepsy. But after a while the books became a window on the world, and not a screen against it. This change doesn't always happen. I think that late adolescent narcotic reading accounts for some of the badness of English departments. As a college student, the boy loves reading and majors in English because he would be reading anyway. Deciding on a career, he takes up English teaching for the same reason. Then in graduate school he is trained to be a scholar, which is painful and irrelevant, and finds he must write papers and publish them to be a professor—and at about this time he no longer requires reading for narcosis, and he is left with nothing but a PhD. And the prospect of fifty years of teaching literature; and he does not even like literature.

Narcotic reading survives the impact of television, because this type of reading has even less reality than melodrama; that is, the reader is in control: Once the characters reach into the reader's feelings, he is able to stop reading, or glance away, or superimpose his own daydream. The trouble with television is that it embodies its own daydream. Literature is often valued precisely because of its distance from the tangible. Some readers prefer looking into the text of a play to seeing it performed. Reading a play, it is possible to stage it oneself by an imaginative act; but it is also possible to remove it from real people. Here is Virginia Woolf, who was lavish in her praise of the act of reading, talking about reading a play rather than seeing it: "Certainly there is a good deal to be said for reading *Twelfth Night* in the book if the book can be read in a garden, with no sound but the thud of an apple falling to the earth, or of the wind ruffling the branches of the trees." She sets her own stage; the play is called *Virginia Woolf Reads Twelfth Night in a Garden*. Piety moves into narcissism, and the high metaphors of Shakespeare's lines dwindle into the flowers of an English garden; actors in ruffles wither, while the wind ruffles branches.

🖉 Text 2   The cat and the grizzly

"Another box of kittens dumped over the fence, Dave," one of our volunteers greeted me one summer morning. I groaned inside. As the founder of Wildlife Images Rehabilitation Center, I had more than enough to do to keep up with the wild animals in our care. But somehow, local people who didn't have the heart to take their unwanted kittens to the pound often dumped them over our fence. They knew we'd try to live-trap them, spay or neuter them, and place them through our network of approximately 100 volunteers.

That day's brood contained four kittens. We managed to trap three of them, but somehow one little rascal got away. In twenty-four acres of park, there wasn't much we could do once the kitten disappeared—and many other animals required our attention. It wasn't long before I forgot completely about the lost kitten as I went about my daily routine.

A week or so later, I was spending time with one of my favorite "guests"—a giant grizzly bear named Griz.

This grizzly bear had come to us as an orphaned cub six years ago, after being struck by a train in Montana. He'd been rescued by a Blackfoot Indian, had lain unconscious for six days in a Montana hospital's intensive care unit, and ended up with neurological damage and a blind right eye. As he recovered, it was clear he was too habituated to humans and too mentally impaired to go back to the wild, so he came to live with us as a permanent resident.

Grizzly bears are not generally social creatures. Except for when they mate or raise cubs, they're loners. But this grizzly liked people. I enjoyed spending time with Griz, giving him personal attention on a regular basis. Even this required care, since a 560 pound creature could do a lot of damage to a human unintentionally.

That July afternoon, I approached his cage for our daily visit. He'd just been served his normal meal—a mix of vegetables, fruit, dog kibble, fish and chicken. Griz was lying down with the bucket between his forepaws, eating, when I noticed a little spot of orange coming out of the blackberry brambles inside the grizzly's pen.

It was the missing kitten. Now probably six weeks old, it couldn't have weighed more than ten ounces at most. Normally, I would have been concerned that the poor little thing was going to starve to death. But this kitten had taken a serious wrong turn and might not even last that long.

What should I do? I was afraid that if I ran into the pen to try to rescue it, the kitten would panic and run straight for Griz. So I just stood back and watched, praying that it wouldn't get too close to the huge grizzly.

But it did. The tiny kitten approached the enormous bear and let out a purr and a mew. I winced. With any normal bear, that cat would be dessert. Griz looked over at him. I cringed as I watched him raise his forepaw toward the cat and braced myself for the fatal blow.

But Griz stuck his paw into his food pail, where he grabbed a piece of chicken out of the bucket and threw it toward the starving kitten.

The little cat pounced on it and carried it quickly into the bushes to eat.

I breathed a sigh of relief. That cat was one lucky animal! He'd approached the one bear of the sixteen we housed that would tolerate him—and the one in a million who'd share lunch.

A couple of weeks later, I saw the cat feeding with Griz again. This time, he rubbed and purred against the bear, and Griz reached down and picked him up by the scruff of his neck. After that, the friendship blossomed. We named the kitten Cat.

These days, Cat eats with Griz all the time. He rubs up against the bear, bats him on the nose, ambushes him, even sleeps with him. And although Griz is a gentle bear, a bear's gentleness is not all that gentle. Once Griz accidentally stepped on Cat. He looked horrified when he realized what he'd done. And sometimes when Griz tries to pick up Cat by the scruff of the cat's neck, he winds up grabbing Cat's whole head. But Cat doesn't seem to mind.

Their love for each other is so pure and simple; it goes beyond size and species. Both animals have managed to successfully survive their rough beginnings. But even more than that, they each seem so happy to have found a friend.

Group discussion

Discuss with your group members how to master the skill of making predictions. To be specific, you need to carry out the following tasks within groups and then hold a cross-group exchange to enrich your findings.

While reading the above two texts, underline the words, phrases or sentences that can trigger your predictions about what happens next or any other thing that may be helpful to your reading. Note down the predictions and their respective triggers in the following table. Have an intra-group discussion to check whether you missed some and try to collect as many predictions as possible.

For example, by reading the title of Text 1, we may expect to learn the author's classification of reading. By reading the first two sentences in Text 1 "Everywhere one meets the idea that reading is an activity desirable in itself. It is understandable that publishers and librarians—and even writers—should promote this assumption, but it is strange that the idea should have general currency", we expect the author to explain what is wrong with the opinion that reading is desirable.

Prediction trigger	Prediction being triggered
four kinds of reading	What is the author's classification of reading?
It is understandable…but it is strange…	What is wrong with the opinion that reading is desirable? Does the variety of reading types (e.g. classification of reading) play a role in it?

Summarize and classify the variety of predictions you have made while reading the above two texts.

For example, we can infer from the titles of the two texts "Four Kinds of Reading" and "The Cat and the Grizzly" that they are respectively expositive and narrative in genre. And the predictions made here can be called genre predictions.

Besides that, we may also classify predictions in terms of form. For instance, "The author is going to elaborate on four kinds of reading" is an assertive prediction; while "How is a cat connected with a grizzly" is a question-type prediction.

There are still some other ways to classify predictions. Are all predictions equally specific? Are you equally sure about each prediction you made?

Please write your answer in the following table by following the examples in it.

Prediction type	Criteria of classification	Example
Genre prediction		four kinds of reading→an expository essay
	Content	
Question-type prediction		The cat and the grizzly → How is a cat connected with a grizzly?
	Form	
	Degree of specificity	

What can trigger predictions? How many types of prediction triggers can you find?

For example, the beginning sentence may trigger a prediction about the content in a paragraph. Therefore, the topic sentence can be regarded as a prediction trigger. Another example is the definite structure "the + noun". In the title of Text 2, "the cat" indicates that there is a cat in the story and he is known and probably close to the writer.

Please put your findings into the following table by following the examples already there.

Prediction trigger type	Example
The topic sentence	Too many intellectuals read in order to reduce images to abstractions. → This paragraph presents a new type of reading which requires intellectual effort in reading.
The + noun	the cat → There is a cat in the story and he is known and probably close to the writer.

Task 4

Is it possible for several (or several types of) predictions to be triggered by a single context clue? Please illustrate your answer with examples from the assigned texts. You may write them down in the following column.

Context clue (prediction trigger):
Prediction 1 and the type of prediction:
Prediction 2 and the type of prediction:

Task 5

How can predictions improve your reading efficiency? To put it another way, what roles do various types of predictions play in reading?

For example, predictions for the genre and the subject matter can help us set proper purposes for reading. When reading the title "Four Kinds of Reading", we may expect to learn the author's classification of reading and his elaboration on each kind of reading. The proper purposes can serve as a good guide to keep us on the right track of capturing the author's main idea and interpreting the text and thus enable us to read efficiently.

Task 6

You cannot ensure that your prediction is always right. Wrong prediction may occur from time to time. In your reading of the above two texts, are there some early predictions being disconfirmed by later reading? Mark those wrong predictions and consider the following questions:

- What do you have to do if some previous predictions are wrong? Will this slow your reading? What lessons can you learn from the wrongly made predictions so as to improve your predicting skill?

- Do wrong predictions always stand as an obstacle to your reading? Can they function positively?

- How do you deal with wrong predictions made on different occasions?

Further practice

☑ Text 3 John Nash

John F. Nash Jr., who revolutionized the mathematical field of game theory, was endowed with a mind that was highly original and deeply troubled. But it became known to most people by Hollywood's description. His mind was beautiful.

Dr. Nash, a Nobel Prize-winning mathematician whose descent into and recovery from mental illness inspired the Academy Award-winning film *A Beautiful Mind*, died May 23 in a two-car accident on the New Jersey Turnpike. He was 86. His wife, Alicia, who was 82, also died.

In 1994, when Dr. Nash received the Nobel Prize in economic sciences, the award marked not only an intellectual triumph but also a personal one. More than four decades earlier, as a Princeton University graduate student, he had produced a 27-page thesis on game theory—in essence, the applied mathematical study of decision-making in situations of conflict—that would become one of the most celebrated works in the field.

Before the academic world could fully recognize his achievement, Dr. Nash descended into a condition eventually diagnosed as schizophrenia. For the better part of 20 years, his once supremely rational mind was beset by delusions and hallucinations.

By the time Dr. Nash emerged from his disturbed state, his ideas had influenced economics, foreign affairs, politics, biology—virtually every sphere of life fueled by competition.

Nasar's book, titled *A Beautiful Mind*, was published in 1998 and adapted for the big screen three years later. The film, although criticized by some for presenting a romanticized version of the mathematician's life, won four Oscars, including for best picture. Portrayed by Russell Crowe,

Dr. Nash became an international celebrity—perhaps the most famous mathematician in recent memory.

The emperor of Antarctica

His mental illness came on when he was about 30, during what might have been one of the richest periods of his career. Dr. Nash was working at the time at the Massachusetts Institute of Technology and was studying quantum theory.

As his condition worsened, Dr. Nash suffered delusions, hallucinations and impressions of being hunted.

He thought that *The New York Times* was publishing messages from extraterrestrials and that he could understand them. He gave a student an intergalactic driver's license, Nasar wrote.

At one point, he declined a prestigious appointment to the University of Chicago because he believed that he was in line to become emperor of Antarctica. At another point, he concluded, according to Nasar, that he was a "messianic figure of great but secret importance" and searched numerals—once the object of his brilliance—for hidden messages.

"I felt like I might get a divine revelation by seeing a certain number; a great coincidence could be interpreted as a message from heaven," Dr. Nash said years later in the PBS "American Experience" documentary "A Brilliant Madness".

He let his hair grow long. He traveled abroad and attempted to give up his U.S. citizenship, and at various times considered himself a Japanese shogun, the biblical figure Job and a Palestinian refugee, among other identities.

"Big Brains"

John Forbes Nash Jr. was born June 13, 1928, in Bluefield, West Virginia. His father was an electrical engineer and his mother was an English and Latin teacher.

As a child, John Jr. acquired a nickname: "Big Brains". His family encouraged education, but he recalled in his Nobel biographical sketch the need to "learn from the world's knowledge rather than from the knowledge of the immediate community".

In 1945, he enrolled at what is now Carnegie Mellon University in Pittsburgh and completed his undergraduate work after switching from chemical engineering to chemistry and finally to mathematics. So great was his progress that he received a master's degree in addition to his bachelor's degree, both in mathematics, upon his graduation in 1948. He then moved to Princeton University, where, as a second-year student, he wrote the thesis that became the intellectual underpinning of his contributions to game theory.

Dr. Nash received his doctorate in 1950, joined the MIT faculty and soon took a research position at the Rand Corp. in California. In that period of his career, he untangled what he described as a "classical unsolved problem" related to differential geometry and to general relativity.

He then returned to MIT, where he met Alicia Larde, a physics student from El Salvador, and they married in 1957. Shortly thereafter, Alicia became pregnant with their son, John Charles Martin Nash, and Dr. Nash began to show signs of mental instability.

During his illness, Dr. Nash was divorced from his wife, moved in and out of hospitals and endured dangerous treatments including insulin-coma therapy. Alicia Nash later took him into her home and cared for him even though they were no longer married.

He spent much of his time on the Princeton campus, where some recognized him as the genius that he was. Others knew him as the Ghost of Fine Hall, a reference to the building that houses the mathematics department.

In time, and seemingly against all odds, he appeared to overcome the illness that had afflicted him for so long. He insisted that he "willed" his recovery.

"I decided I was going to think rationally," Dr. Nash told an interviewer.

Dr. Nash and Alicia were remarried in 2001. "We thought it would be a good idea," she later said. "After all, we've been together most of our lives."

Dr. Nash remarked in his Nobel biographical sketch that his return to rational scientific thought was "not entirely a matter of joy as if someone returned from physical disability to good physical health."

"Without his 'madness'," Dr. Nash wrote, "Zarathustra would necessarily have been only another of the millions or billions of human individuals who have lived and then been forgotten."

Try out the reading skill studied in the previous section on the above text.

Practice word meaning guess while reading the above text.

Look for prediction triggers and then derive sensible predictions from them.

Jot down those predictions and relevant information in the following table.

Trigger	Prediction type	Prediction
Headline	Genre; main idea	News report; an account of his legendary life in memory of John Nash
Headings		

Use examples from the above text to explain how they ease reading burdens such as word meaning guess and improve reading efficiency by enabling quick capture of main ideas, the overall structure and next-to-come events.

Skill acquisition check

At the end of this unit, check whether you have acquired the following skills as expected:

1. To spot context clues for making predictions;

2. To know the different ways to classify predictions and the variety of prediction types;

3. To make different (types of) predictions depending on the features of prediction triggers;

4. To improve reading efficiency from varied aspects by making smart context-sensitive predictions;

5. To view and treat wrong predictions properly.

Unit 3

How to skim and scan what you read

Warm-up

- Do you know what skimming and scanning mean in reading? Have you heard of them before?
- When are the two types of reading usually used? Or when do you prefer skimming/ scanning to word-by-word reading?
- Can you list some features, strengths and weaknesses of the two types of reading?

In-class reading

Skimming refers to reading only for main ideas, ignoring the details, so as to get an overall impression of a text; scanning means seeking from a text answers to specific questions in mind, ignoring all the unrelated information (possibly including main ideas). Granting only a sketchy understanding, neither skimming nor scanning demands much time. On the contrary, they can greatly speed up your reading, and therefore are popular in extensive reading. Diverged as their purposes are, skimming and scanning share a lot in manners and ways of reading. This section presents two texts. You are requested to find answers to the questions attached to each in class quickly. Then join the group or class discussion to reflect on the ways of skimming and scanning, and finish tasks 1 to 4 in the next section.

☑ Text 1 Fake foning

Nowadays, a cellphone service is available to everyone, everywhere. Probably thousands of people have already been using it, but I just discovered it, so I'm going to claim it and also name it: fake foning.

The technology has been working well for me at the office, but there are infinite applications.

Virtually in any public space.

Say you work at a big university with lots of talky faculty members buzzing about. Now, say you need to use the restroom. The trip down the hall will take approximately one hour, because a person can't walk into those talky people without getting pulled aside for a question, a bit of gossip, a new read on a certain line of *Paradise Lost*.

So, a cellphone. Any cellphone. Just pick it up. Don't dial. Just hold that phone to your face and start talking. Walk confidently down the hall engaged in fake conversation, making sure to tailor both the topic and content to the person standing before you whom you are trying to evade.

For standard colleague avoidance, I suggest fake chatting about fake business:

"Yes, I'm glad you called, because we really need to hammer out the details. What's that? Yes, I read Page 12, but if you look at the bottom of 4, I think you can see the problem begin right there."

Be animated. Be engaged in your fake fone conversation. Make eye contact with the people passing, nod to them, gesture keen interest in talking to them at a later time, point to your phone, shrug and move on.

Shoppers should consider fake foning anytime they spot a talky neighbor in the produce department pinching unripe peaches. Without your phone at your face, you'd be in for a 20-minute speech on how terrible the world is.

One important caution about fake foning. The other day I was fake foning my way past a colleague, and he was actually following me to get my attention. I knew he wanted to ask about a project I had not yet finished. I was trying to buy myself some time, so I continued fake foning with my doctor. "So I don't need the operation? Oh, doctor, that is the best news."

And then: Brrrrrrng! Brrrrrmg! Brrrrrmg! My phone started ringing, right there while it was planted on my face. My colleague looked at me, and I at him, and naturally I gasped. "What is the matter with this thing?" I said, pulling the phone away to look at it, and then putting it back to my ear.

"Hello? Are you still there?"

Oops.

Questions:

• What is the author's purpose of writing the passage?

_____

_____

• What is fake foning?

_____

_____

• What are the readers cautioned against when doing fake foning?

_____

_____

⌇ Text 2 Deliver a presentation like Steve Jobs

Our communications coach breaks down the ace presenter's latest Macworld keynote. The result?
A 10-part framework you can use to wow your own audience

When Apple (AAPL) CEO Steve Jobs kicked off this year's Macworld Conference & Expo, he once again raised the bar on presentation skills. While most presenters simply convey information, Jobs also inspires. He sells the steak and the sizzle at the same time, as one reader commented a few years ago.

I analyzed his latest presentation and extracted the 10 elements that you can combine to dazzle your own audience. Bear in mind that Jobs has been refining his skills for years. I broke down his 2007 Macworld keynote in a previous column (BusinessWeek.com, 7/6/07) and in a chapter in my latest book. Still, how he actually arrives at what appear to be effortless presentations bears expanding on and explaining again.

1. Set the theme.

"There is something in the air today." With those words, Jobs opened Macworld. By doing so, he set the theme for his presentation (BusinessWeek.com, 1/15/08) and hinted at the key product announcement—the ultrathin MacBook Air laptop. Every presentation needs a theme, but you don't have to deliver it at the start. Last year, Jobs delivered the theme about 20 minutes into his presentation: "Today Apple reinvents the phone." Once you identify your theme, make sure you deliver it several times throughout your presentation.

2. Demonstrate enthusiasm.

Jobs shows his passion for computer design. During his presentation he used words like "extraordinary" "amazing" and "cool". When demonstrating a new location feature for the iPhone, Jobs said, "It works pretty doggone well." Most speakers have room to add some flair to their presentations. Remember, your audience wants to be wowed, not put to sleep. Next time you're crafting or delivering a presentation, think about injecting your own personality into it. If you think a particular feature of your product is "awesome", say it. Most speakers get into presentation mode and feel as though they have to strip the talk of any fun. If you are not enthusiastic about your own products or services, how do you expect your audience to be?

3. Provide an outline.

Jobs outlined the presentation by saying "There are four things I want to talk about today. So let's get started…" Jobs followed his outline by verbally opening and closing each of the four sections and making clear transitions in between. For example, after revealing several new iPhone features, he said, "The iPhone is not standing still. We keep making it better and better and better. That was the second thing I wanted to talk about today. No. 3 is about iTunes." Make lists and provide your audience with guideposts along the way.

4. Make numbers meaningful.

When Jobs announced that Apple had sold 4 million iPhones to date, he didn't simply leave the number out of context. Instead, he put it in perspective by adding "That's 20,000 iPhones every day, on average." Jobs went on to say, "What does that mean to the overall market?" Jobs detailed the breakdown of the U.S. smart phone market and Apple's share of it to demonstrate just how impressive the number actually is. Jobs also pointed out that Apple's market share equals the share of its top three competitors combined. Numbers don't mean much unless they are placed in context. Connect the dots for your listeners.

5. Try for an unforgettable moment.

This is the moment in your presentation that everyone will be talking about. Every Steve Jobs presentation builds up to one big scene. In this year's Macworld keynote, it was the announcement of MacBook Air. To demonstrate just how thin it is, Jobs said it would fit in an envelope. Jobs drew cheers by opening a manila interoffice envelope and holding the laptop for everyone to see. What is the one memorable moment of your presentation? Identify it ahead of time and build up to it.

6. Create visual slides.

While most speakers fill their slides with data, text and charts, Jobs does the opposite. There is very little text on a Steve Jobs slide. Most of the slides simply show one image. For example, his phrase "The first thing I want to talk to you about today…" was accompanied by a slide with the numeral 1. That's it. Just the number. When Jobs discussed a specific product like the iPhone, the audience saw a slide with an image of the product. When text was introduced, it was often revealed as short sentences (three or four words) to the right of the image. Sometimes, there were no images at all on the slide but a sentence that Jobs had delivered such as "There is something in the air". There is a trend in public speaking to paint a picture for audiences by creating more visual graphics. Inspiring presenters are short on bullet points and big on graphics.

7. Give 'em a show.

A Jobs presentation has ebbs and flows, themes and transitions. Since he's giving his audience a show instead of simply delivering information, Jobs includes video clips, demonstrations and guests he shares the stage with. In his latest keynote, the audience heard from Jim Gianopulos, CEO and chairman of Fox Filmed Entertainment, and Paul Otellini, CEO of Intel (INTC). Enhance your presentations by incorporating multimedia, product demonstrations, or giving others the chance to say a few words.

8. Don't sweat the small stuff.

Despite your best preparation, something might go wrong as it did during the keynote. Jobs was about to show some photographs from a live website, and the screen went black while Jobs waited for the image to appear. It never did. Jobs smiled and said, "Well, I guess Flickr isn't serving up the photos today." He then recapped the new features he had just introduced. That's it. It was no big deal. I have seen presenters get flustered over minor glitches. Don't sweat minor mishaps. Have fun. Few will remember a glitch unless you call attention to it.

9. Sell the benefit.

While most presenters promote product features, Jobs sells benefits. When introducing iTunes movie rentals, Jobs said, "We think there is a better way to deliver movie content to our customers." Jobs explained the benefit by saying "We've never offered a rental model in music because people want to own their music. You listen to your favorite song thousands of times in your life. But most of us watch movies once, maybe a few times. And renting is a great way to do it. It's less expensive, doesn't take up space on our hard drive…" Your listeners are always asking themselves "What's in it for me?" Answer the question. Don't make them guess. Clearly state the benefit of every service, feature or product.

10. Rehearse, rehearse, rehearse.

Steve Jobs cannot pull off an intricate presentation with video clips, demonstrations and outside speakers without hours of rehearsal. I have spoken to people within Apple who tell me that Jobs rehearses the entire presentation aloud for many hours. Nothing is taken for granted. You can see he rehearsed the Macworld presentation because his words were often perfectly synchronized with the images and text on the slides. When Jobs was showing examples of the films that are available on the new iTunes movie rental service, one poster of a particular film appeared at the exact moment he began to talk about it. The entire presentation was coordinated. A Steve Jobs presentation looks effortless because it is well-rehearsed.

Questions:

1. What is the central idea of the passage?

   _____

   _____

2. When encountering a slight hiccup in screen display, what did Steve Jobs say to relieve the embarrassment?

   _____

   _____

3. How many iPhones are sold every day on average, according to Steve Jobs?

   _____

4. Why did Steve Jobs present an interoffice envelope when introducing MacBook Air?

   _____

   _____

Group discussion

After practicing skimming and scanning on the above two texts, you are now required to make some reflections. To be specific, you need to carry out the following tasks within groups and then have an inter-group talk to exchange group findings.

Examine the questions based on the above two texts and separate skimming questions from scanning ones. Underline the words, phrases or sentences in texts that provide answers to those questions. Then fill out the following table to better understand the differences between the two types of reading.

Skimming			Scanning		
Question	Answer	Method	Question	Answer	Method
What is the author's purpose of writing the passage?	Show how to avoid talky acquaintances.	Read through the passage to summarize it.	What is fake foning?	Any cellphone. Just pick it up. Don't dial. Just hold that phone to your face and start talking.	Predict in which part the answer may appear and search that place.

Task 2

Distinguish the answers shown explicitly in the two texts from the implied ones. Is there any possible link between the question type (skimming or scanning) and the explicitness of the answer? Please fill in the blanks in the following table and then answer the question through a comparison of the two columns below.

Question being answered explicitly & the type it falls into	Question being answered implicitly & the type it falls into
What is fake foning? (scanning)	What is the author's purpose of writing the passage? (skimming)

Task 3

To capture the main idea of a passage, is it necessary to read word by word, line by line, and paragraph by paragraph? What are efficient ways of skimming?

> **Hint:** To answer the questions here, you may need to consider the composition of a paragraph and that of a passage. What are necessary components in a paragraph or a passage? How are those components usually organized or structured? Which components are in immediate connection with the main idea and thus may need your special attention? Where are they usually placed in a paragraph/passage? Which parts of a passage/paragraph need reading and which parts can be simply skipped in skimming?

Steps of skimming:
1.　Read and analyze the title (if there is one).
2.
3.
4.

Task 4

How can you quickly find answers to scanning questions in a passage? What context clues may guide you to the source of answers? Examine all the scanning questions in the above two texts for features that determine how the answers may be presented. Make a list of those features and the types of context clues that may direct your attention.

For example, what a person says is likely to be placed within quotation marks. When the scanning question is about someone's quotes, we search first for quotation marks, which are easier to be identified in a piece of writing than his name or his specific words.

Features of scanning questions	Ways to locate answers quickly
About a person's direct statement	Look for quotation marks

Further practice

Try out the two reading skills one more time. Read Text 3 and answer the questions following it. There may be quite a few new words for you in this text. But don't be frightened by them. Being largely irrelevant to the answers to the attached questions, most new words can be simply ignored. Just bear in mind your reading purpose and stick to the ways of doing skimming and scanning discussed in the above section. You will find that this reading task is just a piece of cake.

Text 3 High-tech trash

Will your discarded TV end up in a ditch in Ghana?

June is the wet season in Ghana, but here in Accra, the capital, the morning rain has ceased. As the sun heats the humid air, pillars of black smoke begin to rise above the vast Agbogbloshie Market. I follow one plume toward its source, past lettuce and plantain vendors, past stalls of used tires, and through a clanging scrap market where hunched men bash on old alternators and engine blocks. Soon the muddy track is flanked by piles of old TVs, gutted computer cases, and smashed monitors heaped ten feet (three meters) high. Beyond lies a field of fine ash speckled with glints of amber and green—the sharp broken bits of circuit boards. I can see now that the smoke issues not from one fire, but from many small blazes. Dozens of indistinct figures move among the acrid haze, some stirring flames with sticks, others carrying armfuls of brightly colored computer wire. Most are children.

Choking, I pull my shirt over my nose and approach a boy of about 15, his thin frame wreathed in smoke. Karim says he has been tending such fires for two years. He pokes at one meditatively, and then his top half disappears as he bends into the billowing soot. He hoists a tangle of copper wire off the old tire he's using for fuel and douses the hissing mass in a puddle. With the flame retardant insulation burned away—a process that has released a bouquet of carcinogens and other toxics— the wire may fetch a dollar from a scrap-metal buyer.

Another day in the market, on a similar ash heap above an inlet that flushes to the Atlantic after a downpour, Israel Mensah, an incongruously stylish young man of about 20, adjusts his designer glasses and explains how he makes his living. Each day scrap sellers bring loads of old electronics—from where he doesn't know. Mensah and his partners—friends and family, including two shoeless boys raptly listening to us talk—buy a few computers or TVs. They break copper yokes off picture tubes, littering the ground with shards containing lead, a neurotoxin, and cadmium, a carcinogen that damages lungs and kidneys. They strip resalable parts such as drives and memory chips. Then they rip out wiring and burn the plastic. He sells copper stripped from one scrap load to buy another. The key to making money is speed, not safety. "The gas goes to your nose and you feel something in your head," Mensah says, knocking his fist against the back of his skull for effect. "Then you get sick in your head and your chest." Nearby, hulls of broken monitors float in the lagoon. Tomorrow the rain will wash them into the ocean.

People have always been proficient at making trash. Future archaeologists will note that at the tail end of the 20th century, a new, noxious kind of clutter exploded across the landscape: the digital detritus that has come to be called e-waste.

So what happens to all this junk?

Currently, less than 20 percent of e-waste entering the solid waste stream is channeled through companies that advertise themselves as recyclers, though the number is likely to rise as states like California crack down on landfill dumping. Yet recycling, under the current system, is less benign than it sounds. Dropping your old electronic gear off with a recycling company or at a municipal collection point does not guarantee that it will be safely disposed of. While some recyclers process the material with an eye toward minimizing pollution and health risks, many more sell it to brokers who ship it to the developing world, where environmental enforcement is weak. For people in countries on the front end of this arrangement, it's a handy out-of-sight, out-of-mind solution. Untold tons of e-waste still slip out of European ports, on their way to the developing world.

"We in the developed world get the benefit from these devices," says Jim Puckett, head of Basel Action Network, or BAN, a group that opposes hazardous waste shipments to developing nations. "But when our equipment becomes unusable, we externalize the real environmental costs and liabilities to the developing world."

Asia is the center of much of the world's high-tech manufacturing, and it is here the devices often return when they die. It has long been the world's electronics graveyard. With explosive growth in its manufacturing sector fueling demand, some ports in Asia have become conduits for recyclable scrap of every sort: steel, aluminum, plastic, even paper. Electronic waste carries the lucrative promise of the precious metals embedded in circuit boards.

Some places in Asia had become the dumping ground for massive quantities of electronic junk. Thousands of people—entire families, from young to old—engaged in dangerous practices like burning computer wire to expose copper, melting circuit boards in pots to extract lead and other metals, or dousing the boards in powerful acid to remove gold.

High-tech scrap "imports here started in the 1990s and reached a peak in 2003," says a high school teacher whose students tested the environment around their hometown for toxics from e-waste, "it has been falling since 2005 and now is hard to find."

Yet for some people it is likely too late; a cycle of disease or disability is already in motion. In a spate of studies released last year, scientists documented the environmental plight. The air near some electronics salvage operations that remain open contains the highest amounts of dioxin measured anywhere in the world. Soils are saturated with the chemical, a probable carcinogen that may disrupt endocrine and immune function. High levels of flame retardants called PBDEs— common in electronics, and potentially damaging to fetal development even at very low levels— turned up in the blood of the electronics workers. The high school teacher quoted above says his students found high levels of PBDEs in plants and animals.

One country in Asia may someday succeed in curtailing electronic waste imports. But e-waste flows like water. Shipments that a few years ago might have gone to ports in one country can easily be diverted to friendlier environs in neighbouring countries. "It doesn't help in a global sense for one place like India to become restrictive," says David N. Pellow, an ethnic studies professor at the University of California, San Diego, who studies electronic waste from a social justice perspective. "The flow simply shifts as it takes the path of least resistance to the bottom."

It is next to impossible to gauge how much e-waste is still being smuggled into one country, diverted to other parts of Asia, or—increasingly—dumped in West African countries like Ghana, Nigeria and Ivory Coast.

Ultimately, shipping e-waste overseas may be no bargain even for the developed world. In 2006, Jeffrey Weidenhamer, a chemist at Ashland University in Ohio, bought some cheap, Chinese-made jewelry at a local dollar store for his class to analyze. That the jewelry contained high amounts of lead was distressing, but hardly a surprise; Asian-made leaded jewelry is all too commonly marketed in the U.S. More revealing were the amounts of copper and tin alloyed with the lead. As Weidenhamer and his colleague Michael Clement argued in a scientific paper published this past

July, the proportions of these metals in some samples suggest their source was leaded solder used in the manufacture of electronic circuit boards.

"The U.S. right now is shipping large quantities of leaded materials to Asia, and Asia is the world's major manufacturing center," Weidenhamer says. "It's not all that surprising things are coming full circle and now we're getting contaminated products back." In a global economy, out of sight will not stay out of mind for long.

Questions:

1. What is the subject matter addressed in the passage?

   _____

2. What is the main idea of the passage?

   _____

3. There is another name for "high-tech trash" in the article. What is it?

   _____

Skill acquisition check

At the end of this unit, check whether you have acquired the following skills as expected:

1. To tell the difference between skimming and scanning;

2. To know when to adopt the two types of reading;

3. To learn the variety of ways to carry out a skimming or scanning task;

4. To choose among those ways wisely in light of the particularized contexts so as to apply skimming and scanning efficiently.

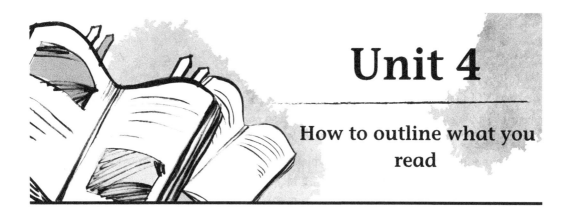

Unit 4

How to outline what you read

Warm-up

- Do you have the habit of writing an outline before composing an essay? Do you know what should be included in an outline? Is there any format you usually follow when writing an outline?

- Outline writing is recommended whenever you prepare for an essay of your own. But is it necessary to make an outline every time you read others'? On what occasions should a reading outline be suggested?

- Compared with writing an outline for your own essay, is there any difference in writing outlines for others'?

In-class reading

While skimming offers you the general idea in a passage, outlining presents a clear picture of its overall organization, covering not only the main idea, but also the major arguments or even supporting details of various levels. For short or simple writing, in which the author's ideas are not complex and can be easily captured and structured, a reading outline may seem redundant. But for long or sophisticated writing, a reading outline can be very helpful in clarifying and documenting the author's thoughts. By enabling you to keep track of the development of the author's ideas, an outline spares your trouble of too much regressive reading and thus indirectly improve the reading efficiency. Therefore, to outline what you read is conditionally welcomed in extensive reading. In this section you are required to read the two texts below and write outlines for them in class.

Note: The reading outline is not considered necessary for short passages. Although not all texts selected in this unit are long enough to justify outline writing, it is believed that you should learn to walk before you run. Therefore, texts are selected and ordered in a way to allow you a step-by-step learning experience.

📖 Text 1 Why so little Chinese in English?

On twitter, a friend asked "Twenty years from now, how many Chinese words will be common parlance in English?" I replied that we've already had 35 years since China's economy was opened, resulting in its stratospheric rise—but almost no recent Chinese borrowings in English.

Many purported experts are willing to explain China to curious (and anxious) westerners. And yet I can't think of even one Chinese word or phrase that has become "common parlance in English" recently. The only word that comes close might be guanxi, the personal connections and relationships critical to getting things done in China. Plenty of articles can be found discussing the importance of guanxi, but the word isn't "common in English" by any stretch.

Most Chinese words now part of English show, in their spelling and meaning, to have been borrowed a long time ago, often from non-Mandarin Chinese varieties like Cantonese. *Kowtow, gung ho and to shanghai* are now impeccably English words we use with no reference to China itself. *Kung fu, tai chi, feng shui* and the like are Chinese concepts and practices westerners are aware of. And of course bok choy, chow mein and others are merely Chinese foods that westerners eat; I would say we borrowed the foods, and their Chinese names merely hitched a ride into English.

Given China's rocket-ride to prominence, why so little borrowing? We import words from other languages that are hard for English-speakers to pronounce. We borrow from languages with other writing systems (Yiddish, Russian, Arabic). We borrow from culturally distant places (India, Japan). We borrow verbs *(kowtow)* and nouns *(tsunami)* and exclamations *(banzai!, oy!)*. We borrow concrete things *(sushi)* and abstract ones *(Schadenfreude, ennui)*. We borrow not only from friends, but from rivals and enemies (*flak* from German in the second world war, *samizdat* from Russian during the cold war, too many words to count from French during the long Anglo-French rivalry).

We've seen a similar film before. Japan's Meiji Reform put quite a few Japanese words and concepts into the Anglophone mind: *kamikaze, futon, haiku, kabuki, origami, karaoke, tycoon, tsunami, jiu-jitsu, zen* and *honcho* are all common English words that nowadays can be used without any reference to Japan. Add to that the more specifically Japanese phenomena well known to the English-speaking world: *karate, judo, sumo, bonsai, manga, pachinko, samurai, shogun, noh* and *kimono*, say, not to mention foods from the bland (tofu) to the potentially fatal (fugu). Of course, Japanese borrowed some of these words from Chinese, like zen (modern Mandarin chán) and tofu (dòufu). But English borrowed them from Japanese, not Chinese.

It seems likely English will borrow from Chinese, too, as trade, cultural and personal connections between China and the West grow. And perhaps there's an elusive "cool" element, a cultural cachet in the West that China has yet to attain. If China gets there one day, this would certainly boost China's linguistic exports. Whether future Chinese borrowings will be new edibles, cultural items or even philosophical terms will depend on China's development and how the West responds. In other words, we should hope Chinese terms we will adopt will be more of the guanxi than of the flak variety.

☑ Text 2 Little match children

Children bear a disproportionate share of the hidden cost of China's growth.

Towards the end of *Jude the Obscure*, Thomas Hardy's final novel, comes one of the most harrowing scenes in English literature. Jude, an itinerant laborer struggling to feed his family, returns home to find his eldest son has hanged himself and his younger siblings from the coat hook on the back of the door. A note says "Done because we are too many".

In June this year China suffered a real-life variant of this terrible scene. In a rural part of Bijie township in Guizhou Province in Southwest China, a brother and three sisters, the oldest 13, the youngest five, died by drinking pesticide. They had been living alone after their mother had disappeared and their father had migrated for work. The 13-year-old boy left a note saying "It is time for me to go—death has been my dream for years".

Three years before that, also in Bijie, five street children died of carbon-monoxide poisoning after they had clambered into a roadside dumpster and lit charcoal to keep themselves warm. Chinese social media drew parallels with the little match girl in Hans Christian Andersen's story of that name: afraid to return home because she has not sold any matches, she freezes to death in the winter night, burning match after match because the light reminds her of her grandmother. It is a well-known tale in China because it is taught in primary schools as an example of the uncaring nature of early capitalism.

Over the past generation, about 270m Chinese laborers have left their villages to look for work in cities. It is the biggest voluntary migration ever. Many of those workers have children; most do not take them along. The Chinese call these youngsters liushou ertong, or left-behind children.

According to the All-China Women's Federation, there were 61m children below the age of 17 left behind in rural areas in 2010. In several of China's largest provinces, including Sichuan and Jiangsu, more than half of all rural children have been left behind. In effect, some villages consist only of children and grandparents. This is a blight on the formative years of tens of millions of people. Alongside the expulsion of millions of peasants from the land they have farmed and the degradation of the country's soil, water and air, this leaving behind is one of the three biggest costs of China's unprecedented and transformative industrialization.

Just over half of the 61m counted in 2010 were living with one parent while the other spouse was away working; 29m had been left in the care of others. Mostly the carers were grandparents, but about 6m were being looked after by more distant relatives or by the state (that number includes orphans and children with disabilities who have been abandoned). There were 2m children who, like the little match children of Bijie, had been left just to fend for themselves.

Not all parents who stick to look for work leave their kids behind: in the 2010 figures, 36m children had gone to live with their migrating families in cities. But this has its own problems; very few of these children can go to a state school or see a state doctor at subsidised prices in their new homes. Moreover, their hard-working parents often cannot look after the children. Without grandparents or a state school to keep an eye on them, such migrant children can be just as neglected as those left behind in the country.

A damaged generation

On top of that there were about 9m left behind in one city when one or both parents had moved to another. Add it all up and, in 2010, 106m children's lives were being profoundly disrupted by their parents' restless search for jobs. For comparison, the total number of children in the United States is 73m. And the proportion of these children who were left behind, rather than migrating with their parents, grew a great deal in the late 2000s.

The experience of those left with one parent while the other is away working is perhaps not so different from that of the children of single parents in the West. But a study by a non-governmental organization, called the Road to School Project, reckons that 10m left-behind children do not see their parents even once a year and 3m have not had a phone call for a year. About a third of left-behind kids see their parents only once or twice a year, typically on Chinese New Year.

Though any child may be left behind, there are some patterns. The youngest children are the most likely to be left, and girls are slightly more likely to be left than boys. This preference for taking boys along means that in cities the preponderance of boys over girls that has been produced by sex-selective abortions is exaggerated further. Anecdotal evidence suggests that an unusual number of left-behind children have siblings. One reason for this is that China's one-child policy has been implemented less strictly in the countryside, and so more rural families have two children to leave behind.

It is not yet possible to say whether the phenomenal level of leaving behind found in the late 2000s persists. There is some evidence that with the slowdown in the economy migrant laborers are starting to drift back to their villages. But even if the trend has slowed, the dislocation still represents a third blow to the traditional Chinese family. First came the one-child-policy. Then the enormously distorted sex ratio. Now a mass abandonment.

Being left behind damages children in many ways. In Cangxi County, Sichuan Province, in Southwest China, the local education authority (as part of a study) gave eight- and nine-year-old left-behind children video cameras and taught them to film their lives. Sun Xiaobing, who is eight years old, is in the charge of her grandparents, but she is left alone for days on end. She shares her lunch with a stray dog to attract its companionship. Her two days of video consist almost entirely of her conversations with farm animals; she has no one else. Wang Kanjun's film is about his little sister. The five-year-old girl spends most of her time at home playing with the phone; she is waiting for her mother to call.

Most left-behind children are lonely. Many live in rural boarding schools far from their villages because, in an attempt to improve educational standards in the countryside, the government shut many village schools down in favor of bigger institutions. About 60% of children in the new boarding schools have been left behind. A non-governmental organization, Growing Home, surveyed them this year and found that they were more introverted than their peers and more vulnerable to being bullied; they also had "significantly higher states of anxiety and depression" than their peers. Many say they do not remember what their parents look like. A few say that they no longer want to see their parents.

In 2010 researchers at the Second Military Medical University in Shanghai studied over 600 children in 12 villages in Shandong Province, in the northeast, half left behind and half not. The difference in the physical condition of the children was minor. But the difference in their school performance was substantial and so was the emotional and social damage to them, as measured by a standard questionnaire. "The psychological effect on left-behind children is huge," argues Tong Xiao, the director of the China Institute of Children and Adolescents. "The kids will have big issues with communications. Their mental state and their development might suffer."

Being brought up by grandparents is a common experience worldwide, and by no means necessarily harmful. But China's rapid development does make it more of a problem now than it was in the past. Unlike their parents, the left-behind children's grandparents are often illiterate; their schooling can suffer accordingly. According to the All-China Women's Federation, a quarter of the grandmothers who are looking after small children never attended school. Most of the rest had only primary education. In one school in Sichuan visited by Save the Children, an international charity, an 11-year-old girl spent most of the lesson caring for her infant sister. As the visitors started to leave, though, she ran up and begged them to look at her homework: she seemed torn between being in loco parentis and a normal 11-year-old.

There are few studies of the health of left-behind children. But given that they account for almost half of all rural children, rural health indicators are a proxy. These are worrying: 12% of rural children under five in China are stunted (i.e. are short for their age)—four times as many as in urban areas; 13% of rural children under five are anaemic, compared with 10% for urban children.

Breastfeeding rates in China are low; only two in seven Chinese children are exclusively breastfed at six months, compared with half in Southeast Asia and two-thirds in Bangladesh. Part of the explanation must be that so many infants are brought up by grandparents. International studies show that breastfeeding during a child's first 1,000 days has lifetime benefits. Children who are not breastfed or get poor food early on do worse at school, are more likely to suffer from serious diseases and have worse job prospects.

Lastly, left-behind children are vulnerable to sexual and other abuse. Back in Bijie, two more left-behind children were found dead in August. One, a disabled 15-year-old girl, had been repeatedly raped by two of her distant relatives. Fearing discovery they had murdered both her and her 12-year-old brother.

Child abuse is distressingly common anyway. An analysis of 47 studies in Chinese and English this year estimated that over a quarter of Chinese children are physically abused at some point in their lives. The left-behind are among the most vulnerable to such abuse, especially those in boarding schools, because any adults who might speak up for them are far away.

Those left behind can be perpetrators of crime as well as victims. Earlier this year a prostitution ring was broken up in Macao. The alleged ringleader turned out to be a 16-year-old boy from Chongqing. Juvenile offences are rising in China, which may well in part be because of the increased numbers of left-behind children. Two-thirds of all Chinese juvenile offenders came from rural areas in 2010, up from half in 2000. When they are brought before the law, left-behind or migrant children are much more likely to go to jail than other children because courts are reluctant to grant probation in the absence of a guardian. In Shanghai, the children of migrant laborers get probation in only 15% of cases, compared with 63% of cases involving local juveniles.

Given the harm that being left behind does to children's health, education and emotional development, it is not hard to imagine that the damage will be felt not just by the left-behind themselves but by society as a whole. The phenomenon is sufficiently recent that there is little compelling evidence of increased criminality, anti-social behavior and so on. And adding to the burdens of the left-behind by prejudging them to be miscreants would clearly add injustice to injury. But in other countries—South Africa, where apartheid often broke families up, is one example being left alone has been found to be a risk factor in children turning to crime.

Leaving such broader consequences aside, the decision to leave behind a child is a hard one. Why do so many migrants make it? A survey by the Center for Child Rights and Corporate Social Responsibility, an NGO, put the question to 1,500 workers in the Pearl River Delta in the south and Chongqing in the southwest. Two-thirds said they would not have enough time to look after them while working in the city; half said it was too expensive to bring up children there.

The long established and valued role Chinese grandparents play in bringing up grandchildren doubtless makes the decision easier for many. And if grandparents are the solution, then leaving behind is a necessary corollary.

It is hard for children registered in a rural area to get state schooling or health care in the city. Private schools that exploit the opportunity this presents are often crowded, substandard and constantly threatened with closure by city governments. On top of this vital school-leaving exams have to be sat where a child is registered. So even if children accompany their parents to the city, they are almost always sent back again at the age of 14 to prepare for the exam.

Wanted: several million social workers

The objective problems of city life are harder to ignore. Many migrant laborers work 12 or more hours a day on construction sites or in export-oriented manufacturing companies. They may commute for four hours more; they may live in dormitories with no provision for children, or where children are not allowed. Understandably, most fear that they will not have enough time to look after their kids.

Zhao Yanjun, who is from Anhui Province in eastern China but works in Fujian Province most of the year, sums up the problems: "I'm really torn about this. I could go back [to Anhui] but I won't have the opportunities and connections I have here. If I bring my son and my wife [to Fujian], one of us will have to quit to look after him, or we'll have to hire a nanny or bring his grandparents here. Any of these choices would be a heavy burden for us."

Reform—already underway—can address some of the problems of the left-behind and those who leave them. But given the underlying factors at work a full response will require China to build a sound child-welfare system.

To its credit, the government has started to make up for lost time. It has set up a pilot program to train "child-welfare directors", otherwise known as barefoot social workers, in five provinces.

The social workers are trained to take the social-welfare system into remote villages. Each looks after between 200 and 1,000 children. So far, the results of the pilot projects are promising. In 120 villages more than 10,000 extra children were enrolled in the state medical scheme between the start of the program, in 2010, and 2012. The school drop-out rate fell by roughly 3%. The government is expanding the pilot program into three more provinces and twice as many villages.

But this only scratches the surface. Even in its expanded form the program will reach roughly 250,000 children, less than 0.5% of all rural left-behind children. A response proportionate to the problem would not just see such interventions hugely increased; it would entail more job-creation in areas where migrants can take all their family members.

At its heart, the problem of the left-behind is one of misplaced hopes. Like so many parents, China's migrants are deferring pleasure now (that of raising their children) for the hope of a better life later (to be bought with the money they earn). One result has been the stunning growth of cities and the income they generate. Another has been a vast disruption of families—and the children left behind are bearing the burden of loss.

Group discussion

This section is designed to help you develop the skill of outlining what you read. With no exception, tasks in this section should be fulfilled in class collaboratively. Exchange opinions with your group members or other groups on proper ways of writing a reading outline under the guidance of the following tasks.

Write outlines for the two texts on your own and then share them within groups. Create a new version combining the strengths of everyone's outline in your group. Read the group outlines to the class and listen carefully to other groups'. Then work collaboratively on a final version by integrating merits of outlines from every group. Present your final version in the columns below.

Outline for Text 1
Title: Main idea:

Outline for Text 2
Title: Main idea:

Task 2

Compare your own draft with the final class version to draw up a list of prominent features for a good reading outline.

Hint: You may need to examine a reading outline from various aspects: What are the components of a reading outline? In what ways are the components connected to one another? What is the best format to present the author's thoughts in a passage? What kind of layout can be most reader-friendly? What language structures are favored to make an outline both clear and brief? To name but a few.

Components	Title, main idea, _____
Logical connection among components	Between title and main idea: Between main idea and first-level arguments: Among first level arguments:
Language features	
Formats	A number-letter outline: A decimal outline:

Task 3

> **Hint:** One of the first level details in Text 2 is something like "Being left behind cause various damages to those children". The second level details elaborating this point include the specified psychological states, physical condition and so on. Does it suffice to stop at the first level detail, or should we go deeper to record some other levels of details in a reading outline? What factors determine the amount of details to be included in a reading outline?

Obligatory components:

Optional components:

Determining factors:

 Task 4

How can you outline a passage efficiently? Reflect on your process of outlining and list the major steps to be followed in writing a reading outline. There are some noteworthy questions for you to consider while carrying out this task.

- When an outline serves to guide writing, the order that ideas/information are presented in the outline should be strictly followed in the forthcoming essay. Is there a similar requirement in outlining others' writing? To put it another way, do you need to list all the ideas/information in their original order? Can information be rearranged or even integrated in a reading outline?

- Do you need to make certain adjustments in the manner of outlining when dealing with passages of different length or complexity? For example, to outline a piece as short and simple as Text 1, do you need to bother considering how many levels of details to be covered? Or, when outlining a passage like Text 2, do you need to bother the main idea of each paragraph and include them all in the outline?

Further practice

☑ Text 3 Coincidences and the meaning of life

The surprising chances of our lives can seem like they're hinting at hidden truths, but they're really revealing the human mind at work.

Towards the end of seventh grade, my middle-school band took a trip to Cedar Point, which was pretty much the theme park to which Midwestern middle school bands traveled. (I imagine it still is.) They had this indoor roller coaster there, called the Disaster Transport. My friends and I were standing in line for this roller coaster, winding up the dimly lit cement steps, when we turned a corner and came across a huge pile of money.

We picked it up and counted it; it was a very specific amount of money. I don't remember now exactly how much, but for the purposes of this retelling, let's say it was $134. That sounds close.

We had barely had time to whiplash from marveling at our good fortune to guiltily suggesting we should find somewhere to turn it in before a group of older kids ahead of us snatched the cash wad out of our hands. They claimed it was theirs; it was not theirs—they counted it in front of us and exchanged "Whoa"s and high fives. We were hapless, gangly middle schoolers (I was growing out my bangs; it was a rough year). They were confident we would do nothing to stop them, and they were right. So that was the end of that.

Until, Part Two:

A little more than a year later, I went to a summer program at Michigan State University, a nerd camp where you take classes like genetics for fun. One evening, as we were sitting around in the common area, chatting and doing homework, I overheard a kid telling his friends how he'd lost a bunch of money last year at Cedar Point.
With very little attempt at chill I interrupted their conversation and grilled him on the particulars.
Was he there on May whatever date I was also there? He was.
Did he lose the money in line for the Disaster Transport? In fact, he did.
How much money did he lose? $134, exactly.

* * *

Though "What are the odds" is pretty much the catchphrase of coincidences, a coincidence is not just something that was unlikely to happen. The overstuffed crate labeled "coincidences" is packed with an amazing variety of experiences, and yet something more than rarity compels us to group them together. They have a similar texture, a feeling that the fabric of life has rippled. The question is where this feeling comes from, why we notice certain ways the threads of our lives collide, and ignore others.

Some might say it's just because people don't understand probability. In their 1989 paper, "Methods for Studying Coincidences", the mathematicians Persi Diaconis and Frederick Mosteller considered defining a coincidence as "a rare event", but decided "this includes too much to permit careful study". Instead, they settled on "A coincidence is a surprising concurrence of events, perceived as meaningfully related, with no apparent causal connection".

From a purely statistical point of view, these events are random, not meaningfully related, and they shouldn't be that surprising because they happen all the time. "Extremely improbable events are commonplace," as the statistician David Hand says in his book *The Improbability Principle*. But humans generally aren't great at reasoning objectively about probability as they go about their everyday lives.

For one thing, people can be pretty liberal with what they consider coincidences. If you meet someone who shares your birthday, that seems like a fun coincidence, but you might feel the same way if you met someone who shared your mother's birthday, or your best friend's. Or if it was the day right before or after yours. So there are several birthdays that person could have that would feel coincidental.

And there are lots of people on this planet—more than 7 billion, in fact. According to the Law of Truly Large Numbers, "with a large enough sample, any outrageous thing is likely to happen," Diaconis and Mosteller write. If enough people buy tickets, there will be a Powerball winner. To the person who wins, it's surprising and miraculous, but the fact that someone won doesn't surprise the rest of us.

Even within the relatively limited sample of your own life, there are all kinds of opportunities for coincidences to happen. When you consider all the people you know and all the places you go and all the places they go, chances are good that you'll run into someone you know, somewhere, at some point. But it'll still seem like a coincidence when you do. When something surprising happens, we don't think about all the times it could have happened, but didn't. And when we include near-misses as coincidences (you and your friend were in the same place on the same day, just not at the same time), the number of possible coincidences is suddenly way greater.

To demonstrate how common unlikely-seeming events can be, mathematicians like to trot out what is called the birthday problem. The question is how many people need to be in a room before there's a 50/50 chance that two of them will share the same birthday. The answer is 23.

"Oh, those guys and their birthdays really get me mad," says Bernard Beitman, a psychiatrist and visiting professor at the University of Virginia, and author of the forthcoming book *Connecting With Coincidence*. That's not the way the average person would frame that question, he says. When someone asks "What are the odds?" odds are they aren't asking "What are the odds that a coincidence of this nature would have happened to anyone in the room?" but more like "What are the odds that this specific thing would happen to me, here and now?" And with anything more complicated than a birthday match, that becomes almost impossible to calculate.

It's true that people are fairly egocentric about their coincidences. The psychologist Ruma Falk found in a study that people rate their own coincidences as more surprising than other people's. They're like dreams—mine is more interesting than yours.

"A coincidence itself is in the eye of the beholder," says David Spiegelhalter, the Winton professor for the public understanding of risk at the University of Cambridge. If a rare event happens in a forest and no one notices and no one cares, it's not really a coincidence.

* * *

I told Spiegelhalter my Cedar Point story on the phone—I couldn't help it. He collects coincidences, see. He has a website where people can submit them, and says he's gotten about 4,000 or 5,000 stories since 2011. Unfortunately, he and his colleagues haven't done much with this treasure trove of information, mostly because a pile of freeform stories is a pretty hard dataset to measure. They're looking for someone to do text-mining on it, but so far all they've been able to analyze is how many coincidences fall into the different categories you can check off when you submit your story:

He says he'd categorize mine as "finding a link with someone you meet." "But it's a very different sort of connection," he says, "not like having lived in the same house or something like that. And it's a very strong one, it's not just like you were both at the theme park. I love that. And you remember it after all this time."

And the craziest thing is not that I found someone's money and then that I was in a room with him a year later, but that I found out about it at all. What if he hadn't brought it up? Or "you might not have heard him if you'd been somewhere slightly away," Spiegelhalter says. "And yet the coincidence would have been there. You would have been six feet away from someone who lost their money. The coincidence in a sense would have physically occurred. It was only because you were listening that you noticed it. And so that's why the amazing thing is not that these things occur, it's that we notice them."

"This is my big theory about coincidences," he continues, "that's why they happen to certain kinds of people."

Beitman in his research has found that certain personality traits are linked to experiencing more coincidences—people who describe themselves as religious or spiritual, people who are self-referential (or likely to relate information from the external world back to themselves), and people who are high in meaning-seeking are all coincidence-prone. People are also likely to see coincidences when they are extremely sad, angry, or anxious.

"Coincidences never happen to me at all, because I never notice anything," Spiegelhalter says. "I never talk to anybody on trains. If I'm with a stranger, I don't try to find a connection with them, because I'm English."

Beitman, on the other hand, says, "My life is littered with coincidences." He tells me a story of how he lost his dog when he was 8 or 9 years old. He went to the police station to ask if they had seen it; they hadn't. Then, "I was crying a lot and took the wrong way home, and there was the dog … I got into [studying coincidences] just because, hey, look Bernie, what's going on here?"

For Beitman, probability is not enough when it comes to studying coincidences. Because statistics can describe what happens, but can't explain it any further than chance. "I know there's something more going on than we pay attention to," he says. "Random is not enough of an explanation for me."

Random wasn't enough for the Swiss psychiatrist Carl Jung either. So he came up with an alternative explanation. Coincidences were, to him, meaningful events that couldn't be explained by cause and effect, which, so far so good, but he also thought that there was another force, outside of causality, which could explain them. This he called "synchronicity," which in his 1952 book, he called an "acausal connecting principle."

Meaningful coincidences were produced by the force of synchronicity, and could be considered glimpses into another of Jung's ideas—the unus mundus, or one world. Unus mundus is the theory that there is an underlying order and structure to reality, a network that connects everything and everyone.

For Jung, synchronicity didn't just account for coincidences, but also ESP (extrasensory perception), telepathy, and ghosts. And to this day, research shows that people who experience more coincidences tend to be more likely to believe in the occult as well.

This is the trouble with trying to find a deeper explanation for coincidences than randomness—it can quickly veer into the paranormal.

* * *

Beitman, like Spiegelhalter, is interested in sorting and labeling different kinds of coincidences, to develop categories "like an early botanist," he says, though his categories are more expansive and include not only things that happen in the world but people's thoughts and feelings as well. In our conversation, he divides coincidences into three broad categories—environment-environment interactions, mind-environment interactions, and mind-mind interactions.

Environment-environment interactions are the most obvious, and easiest to understand. These coincidences are objectively observable. Something, or a series of things, happens in the physical world. You're at a gin joint in Morocco and your long-lost love from Paris shows up. I found some money and a year later I met the person who lost it.

A nurse named Violet Jessop was a stewardess for White Star Line and lived through three crashes of its ill-fated fleet of ocean liners. She was on the Olympic when it collided with the HMS Hawke in 1911. In 1912, she was there for the big one: the Titanic. And four years later, when White Star's Britannic, reportedly improved after its sister ship's disaster, also sank, Jessop was there. And she survived. That one, I guess, is an environment-environment-environment.

Mind-environment coincidences are premonition-esque—you're thinking of a friend and then he/she calls you, for example. But unless you happen to write down "I am thinking of so-and-so [timestamp]" before the call happens, these are cool for the person they happen to, but not really measurable. "We banned premonitions from our site," Spiegelhalter says. "Because, where's the proof? Anybody could say anything."

Another sort of mind-environment interaction is learning a new word and then suddenly seeing it everywhere. Or getting a song stuck in your head and hearing it everywhere you go, or wondering about something and then stumbling onto an article about it. The things on our minds seem to bleed out into the world around us. But, though it makes them no less magical, life's motifs are created not by the world around us, but by humans, by our attention.

This is an effect that the Stanford linguistics professor Arnold Zwicky calls "the frequency illusion," and it's not the same as a premonition. It's just that once you've noticed something, your brain is primed to notice it again the next time you encounter it. A word or a concept you've just learned feels relevant to you—you may have seen it hundreds of times before and just never noticed. But now that you're paying attention, it's more likely to pop out at you the next time it whizzes by.

And then the final category, mind-mind, of course, is straight-up mystical. One example of this is simulpathity, a term Beitman coined to describe feeling the pain or emotion of someone else at a distance. His interest in this particular type of coincidence is deeply personal.

"In San Francisco, in 1973, February 26, I stood at a sink uncontrollably choking," he says, clarifying, "There was nothing in my throat that I knew [of]."

"It was around 11 o'clock in San Francisco. The next day my brother called, and told me my father had died at 2 a.m. in Wilmington, Delaware, which was 11 in San Francisco, and he had died by choking on blood in his throat. That was a dramatic experience for me, and I began to look to see if other people had experiences like this. And many people have."

* * *

This is where we start to leave the realm of science and enter the realm of belief. Coincidences are remarkable in how they straddle these worlds. People have surprising, connective experiences, and they either create meaning out of them, or they don't.

Leaving a coincidence as nothing more than a curiosity may be a more evidence-based mindset, but it's not fair to say that the people who make meaning from coincidences are irrational. The process by which we notice coincidences is "part of a general cognitive architecture which is designed to make sense of the world," says Magda Osman, an associate professor in experimental psychology at Queen Mary University of London. It's the same rational process we use to learn cause and effect. This is one way to scientifically explain how coincidences happen—as byproducts of the brain's meaning-making system.

People like patterns. We look for them everywhere, and by noticing and analyzing them we can understand our world and, to some small degree, control it. If every time you flick a switch, a lamp across the room turns on, you come to understand that that switch controls that lamp.

When someone sees a pattern in a coincidence, "there's no way I can say 'Yes, that was definitely a chance event,' or 'There was an actual causal mechanism for it,' because I'd have to know the world perfectly to be able to say that," Osman says.

Instead what we do is weigh whether it seems likelier that the event was caused by chance, or by something else. If chance is the winner, we dismiss it. If not, we've got a new hypothesis about how the world works.

Take the case of two twins, who were adopted by different families when they were four weeks old. When they were later reunited, their lives had a lot of similarities. They were both named James by their adoptive families, were both married to a Betty and had divorced a Linda. One twin's first son's name was James Alan, the other's was James Allan. They both had adoptive brothers named Larry and pet dogs named Toy. They both suffered from tension headaches, and both vacationed in Florida within three blocks of each other.

You could hypothesize from this that the power of genetics is so strong, that even when identical twins are separated, their lives play out the same way. In fact, the twins were part of a University of Minnesota study on twins reared apart that was asking just that question, though it didn't suggest that there was any gene that would make someone attracted to a Betty, or likely to name a dog Toy.

Drawing inferences from patterns like this is an advantageous thing to do, even when the pattern isn't 100 percent consistent. Take learning language as an example. There isn't going to be a dog, or even a picture of a dog, nearby every time a child hears the word "dog." But if dad points at the family Fido enough times while saying "dog," the kid will learn what the word means anyway.

"Small children are justified in being conspiracy theorists, since their world is run by an inscrutable and all-powerful organization possessing secret communications and mysterious powers—a world of adults, who act by a system of rules that children gradually master as they grow up," write the cognitive scientists Thomas Griffiths and Joshua Tenenbaum in a 2006 study on coincidences.

We retain this capability, even when we're older and have figured out most of these more obvious patterns. It can still be very useful, especially for scientists who are working on unsolved questions, but for most adults in their daily lives, any new coincidental connection is likely to be specious. From a scientific perspective, anyway. If we realize that, then we wave it off as "just a coincidence," or what Griffiths, a professor of psychology and cognitive science at the University of California, Berkeley, calls a "mere coincidence."

On the flip side, for someone who believes in ESP, thinking of a friend right before she calls may not be a coincidence to them at all, but just more evidence to support what they already believe. The same goes for someone who believes in divine intervention—a chance meeting with a long-lost lover may be, to them, a sign from God, not a coincidence at all.

"You really come across a question of just what belief system you have about how reality works," Beitman says. "Are you a person who believes the universe is random or are you a person who believes there's something going on here that maybe we gotta pay more attention to? On the continuum of explanation, on the left-hand side we've got random, on the right-hand side we've got God. In the middle we've got little Bernie Beitman did something here, I did it but I didn't know how I did it."

In the middle zone lie what Griffiths calls "suspicious coincidences."

"To me, that's a key part of what makes something a coincidence—that it falls in that realm between being certain that something is false and being certain that something is true," he says. If enough suspicious coincidences of a certain nature pile up, someone's uncertainty can cross over into belief. People can stumble into scientific discoveries this way—"Hmm, all these people with cholera seem to be getting their water from the same well—or into superstition—"Every time I wear mismatched socks, my meetings go well."

But you can stay in that in-between zone for a long time—suspicious, but unsure. And this is nowhere more obvious than in the coincidences that present as evidence for some kind of hidden but as-yet undiscovered ordering principle for reality, be that synchronicity or a sort of David Mitchell-esque "Everything Is Connected" web that ensnares us in its pattern. Meaningful connections can seem created by design—things are "meant to be," they're happening for a reason, even if the reason is elusive. Or as Beitman puts it, "Coincidences alert us to the mysterious hiding in plain sight."

I suppose no one can prove there isn't such a thing, but it's definitely impossible to prove that there is. So you're left with … not much. Where you fall on the continuum of explanation probably says more about you than it does about reality.

* * *

In *The Improbability Principle*, Hand cites a 1988 U.S. National Academy of Sciences report which concluded that there was "no scientific justification from research conducted over a period of 130 years for the existence of parapsychological phenomena."

"One hundred thirty years!" Hand writes. The fact that people kept trying to find proof for the paranormal was "A testament to the power of hope over experience if there ever was one."

But I disagree. It may be that researching the paranormal is partly an act of hope that you'll find something where no one has found anything before. But it seems like often, experiences are the building blocks of belief in the paranormal, or in an underlying force that organizes reality. Even if they're not doing formal research, people are seeking explanations for their experiences. And structure is a much more appealing explanation than chance.

Where you fall on the chance-structure continuum may have a lot to do with what you think chance looks like in the first place. Research shows that while most people are pretty bad at generating a random string of numbers, people who believe in ESP are even worse. Even more so than skeptics, believers tend to think that repetitions in a sequence are less likely to be random—that a coin flip sequence that went "heads, heads, heads, heads, tails" would be less likely to come up randomly than one that went "heads, tails, heads, tails, heads," even though they're equally probable.

So we have psychology to explain how and why we notice coincidences, and why we want to make meaning from them, and we have probability to explain why they seem to happen so often. But to explain why any individual coincidence happened involves a snarl of threads, of decisions and circumstances and chains of events that, even if one could untangle it, wouldn't tell you anything about any other coincidence.

Jung seems to have been annoyed by this. "To grasp these unique or rare events at all, we seem to be dependent on equally "unique" and individual descriptions," he writes, despairing of the lack of a unifying theory offered by science for these strange happenings. "This would result in a chaotic collection of curiosities, rather like those old natural-history cabinets where one finds, cheek by jowl with fossils and anatomical monsters in bottles, the horn of a unicorn, a mandragora manikin, and a dried mermaid."

This is supposed to be unappealing (surely these things should be put in order!), but I rather like the image of coincidences as a curio cabinet full of odds and ends we couldn't find anywhere else to put. It may not be what we're most comfortable with, but a "chaotic collection of curiosities" is what we've got.

Try out the above discussed reading skill once again.

Do you think a reading outline can be very helpful for you to understand Text 3? Write an outline for it. You may arrange it in the following format.

Title: Coincidences and the Meaning of Life
Main idea:
I.
II.
A.
B.
1.
2.

Exchange your outline with a certain student in your group and check whether his/her outline meets the requirements of a good reading outline listed in the above section. How many levels of details are covered in his/her outline? Is there anything that you consider wrong or inappropriate in his/her outline? Do you have any suggestion for improvement?

Revise your own outline after peer review based on careful consideration of others' suggestions.

Skill acquisition check

At the end of this unit, check whether you have acquired the following skills as expected:

1. To tell when a reading outline is recommended.

2. To learn the variety of outline types such as topic outline, sentence outline, number-letter outline, decimal outline, etc.

3. To know the defining properties of a good outline like parallelism and logical consistency.

4. To decide the degree of specificity (i.e. levels of details to be included) in outline writing.

5. To write a reading outline effectively.

Unit 5

How to read analytically and critically

Warm-up

- If you have studied Unit 1, you must know that one way to guess word meaning is to examine word formation. Can you infer the meaning of "analytically" by breaking it up into its root and suffixes?

- Do you know what the word "analytically" means when it goes with the word "read"? Have you ever heard of "analytical reading" before? Make a guess at the kind of reading it refers to.

- On what occasions do you tend to read critically? Is there any connection between analytical reading and critical reading?

In-class reading

Rosenwasser and Stephen claim in their book *Writing Analytically* (2011) that reading stands at two levels: reading in the literal sense of tackling words on the page; and reading in the sense of gathering data that can be analyzed as primary evidence to produce ideas. Therefore, gaining information or knowledge may not be the ultimate goal of reading; we read to develop our own opinions. To derive one's own ideas from reading requires at least two steps: a clear understanding of the author's thoughts and a comparison between them and what you read from other sources or your personal experiences, feelings, previously gained knowledge, etc. While the former step explains the prime goal of analytical reading, the latter directs us toward critical reading. To put it another way, analytical reading helps readers see through the words to the writer's meaning and avoid their personal misinterpretations; critical reading enables readers to develop their own thoughts by analyzing and examining others' thoughts. In this section you are required to read the following two texts to capture the authors' thoughts and develop your personal views. Then finish tasks 1 to 4 in the next section.

N.B. There is no single way of reading analytically or critically. Just do it in the way that occurs naturally to you.

☑ Text 1 The plot against people

By Russell Baker

Inanimate objects are classified scientifically into three major categories: those that break down, those that get lost, and those that don't work.

The goal of all inanimate objects is to resist man and ultimately to defeat him, and the three major classifications are based on the method each object uses to achieve its purpose. As a general rule, any object capable of breaking down at the moment when it is most needed will do so. The automobile is typical of the category.

With the cunning peculiar to its breed, the automobile never breaks down while entering a filling station which has a large staff or idle mechanics. It waits until it reaches a downtown intersection in the middle of the rush hour, or until it is fully loaded with family and luggage on the Ohio Turnpike. Thus it creates maximum inconvenience, frustration and irritability, thereby reducing its owner's life-span.

Washing machines, garbage disposals, lawn mowers, furnaces, TV sets, tape recorders, slide projectors—all are in league with the automobile to take their turn at breaking down whenever life threatens to flow smoothly for their enemies.

Many inanimate objects, of course, find it extremely difficult to break down. Pliers, for example, and gloves and keys are almost totally incapable of breaking down. Therefore, they have had to evolve a different technique for resisting man.

They get lost. Science has still not solved the mystery of how they do it, and no man has ever caught one of them in the act. The most plausible theory is that they are able to conceal from human eyes.

It is not uncommon for a pair of pliers to climb all the way from the cellar to the attic in its single-minded determination to raise its owner's blood pressure. Keys have been known to burrow three feet under mattresses. Women's purses, despite their great weight, frequently travel through six or seven rooms to find hiding space under a couch.

Scientists have been struck by the fact that things that break down virtually never get lost, while things that get lost hardly ever break down. A furnace, for example, will invariably break down at the depth of the first winter cold wave, but it will never get lost. A woman's purse hardly ever breaks down; it almost invariably chooses to get lost.

Some persons believe this constitutes evidence that inanimate objects are not entirely hostile to man. After all, they point out, a furnace could infuriate a man even more thoroughly by getting lost than by breaking down, just as a glove could upset him far more by breaking down than by getting lost.

Not everyone agrees, however, that this indicates a conciliatory attitude. Many say it merely proves that furnaces, gloves and pliers are incredibly stupid.

The third class of objects—those that don't work—is the most curious of all. These include such objects as barometers, car clocks, cigarette lighters, flashlights and toy-train locomotives. It is inaccurate, of course, to say that they never work. They work once, usually for the first few hours after being brought home, and then quit. Thereafter, they never work again.

In fact, it is widely assumed that they are built for the purpose of not working. Some people have reached advanced ages without ever seeing some of these objects—barometers, for example—in working order.

Science is utterly baffled by the entire category. There are many theories about it. The most interesting holds that the things that don't work have attained the highest state possible for an inanimate object, the state to which things that break down and things that get lost can only aspire.

They have truly defeated man by conditioning him to never expect anything of them. When his cigarette lighter won't light or his flashlight fails to illuminate, it does not raise his blood pressure. Objects that don't work have given man the only peace he receives from inanimate society.

📝 Text 2 Why women aren't funny

(Abridged)

By Christopher Hitchens

Be your gender what it may, you will certainly have heard the following from a female friend who is enumerating the charms of a new (male) squeeze: "He's really quite cute, and he's kind to my friends, and he knows all kinds of stuff, and he's so funny …"However, there is something that you absolutely never hear from a male friend who is hymning his latest (female) love interest: "She's a real honey, has a life of her own … (interlude for attributes that are none of your business) … and, man, does she ever make 'em laugh."

Now, why is this? Why is it the case? I mean, why are women, who have the whole male world at their mercy, not funny? Please do not pretend not to know what I am talking about. All right—try it the other way. Why are men, taken on average and as a whole, funnier than women?

Well, for one thing, they had damn well better be. The chief task in life that a man has to perform is that of impressing the opposite sex, and Mother Nature (as we laughingly call her) is not so kind to men. In fact, she equips many fellows with very little armament for the struggle. An average man has just one, outside chance: He had better be able to make the lady laugh. Making them laugh has been one of the crucial preoccupations of my life. If you can stimulate her to laughter— I am talking about that real, out-loud, head-back, mouth-open-to-expose-the-full-horseshoe-of-lovely-teeth, involuntary, full, and deep-throated mirth; the kind that is accompanied by a shocked surprise and a slight (no, make that a loud) peal of delight—well, then, you have at least caused her to loosen up and to change her expression. I shall not elaborate further.

Women have no corresponding need to appeal to men in this way. They already appeal to men, if you catch my drift. Indeed, we now have all the joy of a scientific study, which illuminates the difference. At the Stanford University School of Medicine, the grim-faced researchers showed 10 men and 10 women a sample of 70 black-and-white cartoons and got them to rate the gags on a "funniness scale." To annex for a moment the fall-about language of the report as it was summarized in Biotech Week:

"The researchers found that men and women share much of the same humour-response system; both use to a similar degree the part of the brain responsible for semantic knowledge and juxtaposition and the part involved in language processing. But they also found that some brain regions were activated more in women. These included the left prefrontal cortex, suggesting a greater emphasis on language and executive processing in women, and the nucleus accumbens … which is part of the mesolimbic reward centre."

"Women appeared to have less expectation of a reward, which in this case was the punch line of the cartoon," said the report's author, Dr. Allan Reiss. "So when they got to the joke's punch line, they were more pleased about it." The report also found that "women were quicker at identifying material they considered unfunny."

Slower to get it, more pleased when they do, and swift to locate the unfunny—for this we need the Stanford University School of Medicine? And remember, this is women when confronted with humor. Is it any wonder that they are backward in generating it?

This is not to say that women are humourless, or cannot make great wits and comedians. And if they did not operate on the humour wavelength, there would be scant point in half killing oneself in the attempt to make them writhe and scream (uproariously). Wit, after all, is the unfailing symptom of intelligence. Men will laugh at almost anything, often precisely because it is—or they are—extremely stupid. Women aren't like that. And the wits and comics among them are formidable beyond compare: Dorothy Parker, Nora Ephron, Fran Lebowitz, Ellen DeGeneres. Greatly daring—or so I thought—I resolved to call up Ms. Lebowitz and Ms, Ephron to try out my theories. Fran responded: "The cultural values are male; for a woman to say a man is funny is the equivalent of a man saying that a woman is pretty. Also, humor is largely aggressive and pre-emptive, and what's more male than that?"

Precisely because humour is a sign of intelligence (and many women believe, or were taught by their mothers, that they become threatening to men if they appear too bright), it could be that in some way men do not want women to be funny. They want them as an audience, not as rivals. And there is a huge, brimming reservoir of male unease, which it would be too easy for women to exploit.

The plain fact is that the physical structure of the human being is a joke in itself: a flat, crude, unanswerable disproof of any nonsense about "intelligent design." The reproductive and eliminating functions were obviously wired together in Hell by some subcommittee that was giggling cruelly as it went about its work.

Men are overawed, not to say terrified, by the ability of women to produce babies. (Asked by a lady intellectual to summarize the differences between the sexes, another bishop responded, "Madam, I cannot conceive.") It gives women an unchallengeable authority. And one of the earliest origins of humour that we know about is its role in the mockery of authority. Irony itself has been called "the glory of slaves." So you could argue that when men get together to be funny and do not expect women to be there, or in on the joke, they are really playing truant and implicitly conceding who is really the boss.

In other words, for women the question of funniness is essentially a secondary one. They are innately aware of a higher calling that is no laughing matter. Whereas with a man you may freely say of him that he is lousy in the sack, or a bad driver, or an inefficient worker, and still wound him less deeply than you would if you accused him of being deficient in the humour department.

If I am correct about this, which I am, then the explanation for the superior funniness of men is much the same as for the inferior funniness of women. Men have to pretend, to themselves as well as to women, that they are not the servants and supplicants. Women have to affect not to be the potentates. This is the unspoken compromise H. L. Mencken described as "the greatest single discovery ever made by man," the realization "that babies have human fathers, and are not put into their mother's bodies by the gods." Anyway, after a certain stage women came to the conclusion that men were actually necessary, and the old form of matriarchy came to a close. People in this precarious position do not enjoy being laughed at, and it would not have taken women long to work out that female humour would be the most upsetting of all.

Childbearing and rearing are the double root of all this. As every father knows, the placenta is made up of brain cells, which migrate southward during pregnancy and take the sense of humor along with them. And when the bundle is finally delivered, the funny side is not always immediately back in view. Is there anything so utterly lacking in humor as a mother discussing her new child? She is unborable on the subject. Even the mothers of other fledglings have to drive their fingernails into their palms and wiggle their toes, just to prevent themselves from fainting dead away at the sheer tedium of it. And as the little ones burgeon and thrive, do you find that their mothers enjoy jests at their expense? I thought not.

Humor, if we are to be serious about it, arises from the ineluctable fact that we are all born into a losing struggle. Those who risk agony and death to bring children into this fiasco simply can't afford to be too frivolous. (And there just aren't that many episiotomy jokes, even in the male repertoire.) I am certain that this is also partly why, in all cultures, it is females who are the rank-and-file mainstay of religion, which in turn is the official enemy of all humor. One tiny snuffle that turns into a wheeze, one little cut that goes septic, one pathetically small coffin, and the woman's universe is left in ashes and ruin. Try being funny about that, if you like. Oscar Wilde was the only person ever to make a decent joke about the death of an infant, and that infant was fictional, and Wilde was (although twice a father) a queer. And because fear is the mother of superstition, and because they are partly ruled in any case by the moon and the tides, women also fall more heavily for dreams, for supposedly significant dates like birthdays and anniversaries, for romantic love, crystals and stones, lockets and relics, and other things that men know are fit mainly for mockery and limericks. Good grief! Is there anything less funny than hearing a woman relate a dream she's just had?

For men, it is a tragedy that the two things they prize the most—women and humour—should be so antithetical. But without tragedy there could be no comedy. My beloved said to me, when I told her I was going to have to address this melancholy topic, that I should cheer up because "women get funnier as they get older."

Observation suggests to me that this might indeed be true, but, excuse me, isn't that rather a long time to have to wait?

Group discussion

You are expected to acquire a general understanding of analytical and critical reading through group discussion in this section. The following tasks are designed to raise your awareness of reading analytically and critically, and to familiarize you with some common and effective methods to do so. As usual, they should be fulfilled in class through collaboration.

Have a group discussion on the subjects, main ideas and major arguments in the above two texts. Then exchange group answers in class. Jot down arguments from each party when divergence occurs.

For example, in Text 1 the author classifies inanimate objects into three types. Some groups may think the three classes are presented in a progressive order from the least irritating to the most. Some other groups may think the other way round (i.e. from the most irritating to the least). Or there may even be a third view—the three classes are randomly listed with no designed sequence. They may find various evidence from the text to argue for their positions.

Text 1	Your group view	Other groups' views
The subject matter		
	Inanimate objects are classified into three types according to the irritating degree (from the _____ irritating to the _____).	
Major arguments		

Text 2	Your group view	Other groups' views
The subject matter		
The main idea		
Major arguments		

Task 2

Discuss the divergent views listed in the above table. Which views make more sense? Argue for the views you hold and refute the others in class. Can the discussion shed light on the ways to read analytically?

For example, groups holding the view that the three classes of inanimate objects are listed in a progressive order in Text 1 may cite the author's words "the most curious" in paragraph 11 as a piece of evidence, while those believing the other way round may use the very last sentence in the text as a refutation (i.e. "Objects that don't work have given man the only peace he receives from inanimate society."). To determine which argument is more sensible, you need to read between the lines and see beyond the literal meaning ("the only peace" is used ironically). And this is exactly what reading analytically requires.

Correct views on the analysis of Text 1	Reasons	Implications for analytical readings
The three classes are listed in a progressive order.	The superlative form in "the most curious" suggests a comparison among the three classes; "The only peace" is used ironically.	Spot key words relevant to the topic; Read between the lines and see beyond the literal meaning.
Correct views on the analysis of Text 2	**Reasons**	**Implications for analytical readings**

Marcus Aurelius once said, "Everything we hear is an opinion, not a fact. Everything we see is a perspective, not the truth." Do you have any doubt/disagreement about the arguments made in the two texts? Please elaborate on the reasons for your doubts/disagreements.

> **Hint:** There are several ways to approach this task. You may examine the ways the authors adopt to justify their theses (e.g. what arguments, evidence or examples do they use to convince readers of their opinions?) and then find the weaknesses or loopholes in these justifications. Or you may jump out of the text itself to analyze what causes the author to write the text in the first place or the historical and cultural context which the text applies to; then examine how the context changes and thus invalidates the thesis made in the text (e.g. can you infer when was the article written? Can the change of time play a role in weakening or strengthening the author's points?). What's more, words often communicate more than the author wants. You may also inspect the text for what the author conveys unconsciously and accidentally and then use the message conveyed against his will to criticize his views.

For example, by entitling Text 2 "Why women aren't funny", the author intends to direct readers' attention to reasons for women being not funny. But the title also shows that he took women's lack of humor for granted. The unjustifiability of this view may direct our attention to his prejudice against women and thus result in the criticism of his being subjective and irrational in writing the text.

Arguments in Text 1	Your doubts/ disagreements	Reasons for your doubts/ disagreements
Arguments in Text 2	**Your doubts/disagreements**	**Reasons for your doubts/ disagreements**

Task 4

Review your criticisms of the two texts and summarize some common ways of reading critically.

For example, from analyzing the title of Text 2, we learn that in order to convince readers, the author may intentionally mislead readers by disguising his opinions as facts. Therefore, to stay vigilant against opinions in the disguise of facts is essential to reading critically.

Ways of reading critically:
1. To keep vigilant against opinions disguised as facts.
2.
3.
4.

Further practice

☑ Text 3 Are tote bags really good for the environment?

By Noah Dillon

They're green in principle, but not in the way people use them. An Object Lesson.

For at least a few decades, Americans have been drilled in the superiority of tote bags. Reusable bags are good, we're told, because they're friendly for the environment. Disposable bags, on the other hand, are dangerous. Municipalities across the country have moved to restrict the consumption of plastic shopping bags to avoid waste. Many businesses have stopped offering plastic sacks, or provide them for a modest but punitive price. Bag-recycling programs have been introduced nationwide.

But canvas bags might actually be worse for the environment than the plastic ones they are meant to replace. In 2008, the UK Environment Agency (UKEA) published a study of resource expenditures for various bags: paper, plastic, canvas, and recycled-polypropylene tote bags. Surprisingly, the authors found that in typical patterns of use and disposal, consumers seeking to minimize pollution and carbon emissions should use plastic grocery bags and then reuse those bags at least once—as trash-can liners or for other secondary tasks. Conventional plastic bags made from high-density polyethylene (HDPE, the plastic sacks found at grocery stores) had the smallest per-use environmental impact of all those tested. Cotton tote bags, by contrast, exhibited the highest and most severe global-warming potential by far since they require more resources to produce and distribute.

Such results feel deeply counterintuitive. HDPE bags seem foreign, artificial. They lodge in trees, catch in the esophagi of animals, fester in landfills, clot cities, and are reduced to small particles floating in ocean gyres—for hundreds of years into the future. But even though they don't easily degrade, they require very few resources to manufacture and transport. They produce less carbon, waste, and byproducts than cotton or paper bags. They're recyclable. They're cheap. For all those reasons, they're ubiquitous. And they remain, long after their usefulness is exhausted.

The UKEA study calculated an expenditure of a little less than two kilograms of carbon per HDPE bag. For paper bags, seven uses would be needed to achieve the same per-use ratio. Tote bags made from recycled polypropylene plastic require 26, and cotton tote bags require 327 uses. (Although they weren't included in the study, one can presume that designer totes, made with leather adornments, metal, and so on drive the required number of uses into basically astronomical numbers.)

Their abundance encourages consumers to see them as disposable, defeating their very purpose.

As the esteem of its environmental benefit has fallen, the tote has simultaneously grown in stature and ubiquity. Many stores offer inexpensive (or even free) reusable bags at the register, stamped with logos. Designers have latched onto the form and increased its stylishness. Totes are handed out as promotional gifts by nonprofits and businesses, a gesture that sends contradictory messages: one of conscientious consumption, another of conspicuous consumption.

Just like plastic bags, totes multiply. In a 2009 article about the bags for Design Observer, the Urban Outfitters designer Dmitri Siegel claimed to have found 23 tote bags in his house, collected from various organizations, stores, and brands. Like plastic sacks, tote bags, too, now seem essentially unending. Because of their ubiquity, tote bags that have been used very little (or not at all) can be found piled on curbs, tossed in trashcans in city parks, in dumpsters, everywhere. Their abundance encourages consumers to see them as disposable, defeating their very purpose.

This low-grade, unfocused mania for averting impending ecological disaster seems to be more harmful than helpful, which is a problem throughout popular environmentalism. Meat eaters decry the water usage demands of almond groves. Conscientiously piled garbage overflows from public trashcans to rot in the street. Studies show that Kenya-grown roses flown to England have a lower carbon footprint than those grown and shipped from Holland, that it's less ecologically damaging for Americans east of the Mississippi to import wine from France than from California. Biodegradable plastics proliferate as single-use containers and utensils, greenly filling the demand for disposable goods rather than questioning it. Fuel economy and emissions standards for cars and trucks are considered, barely, but not those of oil tankers, container ships, military escapades, which can produce tens of millions of times the amount of carbon.

* * *

Siegel identifies designers as particular culprits in the oversaturation of tote bags. He notes that because the bags are large, flat, and easily printed on, they're great for embellishment and product placement. They're given away with purchases at galleries, bookstores, eyeglass boutiques, grocers, tattoo parlors. Plus they've been hyped. He describes the 2007 launch of the "I'm not a plastic bag" tote, by fashion designer Anya Hindmarch:

The bag was originally sold in limited numbers at Hindmarch boutiques, Colette and Dover Street Market in London, but when it went into wide release at Sainsbury's 80,000 people lined up to get one. When the bag hit stores in Taiwan, there was so much demand that the riot police had to be called in to control a stampede, which sent 30 people to the hospital.

Whether they're delicately handled designer goods or a promotional product dirtied by daily wear, few totes are made to last long enough to obtain the number of uses required to reach resource-expenditure parity with the plastic bags they were meant to supplant. Though they promise timelessness and sustainability, they develop holes, straps come undone, seams disintegrate. They become fouled with stains and grime.

Many fashion brands sell bags for hundreds of dollars, with totes tracking the increase in economic inequality. Writing in the Wall Street Journal, Ellen Gamerman cites the same Hindmarch bag as evidence of the problem with turning bags into display symbols:

"Sarah De Belen, a 35-year-old mother of two from Hoboken, N.J., says she uses about 30 or 40 plastic bags at the grocery store every week. Late last year, she saw a woman at the supermarket with a popular canvas tote by London designer Anya Hindmarch and promptly purchased one online for about $45.

The most (or least) virtuous feature of tote bags might be that people don't actually use them.

"But Ms. De Belen says she soon realized she'd need 12 of them to accommodate an average grocery run. 'It can hold, like, a head of lettuce,' she says. Besides, she adds, it's too nice to load up with diapers or dripping chicken breasts."

Every product is manufactured and consumed with some ideal in mind. Pictures of tote bags—such as those from stock photo websites or advertisements—make the ideals we project on them visible. People are depicted carrying fresh fruits and vegetables in their tote bags at a sunny farmers' market. These people are seen in intimate groups. They wear casual, modest, warm-weather clothing. They don't handle digital devices. They take their bags to the beach, the park, art openings, concerts, through cosmopolitan urban communities and idyllic rural escapes. They are fulfilled and creative. They are middle class. They inhabit the landscape of tote-bag dreams: healthy, waste-conscious and ecologically responsible, conservatively ethnically diverse, carefree but productive, connected, affluent, tolerant, adventurous, and optimistic.

In short, they're virtuous.

But the most (or least) virtuous feature of tote bags might be that people don't actually use them. An online poll conducted in 2014 by the marketing research firm Edelman Berland found that about half of respondents typically choose to use plastic over reusable bags, despite also owning reusable bags and recognizing their benefits. Only 20 percent of those polled said that they prefer using plastic bags, but almost half of all respondents said that they usually forego reusable bags even when they're the easier, cheaper option. And the actual practice may be even lower, with use rates for tote bags estimated at about 10 percent.

So long as their owners don't throw them away, their negative impact remains minimized, at least—they might yet be used 327 times. Ecologically speaking, the best practice for tote bags might be one of two extremes: use them all the time, or not at all.

Read Text 3 to practice analytical and critical reading once again.

Collect the author's thoughts and list them in the following column. Try your best not to reduce much the rate of reading while carrying out the task. Make conscious adoption of the ways to read analytically discussed in the above section.

Points made by the author of Text 3:

Read critically and comment on the author's thoughts listed in the above column.

N.B. To read critically merely requires you to reflect and make your own judgment on whether to accept the author' opinions and arguments. It is not a must to criticize and refute (all of) them.

Views to be commented	Your comments

Skill acquisition check

At the end of this unit, check whether you have acquired the following skills as expected:

1. To gain a clear picture of analytical and critical reading and to tell the difference and relation between the two types of reading.

2. To learn the variety of ways to read analytically or critically.

3. To capture the author's views accurately and efficiently.

4. To stay vigilant all the time while reading and develop a habit of critical reading.

Part II
Theme-based Extensive and analytical reading

Crucial as it is to extensive reading, speed is not everything. No matter for what purposes you read, a proper understanding of the contents is an elementary requirement. Therefore, reading extensively is not completely incompatible with reading analytically.

In this part, you are expected to read extensively and analytically so as to lay the foundations for critical reading. It is hoped that through content-based extensive reading you will gradually develop the habit of thinking analytically and critically.

All the units below feature themed reading. Being composed of one to several texts, each unit centers on a single topic. You need to gather information or ideas from the text(s) in order to produce your own thoughts on the topic. As a textbook advocating enquiry-based learning, it offers no background information or text analysis. Various tasks at different stages of reading are designed to guide you to do the learning on your own.

Preliminaries

Different from Part I, in which reading tasks are mainly done in class, Part II demands more pre-class reading and preparation. You are expected to read the texts and finish the pre-class reading tasks collaboratively before class.

Unit 6

On extensive reading

Pre-class reading tasks

At the beginning of Part II, three texts are presented to elaborate on the topic "what is extensive reading". You are required to read them in advance and then carry out the following tasks collaboratively with your group members before class.

Summarize properties that can define extensive reading.

In what ways do the three texts enrich your understanding of extensive reading? List all the new knowledge you acquire from them on extensive reading.

Tell the difference of the three texts in terms of writing style. What type of writing does each belong to, informative, argumentative, or neither? Are they written in the same degree of formality? Which one sounds more casual or colloquial? Can you guess where each of them comes from, an online course, an encyclopedia, or an academic journal?

⌇ Text 1 What is extensive reading?

By Mark Wilbur

In my last article, I talked about intensive reading. Hopefully, I've convinced some of you that languages are too complex to learn properly by memorizing new vocabulary and grammar structures. Now, I'll describe extensive reading. What is extensive reading? In short, extensive reading is everything that intensive reading is not. It is not "hard" material. It is not tedious. It is not slow. Unfortunately it is also not very common in the ESL classroom, either.

What kinds of materials are suitable?

The most important thing about choosing materials for extensive reading is that they are at least 98% comprehensible to the students. There should be very little new vocabulary and very little new grammar. One or two new words per page and maybe one new sentence structure per session would be ideal. If the students can already understand that much of the text, new words can often be learned entirely through context. If these few new words appear again and again throughout the text, all the better. Words learned like this aren't learned all at once, of course. Students start with a fuzzy understanding of a new word, which gradually gets clearer and clearer as they encounter it again and again in new contexts. This may seem like a slow way to go, but as I argued in my intensive reading article, there really is no short-cut. Translations accompanied by a few example sentences are never enough alone.

How much should they read?

Assuming, as I did in my last article, that they have an hour a day, they should read at least 25 pages a day. If they only have half an hour to spend on reading, then they need to read at least 10 pages. This may seem like a lot and, if the students are at a level where they can read normal paperback books with few pictures, it is. A native reader typically reads 40 to 100 pages per hour. There are two reasons for requiring so much. First of all, it forces them to use dictionaries sparingly. As any student of Chinese knows, every 5 minutes spent looking through a dictionary is another 5 minutes in which very little language is acquired. The second reason to read so much is that reading too slowly interferes with comprehension. In normal reading, there are certain neurological processes at work that depend on sufficient reading speed (Day and Bamford, 1998). According to Nuttall, "speed, enjoyment and comprehension are closely linked with one another" (1996: 128). When adults read in their own languages, they take in entire phrases at a time, not individual words. If an L2 learner reads too slowly, word by word, it is even possible to forget the meaning of the first few words in a sentence before reading the last.

What are the benefits?

It seems obvious that it is better for a student to learn 20 new words while reading 20 pages of a fairly easy and interesting text, than it is to spend 20 minutes memorizing the same words and then struggle through 2 difficult, boring paragraphs and then do various grammar and translation drills. (For a look at one such difficult text look at page four of this report.) However, I'll outline the main points below:

It can provide "massive comprehensible input"

It can enhance learners' general language competence

It can increase knowledge of previously learned vocabulary

It leads to improvement in writing

It can motivate learners to read

It teaches learners about the culture of the target language users, which will allow learners to more easily join the L2 speech community

It can consolidate previously learned language

It helps to build confidence with extended texts

It facilitates the development of prediction skills

How can these benefits be maximized?

Remember that newly acquired vocabulary is fragile. Therefore, the most important vocabulary to use is the vocabulary just learned. Obviously, you don't want to introduce too much new vocabulary at one time, either. Aside from making sure that the difficulty of your texts is appropriate, it is also important to make sure that they are interesting to the students. The more interesting the texts are, the more the students will like reading (and the language in general), and the sooner they will start doing voluntary reading on their own. See this diary of a JFL (Japanese as a foreign language) learner's extensive reading experiences.

What are the difficulties?

Using extensive reading in a classroom is, by nature, a difficult thing to do. Different students are at different levels. It takes some work to make a viable curriculum in which not everyone is necessarily reading the same thing at the same time. Some students, who have been studying a foreign language for a while in a traditional class, resist extensive reading at first. They feel that if it isn't hard, it isn't "real learning". It is absolutely vital to explain the rationale and benefits to them. Most difficult of all, particularly in an EFL as opposed to an ESL environment, is getting the appropriate reading materials.

☑ Text 2 Extensive reading: why? and how?

By Timothy Bell

Abstract

An extensive reading program was established for elementary level language learners at the British Council Language Center in Sanaa, Yemen. Research evidence for the use of such programs in

EFL/ESL contexts is presented, emphasizing the benefits of this type of input for students' English language learning and skills development. Practical advice is then offered to teachers worldwide on ways to encourage learners to engage in a focused and motivating reading program with the potential to lead students along a path to independence and resourcefulness in their reading and language learning.

Introduction: The Reading Program

An extensive reading program was established at the British Council Language Center in Sanaa, Yemen. An elementary level class of government employees (age range 17-42) was exposed to a regime of graded readers, which was integrated into normal classroom teaching. Students followed a class reader, had access to a class library of graded readers, and had classes in the British Council library, which gave them access to a collection of 2000 titles. Questionnaires were used to examine students' reading interests, habits and attitudes, both prior to, and following the program. The class library contained 141 titles in the published readers of some major publishers (see inventory of titles in Bell, 1994). Familiar titles (e.g. popular Arab folk tales) were selected for both the class readers and the class library, so as to motivate the students to read. These titles proved very popular, as did the practice of reading aloud to the class.

Students' reading was carefully monitored; formal and informal records being kept both by the researcher, and by the students themselves. Reading diaries and book reports were used, together with a card file system to document the program and record both the titles read and students' written comments on the books. A wall chart acted as a focal point for in-class reading, discussion and exchange of titles. Reader interviews were conducted throughout the program, which ran for a period of six months over the course of two semesters. Students became actively involved in running the class library; tables were arranged and titles displayed attractively during the periods set aside for the reading program. Students were taken into the main British Council library for one lesson a week, during which they participated in controlled twenty-minute sessions of USSR (uninterrupted sustained silent reading) (cf. Davis, 1995).

With reference to research evidence, we now turn to the role of extensive reading programs in fostering learners' progress in reading development and improvement.

The Role of Extensive Reading in Language Learning

1. It can provide 'comprehensible input'

In his 1982 book, Krashen argues that extensive reading will lead to language acquisition, provided that certain preconditions are met. These include adequate exposure to the language, interesting material, and a relaxed, tension-free learning environment. Elley and Manghubai (1983:55) warn that exposure to the second language is normally "planned, restricted, gradual and largely artificial." The reading program provided in Yemen, and the choice of graded readers in particular, was intended to offer conditions in keeping with Krashen's model.

2. It can enhance learners' general language competence

Grabe (1991:391) and Paran (1996:30) have emphasized the importance of extensive reading in providing learners with practice in automaticity of word recognition and decoding the symbols on the printed page (often called bottom-up processing). The book flood project in Fiji (Elley & Manghubai: op cit.), in which Fijian school children were provided with high-interest storybooks, revealed significant post treatment gains in word recognition and reading comprehension after the first year, and wider gains in oral and written skills after two years.

3. It increases the students' exposure to the language

The quality of exposure to language that learners receive is seen as important to their potential to acquire new forms from the input. Elley views provision of large quantities of reading material to children as fundamental to reducing the 'exposure gap' between L1 learners and L2 learners. He reviews a number of studies with children between six and twelve years of age, in which subjects showed rapid growth in language development compared with learners in regular language programs. There was a "spread of effect from reading competence to other language skills - writing, speaking and control over syntax," (Elley 1991:404).

4. It can increase knowledge of vocabulary

Nagy & Herman (1987) claimed that children between grades three and twelve (US grade levels) learn up to 3000 words a year. It is thought that only a small percentage of such learning is due to direct vocabulary instruction, the remainder being due to acquisition of words from reading. This suggests that traditional approaches to the teaching of vocabulary, in which the number of new words taught in each class was carefully controlled (words often being presented in related sets), is much less effective in promoting vocabulary growth than simply getting students to spend time on silent reading of interesting books.

5. It can lead to improvement in writing

Stotsky (1983) and Krashen (1984) reviewed a number of L1 studies that appear to show the positive effect of reading on subjects' writing skills, indicating that students who are prolific readers in their pre-college years become better writers when they enter college. L2 studies by Hafiz & Tudor (1989) in the UK and Pakistan, and Robb & Susser (1989) in Japan, revealed more significant improvement in subjects' written work than in other language skills. These results again support the case for an input-based, acquisition-oriented reading program based on extensive reading as an effective means of fostering improvements in students writing.

6. It can motivate learners to read

Reading material selected for extensive reading programs should address students' needs, tastes and interests, so as to energize and motivate them to read the books. In the Yemen, this was achieved through the use of familiar material and popular titles reflecting the local culture (e.g. Aladdin and His Lamp). Bell & Campbell (1996, 1997) explore the issue in a South East Asian context, presenting various ways to motivate learners to read and explaining the role of extensive reading and regular use of libraries in advancing the reading habit.

7. It can consolidate previously learned language

Extensive reading of high-interest material for both children and adults offers the potential for reinforcing and recombining language learned in the classroom. Graded readers have a controlled grammatical and lexical load, and provide regular and sufficient repetition of new language forms (Wodinsky & Nation 1988).Therefore, students automatically receive the necessary reinforcement and recycling of language required to ensure that new input is retained and made available for spoken and written production.

8. It helps to build confidence with extended texts

Much classroom reading work has traditionally focused on the exploitation of shorts texts, either for presenting lexical and grammatical points or for providing students with limited practice in various reading skills and strategies. However, a large number of students in the EFL/ESL world require reading for academic purposes, and therefore need training in study skills and strategies for reading longer texts and books. Kembo (1993) points to the value of extensive reading in developing students' confidence and ability in facing these longer texts.

9. It encourages the exploitation of textual redundancy

Insights from cognitive psychology have informed our understanding of the way the brain functions in reading. It is now generally understood that slow, word-by-word reading, which is common in classrooms, impedes comprehension by transferring an excess of visual signals to the brain. This leads to overload because only a fraction of these signals need to be processed for the reader to successfully interpret the message. Kalb (1986) refers to redundancy as an important means of processing, and to extensive reading as the means of recognizing and dealing with redundant elements in texts.

10. It facilitates the development of prediction skills

One of the currently accepted perspectives on the reading process is that it involves the exploitation of background knowledge. Such knowledge is seen as providing a platform for readers to predict the content of a text on the basis of a pre-existing schema. When students read, these schema are activated and help the reader to decode and interpret the message beyond the printed words. These processes presuppose that readers predict, sample, hypothesize and reorganize their understanding of the message as it unfolds while reading (Nunan 1991: 65-66).

Practical Advice on Running Extensive Reading Programs

1. Maximize Learner Involvement

A number of logistical hurdles have to be overcome in order to make an extensive reading program effective. Books need to be transported, displayed and collected at the end of each reading session. Considerable paperwork is required to document the card file system, reading records, inventories, book reports and in maintaining and updating lists of titles. Students should therefore be encouraged to take an active role in the management and administration of the reading program. In the Yemen program, students gained a strong sense of ownership through running the reading resources in an efficient, coordinated and organized manner.

2. The Reader Interview

Regular conferencing between teacher and student played a key role in motivating students in the Yemen to read the books. This enabled effective monitoring of individual progress and provided opportunities for the teacher to encourage students to read widely, show interest in the books being read, and to guide students in their choice of titles. By demonstrating commitment in their own reading, teachers can foster positive attitudes to reading, in which it is no longer viewed as tedious, demanding, hard work, but as a pleasurable part of their learning.

3. Read Aloud to the Class

In the Yemen study, reader interviews conducted with students revealed the popularity of occasions when the teacher read aloud to the class. The model of pronunciation provided acted as a great motivator, encouraging many students to participate in classroom reading. Students gained confidence in silent reading because they were able to verbalize sounds they previously could could not recognize. This resulted in wider reading by some of the weaker readers in the class. Often thought of as bad practice, reading aloud should play a full part in motivating the emerging reader to overcome the fear of decoding words in an unfamiliar script.

4. Student Presentations

Short presentations on books read played an absolutely crucial role in the program and students frequently commented on the value of oral work in class for exchanging information about the books. The reader interviews revealed that most of the book choices made by students resulted from recommendations made by friends and not by the teacher. This demonstrates that given the right preparation, encouragement, sense of ownership and belonging, an extensive reading program will achieve a direction and momentum governed by the learners themselves; a large step in the promotion of student independence and autonomy.

5. Written Work Based on the Reading

Effective reading will lead to the shaping of the reader's thoughts, which naturally leads many learners to respond in writing with varying degrees of fluency. Elementary level students can be asked simply to write short phrases expressing what they most enjoyed about a book they read, or to record questions they wish to ask the teacher or other students in class. With intermediate students, book reports may be used, with sections for questions, new vocabulary, and for recording the main characters and events. At this level, summary writing is also a valuable practice because it allows learners to assert full control, both of the main factual or fictional content of a book, and of the grammar and vocabulary used to express it. Advanced students can be asked to write compositions, which, by definition, are linguistically more demanding written responses to the reading material.

6. Use Audio Material in the Reading Program

The use of audio recordings of books read aloud and of graded readers on cassette proved very popular with the students in Yemen, and is advocated for wide application. Listening material provided the learners with a model of correct pronunciation which aided word recognition, and exposed students to different accents, speech rhythms and cadences. Student confidence in their ability to produce natural speech patterns and to read along with the voice of a recorded speaker is central to maintaining their motivation to master the language as a medium for talking about their reading.

7. Avoid the Use of Tests

Extensive reading programs should be "without the pressures of testing or marks" (Davis 1995:329). The use of tests runs contrary to the objective of creating stress-free conditions for pleasure reading because it invokes images of rote learning, vocabulary lists, memorization and homework. Extensive reading done at home should be under the learner's control and not an obligation imposed by the teacher. By their very nature, tests impose a rigor on the learning process, which the average student will never equate with pleasure.

8. Discourage the Over-Use of Dictionaries

While dictionaries certainly have a place in the teaching of reading, it is probably best located in intensive reading lessons, where detailed study of the lexical content of texts is appropriate. If learners turn to the dictionary every time they come across an unfamiliar word, they will focus only on the language itself, and not on the message conveyed. This habit will result in slow, inefficient reading and destroy the pleasure that reading novels and other literature are intended to provide. Summarizing comments on the extensive reading done by his subjects, Pickard (1996:155) notes that "Use of the dictionary was sparing, with the main focus on meaning".

9. Monitor the Students' Reading

In order to run an extensive reading program successfully, effective monitoring is required, both to administer the resources efficiently, and to trace students' developing reading habits and interests. In the Yemen program, a card file system was used to record titles and the dates the books were borrowed and returned. Input from the monitoring process helps us to record students' progress, maintain and update an inventory of titles, and locate and select new titles for the class library. It therefore serves both the individual needs of the reader and the logistical task of managing the reading resources.

10. Maintain the Entertainment

This is perhaps the most important aspect of the program to emphasize. Teachers need to invest time and energy in entertaining the participants by making use of multimedia sources to promote the books (e.g. video, audio, CD ROM, film, etc.). They should also exploit the power of anecdote by telling the students about interesting titles, taking them out to see plays based on books, exploiting posters, leaflets, library resources, and even inviting visiting speakers to give a talk in class on a book they have read recently. In these ways, teachers can maintain student motivation to read and secure their full engagement in the enjoyment the program provides.

Conclusion

Tsang's (1996) study, carried out in Hong Kong secondary schools, provided further persuasive evidence of the effectiveness of extensive reading in fostering learners' language development. He found that "the reading program was significantly more effective than the writing program" (1996:225). Extensive reading programs can provide very effective platforms for promoting reading improvement and development from elementary levels upwards. Although they do require a significant investment in time, energy and resources on the part of those charged with managing the materials, the benefits in terms of language and skills development for the participating learners far outweigh the modest sacrifices required. If such programs receive institutional support and can be integrated into the curriculum so that they become agreed school policy, as suggested in Davis (1995), they will likely be more readily and widely adopted, particularly in countries where material and financial resources are adequate.

Text 3 Extensive reading

Extensive reading (or free reading, book flood, reading for pleasure) is a way of language learning, including foreign language learning, through large amounts of reading. As well as facilitating acquisition and learning of vocabulary, it is believed to increase motivation through positive affective benefits. Proponents such as Krashen (1989) claim that reading alone will increase encounters with unknown words, bringing learning opportunities by inferencing. The learner's encounters with unknown words in specific contexts will allow the learner to infer and thus learn those words' meanings. While the mechanism is commonly accepted as true, its importance in language learning is disputed. (Cobb 2007)

In language learning, extensive reading is contrasted with intensive reading, which is slow, careful reading of a small amount of difficult text—it is when one is "focused on the language rather than the text". Extensive and intensive reading are two approaches to language learning and instruction, and may be used concurrently; intensive reading is however the more common approach, and often the only one used.

Concepts

Free voluntary reading refers to using extensive reading in language education. Students are free to choose a book that they like and are allowed to read it at their own pace. The aim of a free voluntary reading program is to help students to enjoy reading, so assessment is usually minimized or eliminated entirely.

The idea behind extensive reading is that a lot of reading of interesting material that is slightly below, at, or barely above the full comprehension level of the reader will foster improved language skills. Graded readers are often used. For foreign-language learners, some researchers have found that the use of glosses for "difficult" words is advantageous to vocabulary acquisition (Rott, Williams & Cameron 2002) but at least one study finds it has no effect (Holley & King 2008). A number of studies report significant incidental vocabulary gain in extensive reading in a foreign language (Huckin & Coady 1999). Advocates claim it can enhance skill in speaking as well as in reading.

Day and Bamford (1988) gave a number of traits common or basic to the extensive reading approach. Students read as much as possible. Reading materials are well within the reader's grammatical and vocabulary competence. The material should be varied in subject matter and character.

Students choose their own reading material and are not compelled to finish uninteresting materials. Reading material is normally for pleasure, information or general understanding; reading is its own reward with few or no follow-up exercises after reading; reading is individual and silent. Reading speed is usually faster when students read materials they can easily understand.

The teacher is a role model who also orients the students to the goals of the program, explains the idea and methodology, keeps records of what has been read, and guides students in material selection and maximizing the effect of the program.

Some recent practitioners have not followed all of these traits, or have added to them, for example, requiring regular follow-up exercises such as story summaries or discussions and the use of audio materials in tandem with the readings (Bell 1998).

Graded reader series

A graded reader series of books that increase in difficulty from shorter texts using more common words in the first volumes, to longer texts with less common vocabulary in later volumes. Cobb (2008) cites Oxford's Bookworm series, which includes the 2,500 most frequent words, The Longman Bridge Series (1945), with a systematic grading up to 8,000 words, now out of print, and the Penguin/Longman Active Reading series with its 3,000 word-family target.

Many series of graded readers exist in English, and series exist also in French, German, Italian, and Spanish. As of 2008, readers are notably absent or scarce in Russian, Arabic, Japanese, and Mandarin Chinese, though since 2006, an extensive reader series is available in Japanese. English readers have primarily been produced by British publishers, rather than American or other Anglophone nations. As of 1997, only one small series (15 volumes) was published in the United States, and a few in Europe outside the UK, with the majority in the UK.

Translation of modern literature

For advocates of extensive reading, lack of reading selection is an acute issue in classical languages such as Latin—the main readings available being quite difficult and are perceived as dry. To increase the available literature and make more light selection available, modern literature (particularly children's literature, comics, and genre fiction) may be translated into classical languages—see list of Latin translations of modern literature for examples in Latin. As F. W. Newman writes in his introduction to a Latin translation of Robinson Crusoe:

No accuracy of reading small portions of Latin will ever be so effective as extensive reading; and to make extensive reading possible to the many, the style ought to be very easy and the matter attractive.

Threshold

Laufer suggest that 3,000 word families or 5,000 lexical items are the threshold (Laufer 1997). Coady & Nation (1998) suggest 98% of lexical coverage and 5,000 word families or 8,000 items for a pleasurable reading (Coady & Huckin 1997, p. 233). After this threshold, the learner leaves the beginner paradox, and enters a virtuous circle (Coady & Huckin 1997, p. 233). Then, extensive reading becomes more efficient.

Limits

Cobb (2007), McQuillan & Krashen (2008), and Cobb (2008) offer contrasting perspectives. All agree on the need of lexical input, but Cobb (2007; 2008) supported by Parry (1997) denounces the sufficiency of extensive reading, the current lexical expansion pedagogy, and especially for confirmed learners. According to Cobb (2007), Krashen (1989)'s Input Hypothesis states that extensive reading generates a continuous hidden learning (lexical input), eventually "doing the entire job" of vocabulary acquisition. This hypothesis is without empirical evidence, neither on the extent (% of global vocabulary acquisition), nor on the sufficiency of extensive reading for lexicon learning (Cobb 2007).

Cobb (2007) thus proposed a computer-based study to quantitatively assess the efficiency of extensive reading. Cobb estimated the reading quantity of common learners within the L2 language (~175,000 words over 2 years), then randomly took 10 words in each of the 1st thousand most frequent words, the 2nd thousand, and the 3rd thousand, to see how many times those words would appear. Those results should be higher than 6 to 10 encounters, the number need for stable initial word learning to occur.

Cobb (2007) summarizes as following: "[the quantitative study] shows the extreme unlikelihood of developing an adequate L2 reading lexicon [above 2,000 words families] through reading alone, even in highly favorable circumstances" since "for the vast majority of L2 learners, free or wide reading alone is not a sufficient source of vocabulary knowledge for reading". Thereafter, Cobb restated the need of lexical input, and stated the possibility to increase it using computing capabilities.

McQuillan & Krashen (2008) answer that learners may read far more than 175,000 words but rather +1,000,000 words in 2 years, but Cobb (2008) counters that view as being based on excessively successful cases of reading oversimplified texts. Experiments cited by McQuillan & Krashen use easy and fast to read texts, but not material suitable for discovering new vocabulary; unsimplified texts are far harder and slower to read.

Advocacy and Support Organizations

The Extensive Reading Foundation is a not-for-profit, charitable organization whose purpose is to support and promote extensive reading. One Foundation initiative is the annual Language Learner Literature Award for the best new works in English. Another is maintaining a bibliography of research on extensive reading. The Foundation is also interested in helping educational institutions set up extensive reading programs through grants that fund the purchase of books and other reading material.

The Extensive Reading Special Interest Group (ER SIG) of The Japan Association for Language Teaching (JALT) is a not-for-profit organization which exists to help promote Extensive Reading in Japan. Via a website, the publications Extensive Reading in Japan and Journal of Extensive Reading, presentations throughout Japan, and other activities the ER SIG aims to help teachers set up and make the most of their ER programs and ER research projects.

Classroom activities

Text analysis

1. What is extensive reading? What properties are essential to extensive reading in language education?

2. Are the three texts equally convincing to you? What can contribute to the cogency of informative writing?

Class discussion

1. Have you had any misunderstanding of extensive reading before reading these texts? In what ways do these texts correct your view on extensive reading?

2. What do you think are the major differences between extensive reading introduced in this unit and intensive reading you have been practicing in other reading classes?

Critical thinking

Helpful as it is, Wikipedia is not considered authoritative, so we should always read with caution. What's more, authors may have divergent or opposite views on the same topic. So there may be mistakes or inconsistent/confusing points made in the three texts. Do you have any doubt on the information shown in the three texts as to what extensive reading is or requires?

Remember: To avoid subjectivity in critical thinking, you have to present your doubts with solid evidence.

Class debate

Considering the various constraints on extensive reading, such as free choices of reading pace, material, etc., you may find it worth thinking whether extensive reading can be taught in class. Discuss with your teammates and take a stance on this issue and prepare for an inter-group debate.

Proposition: Extensive reading can be taught in class.

Opposition: Extensive reading cannot be taught in class.

Remember: Debating must be interactive. You should engage with your opponents by rebutting their arguments, instead of merely stating your own. Don't stick rigidly to what you have prepared.

Group discussion and presentation

Given the fact that extensive reading ability is considered indispensable to English majors and the course cannot be removed from the college curriculum in China, we should think hard on how to make the best of the course, rather than emphasize the incompatibility between the notion of extensive reading and the classroom atmosphere. Hold a group discussion on the dilemma faced by the extensive reading course in China. Can you propose some possible solutions to it? What should the course offer? What objectives should be set for the course? What criteria should be taken for the selection of reading materials? And so on. Prepare to present your group ideas in front of other groups.

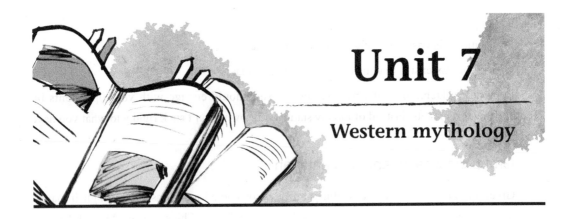

Unit 7

Western mythology

Pre-class reading tasks

In this unit, you will read a love story from Roman mythology. Do some research on mythology with your group members and prepare for the following questions before class.

Task 1

How is mythology commonly defined? Can the Bible be categorized into mythology?

Task 2

Can you name some world-famous mythologies? In what ways does the Chinese mythology resemble and differ from western mythologies?

Task 3

Do you know how Roman mythology is related to Greek mythology? Is the following myth from Roman mythology or the Greek mythology?

Make a name list of all the gods involved in the following myth. Then find their corresponding names in Greek mythology and also what they are respectively in charge of.

Task 4

If you google the title of the following text, you may find many versions of the myth. They may be slightly different in terms of plot, language and so on. And none of them can be regarded as authentic. Do you know why there is no authentic version for any myth?

☑ Text   Cupid and Psyche

By Lucius Apuleius

A certain king and queen had three daughters. The charms of the two elder were more than common, but the beauty of the youngest was so wonderful that the poverty of language is unable to express its due praise. The fame of her beauty was so great that strangers from neighboring countries came in crowds to enjoy the sight, and looked on her with amazement, paying her that homage which is due only to Venus herself. In fact Venus found her altars deserted, while men turned their devotion to this young virgin. As she passed along, the people sang her praises, and strewed her way with chaplets and flowers.

This homage to the exaltation of a mortal gave great offense to the real Venus. Shaking her ambrosial locks with indignation, she exclaimed, "Am I then to be eclipsed in my honors by a mortal girl? But she shall not so quietly usurp my honors. I will give her cause to repent of so unlawful a beauty."

Thereupon she calls her winged son Cupid, mischievous enough in his own nature, and rouses and provokes him yet more by her complaints. She points out Psyche to him and says, "My dear son, punish that contumacious beauty; give your mother a revenge as sweet as her injuries are great; infuse into the bosom of that haughty girl a passion for some low, mean, unworthy being."

Cupid prepared to obey the commands of his mother. There are two fountains in Venus's garden, one of sweet waters, the other of bitter. Cupid filled two amber vases, one from each fountain, and suspending them from the top of his quiver, hastened to the chamber of Psyche, whom he found asleep. He shed a few drops from the bitter fountain over her lips, though the sight of her almost moved him to pity; then touched her side with the point of his arrow. At the touch she awoke, and opened eyes upon Cupid (himself invisible), which so startled him that in his confusion he wounded himself with his own arrow. Heedless of his wound, his whole thought now was to repair the mischief he had done, and he poured the balmy drops of joy over all her silken ringlets.

Psyche, henceforth frowned upon by Venus, derived no benefit from all her charms. True, all eyes were cast eagerly upon her, and every mouth spoke her praises; but neither king, royal youth, nor plebeian presented himself to demand her in marriage. Her two elder sisters of moderate charms had now long been married to two royal princes; but Psyche, in her lonely apartment, deplored her solitude, sick of that beauty which, while it procured abundance of flattery, had failed to awaken love.

Her parents, afraid that they had unwittingly incurred the anger of the gods, consulted the oracle of Apollo, and received this answer, "The virgin is destined for the bride of no mortal lover. Her future husband awaits her on the top of the mountain. He is a monster whom neither gods nor men can resist."

This dreadful decree of the oracle filled all the people with dismay, and her parents abandoned themselves to grief. But Psyche said, "Why, my dear parents, do you now lament me? You should rather have grieved when the people showered upon me undeserved honors, and with one voice called me a Venus. I now perceive that I am a victim to that name. I submit. Lead me to that rock to which my unhappy fate has destined me."

Accordingly, all things being prepared, the royal maid took her place in the procession, which more resembled a funeral than a nuptial pomp, and with her parents, amid the lamentations of the people, ascended the mountain, on the summit of which they left her alone, and with sorrowful hearts returned home.

While Psyche stood on the ridge of the mountain, panting with fear and with eyes full of tears, the gentle Zephyr raised her from the earth and bore her with an easy motion into a flowery dale. By degrees her mind became composed, and she laid herself down on the grassy bank to sleep.

When she awoke refreshed with sleep, she looked round and beheld near a pleasant grove of tall and stately trees. She entered it, and in the midst discovered a fountain, sending forth clear and crystal waters, and fast by, a magnificent palace whose august front impressed the spectator that it was not the work of mortal hands, but the happy retreat of some god. Drawn by admiration and wonder, she approached the building and ventured to enter.

Every object she met filled her with pleasure and amazement. Golden pillars supported the vaulted roof, and the walls were enriched with carvings and paintings representing beasts of the chase and rural scenes, adapted to delight the eye of the beholder. Proceeding onward, she perceived that besides the apartments of state there were others filled with all manner of treasures, and beautiful and precious productions of nature and art.

While her eyes were thus occupied, a voice addressed her, though she saw no one, uttering these words, "Sovereign lady, all that you see is yours. We whose voices you hear are your servants and shall obey all your commands with our utmost care and diligence. Retire, therefore, to your chamber and repose on your bed of down, and when you see fit, repair to the bath. Supper awaits you in the adjoining alcove when it pleases you to take your seat there."

Psyche gave ear to the admonitions of her vocal attendants, and after repose and the refreshment of the bath, seated herself in the alcove, where a table immediately presented itself, without any visible aid from waiters or servants, and covered with the greatest delicacies of food and the most nectareous wines. Her ears too were feasted with music from invisible performers; of whom one sang, another played on the lute, and all closed in the wonderful harmony of a full chorus.

She had not yet seen her destined husband. He came only in the hours of darkness and fled before the dawn of morning, but his accents were full of love, and inspired a like passion in her. She often begged him to stay and let her behold him, but he would not consent. On the contrary he charged her to make no attempt to see him, for it was his pleasure, for the best of reasons, to keep concealed.

"Why should you wish to behold me?" he said. "Have you any doubt of my love? Have you any wish ungratified? If you saw me, perhaps you would fear me, perhaps adore me, but all I ask of you is to love me. I would rather you would love me as an equal than adore me as a god."

This reasoning somewhat quieted Psyche for a time, and while the novelty lasted she felt quite happy. But at length the thought of her parents, left in ignorance of her fate, and of her sisters, precluded from sharing with her the delights of her situation, preyed on her mind and made her begin to feel her palace as but a splendid prison. When her husband came one night, she told him her distress, and at last drew from him an unwilling consent that her sisters should be brought to see her.

So, calling Zephyr, she acquainted him with her husband's commands, and he, promptly obedient, soon brought them across the mountain down to their sister's valley. They embraced her and she returned their caresses.

"Come," said Psyche, "enter with me my house and refresh yourselves with whatever your sister has to offer."

Then taking their hands she led them into her golden palace, and committed them to the care of her numerous train of attendant voices, to refresh them in her baths and at her table, and to show them all her treasures. The view of these celestial delights caused envy to enter their bosoms, at seeing their young sister possessed of such state and splendor, so much exceeding their own.

They asked her numberless questions, among others what sort of a person her husband was. Psyche replied that he was a beautiful youth, who generally spent the daytime in hunting upon the mountains.

The sisters, not satisfied with this reply, soon made her confess that she had never seen him. Then they proceeded to fill her bosom with dark suspicions. "Call to mind," they said, "the Pythian oracle that declared you destined to marry a direful and tremendous monster. The inhabitants of this valley say that your husband is a terrible and monstrous serpent, who nourishes you for a while with dainties that he may by and by devour you. Take our advice. Provide yourself with a lamp and a sharp knife; put them in concealment that your husband may not discover them, and when he is sound asleep, slip out of bed, bring forth your lamp, and see for yourself whether what they say is true or not. If it is, hesitate not to cut off the monster's head, and thereby recover your liberty."

Psyche resisted these persuasions as well as she could, but they did not fail to have their effect on her mind, and when her sisters were gone, their words and her own curiosity were too strong for her to resist. So she prepared her lamp and a sharp knife, and hid them out of sight of her husband. When he had fallen into his first sleep, she silently rose and uncovering her lamp beheld not a hideous monster, but the most beautiful and charming of the gods, with his golden ringlets wandering over his snowy neck and crimson cheek, with two dewy wings on his shoulders, whiter than snow, and with shining feathers like the tender blossoms of spring.

As she leaned the lamp over to have a better view of his face, a drop of burning oil fell on the shoulder of the god. Startled, he opened his eyes and fixed them upon her. Then, without saying a word, he spread his white wings and flew out of the window. Psyche, in vain endeavoring to follow him, fell from the window to the ground.

Cupid, beholding her as she lay in the dust, stopped his flight for an instant and said, "Oh foolish Psyche, is it thus you repay my love? After I disobeyed my mother's commands and made you my wife, will you think me a monster and cut off my head? But go; return to your sisters, whose advice you seem to think preferable to mine. I inflict no other punishment on you than to leave you for ever. Love cannot dwell with suspicion." So saying, he fled away, leaving poor Psyche prostrate on the ground, filling the place with mournful lamentations.

When she had recovered some degree of composure she looked around her, but the palace and gardens had vanished, and she found herself in the open field not far from the city where her sisters dwelt. She repaired thither and told them the whole story of her misfortunes, at which, pretending to grieve, those spiteful creatures inwardly rejoiced.

"For now," said they, "he will perhaps choose one of us." With this idea, without saying a word of her intentions, each of them rose early the next morning and ascended the mountain, and having reached the top, called upon Zephyr to receive her and bear her to his lord; then leaping up, and not being sustained by Zephyr, fell down the precipice and was dashed to pieces.

Psyche meanwhile wandered day and night, without food or repose, in search of her husband. Casting her eyes on a lofty mountain having on its brow a magnificent temple, she sighed and said to herself, "Perhaps my love, my lord, inhabits there," and directed her steps thither.

She had no sooner entered than she saw heaps of corn, some in loose ears and some in sheaves, with mingled ears of barley. Scattered about, lay sickles and rakes, and all the instruments of harvest, without order, as if thrown carelessly out of the weary reapers' hands in the sultry hours of the day.

This unseemly confusion the pious Psyche put an end to, by separating and sorting everything to its proper place and kind, believing that she ought to neglect none of the gods, but endeavor by her piety to engage them all in her behalf. The holy Ceres, whose temple it was, finding her so religiously employed, thus spoke to her, "Oh Psyche, truly worthy of our pity, though I cannot shield you from the frowns of Venus, yet I can teach you how best to allay her displeasure. Go, then, and voluntarily surrender yourself to your lady and sovereign, and try by modesty and submission to win her forgiveness, and perhaps her favor will restore you the husband you have lost."

Psyche obeyed the commands of Ceres and took her way to the temple of Venus, endeavoring to fortify her mind and ruminating on what she should say and how best propitiate the angry goddess, feeling that the issue was doubtful and perhaps fatal.

Venus received her with angry countenance. "Most undutiful and faithless of servants," said she, "do you at last remember that you really have a mistress? Or have you rather come to see your sick husband, yet laid up of the wound given him by his loving wife? You are so ill favored and disagreeable that the only way you can merit your lover must be by dint of industry and diligence. I will make trial of your housewifery." Then she ordered Psyche to be led to the storehouse of her temple, where was laid up a great quantity of wheat, barley, millet, vetches, beans, and lentils prepared for food for her pigeons, and said, "Take and separate all these grains, putting all of the same kind in a parcel by themselves, and see that you get it done before evening." Then Venus departed and left her to her task.

But Psyche, in a perfect consternation at the enormous work, sat stupid and silent, without moving a finger to the inextricable heap.

While she sat despairing, Cupid stirred up the little ant, a native of the fields, to take compassion on her. The leader of the anthill, followed by whole hosts of his six-legged subjects, approached the heap, and with the utmost diligence taking grain by grain, they separated the pile, sorting each kind to its parcel; and when it was all done, they vanished out of sight in a moment.

Venus at the approach of twilight returned from the banquet of the gods, breathing odors and crowned with roses. Seeing the task done, she exclaimed, "This is no work of yours, wicked one, but his, whom to your own and his misfortune you have enticed." So saying, she threw her a piece of black bread for her supper and went away.

Next morning Venus ordered Psyche to be called and said to her, "Behold yonder grove which stretches along the margin of the water. There you will find sheep feeding without a shepherd, with golden-shining fleeces on their backs. Go, fetch me a sample of that precious wool gathered from every one of their fleeces."

Psyche obediently went to the riverside, prepared to do her best to execute the command. But the river god inspired the reeds with harmonious murmurs, which seemed to say, "Oh maiden, severely tried, tempt not the dangerous flood, nor venture among the formidable rams on the other side, for as long as they are under the influence of the rising sun, they burn with a cruel rage to destroy mortals with their sharp horns or rude teeth. But when the noontide sun has driven the cattle to the shade, and the serene spirit of the flood has lulled them to rest, you may then cross in safety, and you will find the woolly gold sticking to the bushes and the trunks of the trees."

Thus the compassionate river god gave Psyche instructions how to accomplish her task, and by observing his directions she soon returned to Venus with her arms full of the golden fleece; but she received not the approbation of her implacable mistress, who said, "I know very well it is by none of your own doings that you have succeeded in this task, and I am not satisfied yet that you have any capacity to make yourself useful. But I have another task for you. Here, take this box and go your way to the infernal shades, and give this box to Proserpine and say, 'My mistress Venus desires you to send her a little of your beauty, for in tending her sick son she has lost some of her own.' Be not too long on your errand, for I must paint myself with it to appear at the circle of the gods and goddesses this evening."

Psyche was now satisfied that her destruction was at hand, being obliged to go with her own feet directly down to Erebus. Wherefore, to make no delay of what was not to be avoided, she goes to the top of a high tower to precipitate herself headlong, thus to descend the shortest way to the shades below. But a voice from the tower said to her, "Why, poor unlucky girl, do you design to put an end to your days in so dreadful a manner? And what cowardice makes you sink under this last danger who have been so miraculously supported in all your former?" Then the voice told her how by a certain cave she might reach the realms of Pluto, and how to avoid all the dangers of the road, to pass by Cerberus, the three-headed dog, and prevail on Charon, the ferryman, to take her across the black river and bring her back again. But the voice added, "When Proserpine has given you the box filled with her beauty, of all things this is chiefly to be observed by you, that you never once open or look into the box nor allow your curiosity to pry into the treasure of the beauty of the goddesses."

Psyche, encouraged by this advice, obeyed it in all things, and taking heed to her ways traveled safely to the kingdom of Pluto. She was admitted to the palace of Proserpine, and without accepting the delicate seat or delicious banquet that was offered her, but contented with coarse bread for her food, she delivered her message from Venus. Presently the box was returned to her, shut and filled with the precious commodity. Then she returned the way she came, and glad was she to come out once more into the light of day.

But having got so far successfully through her dangerous task a longing desire seized her to examine the contents of the box. "What," said she, "shall I, the carrier of this divine beauty, not take the least bit to put on my cheeks to appear to more advantage in the eyes of my beloved husband!" So she carefully opened the box, but found nothing there of any beauty at all, but an infernal and truly Stygian sleep, which being thus set free from its prison, took possession of her, and she fell down in the midst of the road, a sleepy corpse without sense or motion.

But Cupid, being now recovered from his wound, and not able longer to bear the absence of his beloved Psyche, slipping through the smallest crack of the window of his chamber which happened to be left open, flew to the spot where Psyche lay, and gathering up the sleep from her body closed it again in the box, and waked Psyche with a light touch of one of his arrows. "Again," said he, "have you almost perished by the same curiosity. But now perform exactly the task imposed on you by my mother, and I will take care of the rest."

Then Cupid, as swift as lightning penetrating the heights of heaven, took his case to Jupiter, who gave his consent in return for Cupid's future help whenever a choice maiden catches his eye. Jupiter had Mercury convene an assembly of the gods in the theater of heaven, where he made a public statement of approval, warned Venus to back off, and gave Psyche ambrosia, the drink of immortality, so the couple could be united in marriage as equals. Their union, he said, would redeem Cupid from his history of provoking adultery and sordid liaisons.

Psyche became at last united to Cupid, and in due time they had a daughter born to them whose name was Pleasure.

Classroom activities
Story-telling and performance

One volunteer group is needed to retell the myth and divide it into parts. The other groups may choose from those parts to stage in class. The various parts should be staged in time order. The performance of each group will be graded based on the acting skills and the appropriateness of lines they write for different characters.

Language analysis

Do you think the myth is hard to read? Exemplify the language features that make the text unintelligible? Are those features expected from myth-writing?

Group-based text analysis and critical thinking

1. The myth can be read as allegory. What is the dominant moral conveyed here?

2. Different from God in Christianity, Greek and Roman gods have human characteristics and features. You may learn more about western people through reading those myths. For example, the origin of individualism in western society can be traced back to Greek and Roman mythology. Analyze the personalities of various gods presented in this myth and then comment on them (What do you think of those gods? What can you learn from the analysis of their personalities? etc.).

Class discussion

1. Zephyr, who picks up the fearful girl Psyche on the ridge of the mountain and takes her gently to Cupid's palace in the myth, is the god of the west wind. Can you recite some Chinese and western poems with lines containing the words *west wind*. Why does the piercingly cold west wind in Chinese people's eyes enjoy a gentle image in western mythology? What is the factor leading to the cultural difference here?

2. Have you heard of fairy tales like *Beauty and the Beast* and *Cinderella*? There is a close linkage between the two stories and the myth presented in this unit. Actually the former derives from the latter. List the various aspects in which the two fairy tales resemble the myth.

3. The importance of Greek and Roman mythology (as well as the Bible) in western culture is sometimes compared to that of Confucianism in Chinese. Does the analysis of the above myth shed some light on the understanding of this analogy? Explain your understanding of it.

Group discussion and presentation

Greek and Roman mythology has exerted great influence on western arts and literature. Take the myth in this unit as an example, many artists are obsessed with a special episode in it— *Psyche discovers Cupid*. The following are an oil painting and a sculpture created to re-present the episode. Compare the two artworks, tell the difference between them, and share your appreciation of them in class with other students (viz. in what ways you find them appealing).

Cupid and Psyche by Giuseppe Crespi

Cupid and Psyche by Reinhold Begas

Unit 8

Pollution: Who to blame?

Pre-class reading tasks

In this unit, you will read three texts on pollution or that in China. The texts feature different writing styles and present divergent views on (or answers to) culprits of pollution. The following are pre-class reading tasks for your study groups.

Read the following texts and compare them from whatever perspectives you may think of, such as the text type, purpose of writing, keynote of writing, etc.

Explore the three authors' views on major causes of China's smog/pollution and on the parties responsible for it.

Pollution in China is a quite complicated issue. Find more articles on this topic to collect enough information to enable you to comment on the authors' opinions and develop your own. Prepare for a presentation in class.

✍ Text 1 Smog

Smog is the hazy, unhealthy polluted air that accumulates over cities and other regions under certain conditions.

Modern smog is derived primarily from precursor chemical pollutants, emitted to the atmosphere from vehicular internal combustion engines and industrial plants, that react in the atmosphere with sunlight to produce secondary chemical pollutants that also combine with the precursor emissions to form the components of what is called photochemical smog.

Origin of the term "smog"

The word smog is a blend of the words smoke and fog. Coinage of the term is generally attributed to Dr. Henry Antoine des Voeux in his 1905 paper, "Fog and Smoke" for a meeting of the Public Health Congress in London. The July 26, 1905 edition of the Daily Graphic, a London newspaper, quoted des Voeux: "... he said it required no science to see that there was something produced in great cities which was not found in the country, and that was smoky fog, or what was known as 'smog'." The next day, the Globe newspaper remarked that "Dr. des Voeux did a public service in coining a new word for the London fog."

Atmospheric chemistry involved in smog formation

Originally, Dr. des Voeux's term smog referred to a mixture of smoke, sulfur dioxide (SO_2) and fog that was once prevalent in London when coal with a high sulfur content was widely used throughout the city as heating fuel. The dark, sulfurous London smog caused reduced visibility, respiratory problems and had a noticeable deleterious effect on human health. The Great Smog of 1952 darkened the streets of London and killed approximately 4,000 people in a 4-day period (another 8,000 died from its effects in the following months). The type of smog experienced in London many decades ago is no longer encountered since other fuels have largely replaced the wide-spread use of high-sulfur coal for heating.

Photochemical smog is chemically quite different than the old London-type smog and has a long history. In 1542, when exploring what is now Southern California, Juan Rodriguez Cabrillo named San Pedro Bay the "Bay of Smokes" because of the thick haze that covered the area. Complaints of eye irritation from the polluted air in Los Angeles date back to the late 1860s. In the 1940s, photochemical smog first became apparent in Los Angeles and other large cities on sunny days, although none of those cities had any significant use of coal for heating fuel or for industrial activities.

Photochemical smog is a daytime phenomenon that occurs mostly during warm, sunny summertime days and is characterized by a brown haze that reduces visibility and contains oxidants, such as ozone (O_3), that cause respiratory problems, eye irritation and damage to plants. It is a mixture of variable amounts of ozone, reactive hydrocarbons, nitrogen oxide (NO), nitrogen dioxide (NO_2), aldehydes, peroxyacetyl nitrate (PAN), particulate matter and other components. By contrast, the London-type smog (also referred to as "classic smog") occurs mostly during cold winter days and consists primarily of a mixture of sulfur dioxide and particulate matter (i.e., "soot") usually derived from burning coal.

Photochemical smog precursor pollutants

The chemistry involved in the formation of smog is highly complex and involves many different reactions (see the diagram). The three major ingredients required to form photochemical smog are solar energy (i.e., sunlight), reactive hydrocarbons and nitrogen oxide, the latter two being referred to as the precursor pollutants. As shown in the diagram, the two precursors enter the atmosphere as gases emitted for the most part from vehicular internal combustion engines fuelled by gasoline and diesel oil. To a much lesser extent, nitrogen oxide is also emitted from industrial combustion sources, and reactive hydrocarbons are emitted by evaporation from the handling and storage of volatile hydrocarbons such as gasoline, solvents, some pesticides and some paints. Biogenic sources such as pine trees and certain other trees are also a source, though of relatively minor importance, of reactive hydrocarbon emissions such as isoprene and α-pinene.

Simplified chemistry of photochemical smog formation

In the simplified schematic overview depicted in the adjacent diagram, the major chemical reactions that contribute to the formation of photochemical smog include the following:

The gaseous precursor nitrogen oxide, emitted primarily from vehicular internal combustion engines, is oxidized to produce gaseous nitrogen dioxide.

The gaseous nitrogen dioxide is broken down by solar energy from sunlight to produce gaseous nitrogen oxide and atomic oxygen (O, an oxygen radical). This process is referred to as photolysis and hence the term "photochemical smog".

The atomic oxygen reacts with gaseous atmospheric oxygen (O_2) to form gaseous ozone (O_3).

The gaseous ozone also oxidizes gaseous nitrogen oxide to form gaseous nitrogen dioxide and gaseous oxygen.

The gaseous precursor reactive hydrocarbons (RH), emitted primarily from vehicular internal combustion engines, reacts with atomic oxygen, atmospheric oxygen and ozone to produce various highly reactive hydrocarbon free radicals (RO•2).

The hydrocarbon free radicals then react with other species such as nitrogen dioxide to form peroxyacetyl nitrate (PAN), aldehydes and other smog components.

The various products produced or formed from the precursor pollutants are referred to as secondary pollutants. All of the above chemical reactions (as well as others) occur more or less simultaneously during sunny, summertime days in most large cities with a great number of automobiles and other vehicles.

Photochemical smog

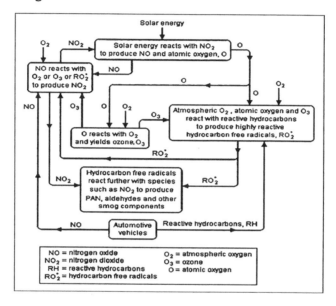

Health effects

Photochemical smog constitutes a serious health problem in most large cities. It is especially harmful for senior citizens, children, and people with heart and lung conditions such as emphysema, bronchitis, and asthma. It can inflame breathing passages, decrease the lungs' working capacity, cause shortness of breath, pain when inhaling deeply, wheezing, and coughing. It can cause eye and nose irritation and it dries out the protective membranes of the nose and throat. In general, it interferes with the body's ability to fight infection, thereby increasing susceptibility to illness.

The table explains the Air Quality Index (AQI) ranges used by the U.S. Environmental Protection Agency (U.S. EPA) and their corresponding health effect categories and color codes. The U.S. EPA's AQI is also known as the Pollution Standards Index (PSI). A national map of the United States containing daily AQI forecasts across the nation, using that same color-coding, is published online jointly by the U.S. EPA and the National Oceanic and Atmospheric Administration (NOAA).

United States' AQI（Air Quality Index）

Air Quality Index	Air Quality Category
0–50	Good
51–100	Moderate
101–150	Unhealthy for Sensitive Groups
151–200	Unhealthy
201–300	Very Unhealthy
301–500	Hazardous

If multiple pollutants are measured at a monitoring site, then the largest or "dominant" AQI value is reported for the location.

The U.S. EPA has developed conversion calculators, available online, for the conversion of AQI values to concentration values and for the reverse conversion of concentrations to AQI values.

The South Coast Air Quality Management District (SCAQMD) of Southern California has published an excellent, comprehensive discussion of the undesirable health effects caused by air pollution. It also includes an extensive listing and discussion of the many medical health effect studies of pollution performed during the past decades starting around 1950.

Areas affected

Smog can form in almost any location where the level of air pollutants is high, and it is more likely to occur during periods of warm, sunny weather when the upper air is warm enough to inhibit vertical circulation. It often persists for extended time periods over densely populated cities, such as Athens, Beijing, Berlin, Cairo, Hong Kong, Kuala Lumpur, London, Los Angeles, Milan, Moscow, New York, Paris, Rome, São Paulo, Seoul and Shanghai. Smog is especially prevalent in geologic basins encircled by hills or mountains.

England

In 1306, concerns over air pollution were sufficient for Edward I to briefly ban coal fires in

London. In 1661, John Evelyn, the noted English diarist of his day, published Fumifugium in which he suggested the widespread planting of fragrant trees, shrubs and flowers around London so as to counteract the foul effects of the smoke from coal-burning.

In the 1800s, more than a million London residents were burning coal, and winter "fogs" became more than a nuisance. An 1873 coal-smoke saturated fog, thicker and more persistent than natural fog, hovered over the city for days. As now known from subsequent epidemiological findings, the fog caused 268 deaths from bronchitis. Another fog in 1879 lasted from November to March, four long months darkened skies and gloom. Severe episodes of smog continued even into the 20th centuries and were nicknamed "pea-soupers".

As discussed earlier above, the Great Smog of 1952 killed approximately 4,000 people in the short time of 4 days and a further 8,000 died from its effects in the following months. That finally prompted real legislative reform. In 1956, the Clean Air Act 1956, sponsored by the Ministry of Housing and Local Government in England and the Department of Health in Scotland, was enacted by the Parliament of the United Kingdom and introduced smokeless zones in London. It was in effect until 1964 and consequently reduced the sulfur dioxide levels in London's air to the point that made the intense and persistent London smog a thing of the past. It was after this that the great clean-up of London began and buildings recovered their original clean stone façades which, during two centuries, had gradually blackened.

However, photochemical smog still does occur in modern London.

European Union

The European Union (EU) is composed of 27 member states and was established by the Treaty of Maastricht in 1993. Its executive functions are performed by the European Commission and to a limited extent by the European Council.

The large cities within the EU, such as Athens, Berlin, Milan, Paris, Rome and others, all experience episodes of photochemical smog in varying degrees of severity and especially so in the summer months.

The EU uses the ground-level atmospheric ozone concentration as an indicator of air quality and has adopted these limiting ozone values:

Target value (TV): 120 µg/m³ for 1 hour averaging time for 8-hour average, daily maximum. Not to be exceeded more than 25 days per year. Defined as the target value for the protection of human health.

Information threshold (IT): 180 μg/m^3 for 1 hour averaging time. Defined as the level beyond which there is a risk to human health from brief exposure for particularly sensitive sections of the population. Any exceedance of this threshold should be reported by the member state in which it occurs to the European Commission.

Alert threshold (AT): 240 μg/m3 for 1 hour averaging time. Defined as the level beyond which there is a risk to human health from brief exposure for the general population. If exceeded in a member state, national authorities of the member state are required to warn the public and give advice.

According to a recent report by the European Environmental Agency (EEA), the overall area of the EU that experiences exceedances of the ozone target value has declined by 60% during the period from 2006–2009. The executive summary of that report states: In contrast to previous summers, in 2009 there were no pan-European multi-day episodes. Summer 2009 was characterized by ozone episodes of two to five days followed by spells with few exceedances. However, the executive summary also states that a significant area of the EU still experienced exceedance of the ozone target value.

Russia

In early August 2010, the city of Moscow was covered by a heavy, dark smog caused by extensive wildfires across much of western Russia, turning the city's buildings into blurs, grounding air flights, and forcing the city's residents and tourists to wear surgical masks. At the beginning of August, forest fires in Russia exceeded 100, 000 hectares which by August 21 had decreased to 7,000 hectares according to the Emergencies Ministry.

The head of the Moscow's health department said that the abnormal heat and smog coming from fires had seriously exacerbated the environmental conditions in Moscow and "The death rate has doubled in the city. The regular daily death rate in Moscow is 360—380. We had about 700 deaths today."

Some airborne pollutants were four times higher than normal, the worst concentrations seen to date according to city health officials. The concentrations appeared likely to get even worse as the state news agency, ITAR-Tass, reported that the smoke was thickening.

Ruhr Valley Incident of 1985

The Ruhr district, located in the Rhine river valley of western Germany, is an urban area in the state of North Rhine-Westphalia. With a population of about 7 million (2008) and an area of 4,435 square kilometers (1,713 square miles), it is the largest urban area in Germany. Historically, it has been a heavily industrialized area that experienced decades of polluted air containing smoke and high amounts of sulfur dioxide—the key ingredients of London-type smog.

In January of 1985, the Ruhr district experienced an extended episode of London-type smog that lasted 5 days with the 24-hour averages of sulfur dioxide in the air as high as 0.8 mg/m3 and particulate matter as high as 0.6 mg/m3, both primarily derived from the extensive burning of coal by the area's steel mills and other industries. In the 5 days of the episode, the daily death rate increased by 8% and the hospital admissions for respiratory and cardiovascular problems increased by 15%.

During the smog episode, a smog alarm was called, personal automobile driving was banned and many schools were closed.

Iran

In December 2005, schools and public offices had to close in Tehran, Iran, and 1600 people were taken to hospital, in a severe smog blamed largely on automobile exhausts.

Mexico

Mexico City is located in the tropical latitudes on a high plain at an altitude of 2,200 meters, and is surrounded on three sides by mountains that reach elevations of 5,000 meters. The major sources of air pollutants within Mexico City's urban area include exhaust from 3.5 million vehicles, thousands of industries, and mineral dust. The ancient lakebed valley in which the city is situated became a major source of dust when it was drained in the 16th century. The area is known as the Valley of Mexico, sometimes called the Bowl of Mexico.

Due to its location in a highland bowl, cold air sinks down onto the urban area of Mexico City, trapping industrial and vehicle pollution underneath and, as a result, the city has one of the world's worst air pollution problems. Within one generation, the city has changed from being known for some of the cleanest air of the world into one with some of the worst pollution, with pollutants like nitrogen dioxide measured at twice or thrice the level of international standards. Since solar radiation does not vary significantly with season at tropical latitudes, photochemical smog is present over the city much of the year.

Southeast Asia

Southeast Asia consists of a mainland section and a maritime section. The mainland section includes Mayanmar, Cambodia, Laos, Thailand, Vietnam and Peninsular Malaysia and the maritime section includes Brunei, East Malaysia, East Timor, Indonesia, Philippines, and Singapore. The large cities in Southeast Asia have been plagued by smoky haze and photochemical smog ever since the late 1990s. The primary cause of the smoky haze have been the extensive forest fires occurring in Indonesia. Farmers and plantation owners are said to be responsible for the fires, which they use to clear tracts of land for further plantings. Other contributing factor are that El Niño conditions have created some very dry seasons with very little rainfall and the peat swamps that underlie the Indonesian forests and add fuel to the fires.

One of the recent major occurrences of smoky haze in Malaysia, Singapore and other parts of Southeast Asia occurred in October 2006 and was caused by smoke from forest fires in Indonesia being blown across the Straits of Malacca by south-westerly winds.

Since December 1997, member countries of the Association of Southeast Asia Nations (ASEAN) have been undertaking joint efforts in monitoring, preventing and mitigating transboundary haze pollution resulting from land and forest fires, guided by the Regional Haze Action Plan (RHAP) that was endorsed by the ASEAN Environment Ministers. In addition, the ASEAN Agreement on Transboundary Haze Pollution (or ASEAN Haze Agreement) was adopted in June 2002 and comprehensively addresses all aspects of fire and haze including prevention, emphasizing the underlying causes, monitoring, and mitigation.

In addition to the smoky haze caused by the forest fires, they have resulted in large amounts of the photochemical smog precursor, nitrogen oxide, entering the atmosphere. That, coupled with the great numbers of automobiles and other vehicles used in the large cities of Southeast Asia, has resulted in those cities being subjected to photochemical smog as well as hazy smoke.

United States

The U.S. EPA has designated over 300 U.S. counties in the United States to be "non-attainment areas" for one or more air pollutants, meaning that they have failed to attain and maintain the National Ambient Air Quality Standards as required by the Clean Air Act enacted by the U.S. Congress . The non-attainment areas are largely clustered around large metropolitan areas, with the largest contiguous non-attainment zones being in California and the Northeast, as can be seen in the map below. Various U.S. and Canadian government agencies collaborate to produce real-time air quality maps and forecasts.

Located in low basins surrounded by mountains, Los Angeles and the San Joaquin Valley are known for their photochemical smog. The millions of vehicles in these basins, plus the added effects of the port complex in Los Angeles, result in the accumulation of photochemical smog precursors and subsequently to the formation of photochemical smog. Strict regulations by the California Air Resources Board and other California government agencies overseeing this problem have reduced the number of smog alerts from several hundred annually to just a few. However, these geographically predisposed smog areas still have air pollution levels that are a pressing issue for the more than 25 million people who live there.

Text 2 China fights uphill battle against air pollution

(Adapted)

By Xinhua

Although China has made achievements in air pollution control in recent years, a tough battle remains, minister of environmental protection Li Ganjie has said.

Speaking at a press conference in Beijing Monday, Li said from 2013 to 2016, the density of PM2.5 fell 33 percent in the Beijing-Tianjin-Hebei region.

PM2.5 density measures the concentration of small particles in the air and is often used as a gauge of smog.

Figures in the Yangtze River and Pearl River deltas dropped 31.3 percent and 31.9 percent respectively during the same period, according to Li.

However, the Beijing-Tianjin-Hebei region has seen a rebound in PM2.5 and PM10 density in the first half of the year, with the two indicators up 14.3 and 13.2 percent, compared to the same period last year.

In January 2013, most parts of northern China were hit by severe air pollution, with Beijing enveloped by heavy smog for more than 20 days during the month.

In 2013, PM2.5 density became an important indicator to gauge air quality across China. Since then, the Chinese government has made a series of policies to reduce air pollution.

After three years of efforts, the average density of PM2.5 in Beijing dropped to 73 micrograms per cubic meters, down 18 percent from 2013 levels. Heavy air pollution days in Beijing dropped from 58 days in 2013 to 39 days in 2016, according to the Air Quality Index (AQI).

Under Chinese air quality standards, an AQI below 100 is defined as a good air quality day. An average daily AQI above 200 indicates heavy air pollution. People including children and elderly people are suggested not to participate in outside activities.

In 2016, the average concentration of PM2.5 in Tianjin city was 69 micrograms per cubic meters and 70 in Hebei Province, falling by 28.1 and 35.2 percent respectively, compared with 2013.

Nationwide, air quality in some 338 cities at the prefecture level and above has improved, according to the Ministry of Environmental Protection (MEP).

Since coal burning is the primary source of air pollution in the Beijing-Tianjin-Hebei region, the area has started to reduce and ban coal use.

For instance, the volume of coal consumption in Beijing was 23 million tonnes in 2013, the figure declined to below 10 million tonnes this year. According to a plan revealed in 2014, Beijing will ban coal use in its downtown areas in 2020, covering Dongcheng, Xicheng, Chaoyang, Haidian, Fengtai and Shijingshan districts.

Shu Yinbiao, chairman of the State Grid, said the State Grid would help promote clean energy heating in north China in the winter. Some areas in Beijing and Tianjin will become "coal free zones."

Nearly 200,000 households in Wuqing District of Tianjin will bid farewell to an era of burning coal for heating and cooking. More than 1.2 million households in Langfang and Baoding cities of Hebei will use clean energy by the end of October.

He Hong, a scientist at the Chinese Academy of Sciences, said air pollution in China was caused by multiple reasons, such as the development of industries and the surge of vehicles, which generate massive emissions.

"But it is different from the air pollution that appeared in London and Los Angeles in the twentieth century. Smoke in London was mainly caused by burning coal, while in Los Angeles it was mainly because of too many vehicles," He added.

Areas affected by air pollution in China are much larger than those cities in Britain and the United States. "Addressing air pollution in China is much more complicated than that in European and American countries. And it's also hard to solve the problem in a short term," He said.

Actually, "no country in history has emerged as a major industrial power without creating a legacy of environmental damage that can take decades and big dollops of public wealth to undo. Britain, the United States and Japan polluted their way to prosperity and worried about environmental damage only after their economies matured and their urban middle classes demanded blue skies and safe drinking water. But just as the speed and scale of China's rise as an economic power have no clear parallel in history, so its pollution problem has shattered all precedents. 'It is a very awkward situation for the country because our greatest achievement is also our biggest burden,' says Wang Jinnan, one of China's leading environmental researchers. Environmental degradation is now so severe, with such stark domestic and international repercussions, that pollution poses not only a major long-term burden on the Chinese public but also an acute challenge to the government. China is more like a teenage smoker with emphysema. The costs of pollution have mounted well before it is ready to curtail economic development. 'Typically, industrial countries deal with green problems when they are rich,' said Ren Yong, a climate expert at the Center for Environment and Economy in Beijing. 'We have to deal with them while we are still poor. There is no model for us to follow.'" (Kahn & Yardley, 2007, *The New York Times*)

Li stressed that China was determined to fight against air pollution.

The MEP has launched a campaign against heavy air pollution in autumn and winter in the Beijing-Tianjin-Hebei region and surrounding areas from 2017 to 2018, according to Li. The campaign will mainly focus on curbing pollution by industrial enterprises, cutting coal consumption and improving emergency responses to heavy pollution weather.

"'Beijing has imposed strict measures to curb pollution emissions since 2017 and strengthened their implementation since September. Joint efforts have been made by every involved department and district,' the municipal environmental authority said. To date, Beijing has phased out 374,000 old vehicles with heavy exhaust emissions. And 5,829 polluting companies, which were exposed by environmental inspectors from the ministry, were shut down, it said. The capital's environmental authority has levied fines of 145 million yuan (US$21.8 million) on more than 3,000 polluting companies in the first three quarters, an 86.2 percent increase of total fines in the same period last year." (Zheng Jinran, 2017, *China Daily*)

⚓ Text 3　China: Ecological civilization rising?

By John Fullerton

1　Returning to China for the first time in a quarter century this month was equally awe inspiring and terrifying. The observation deck of the truly gorgeous Shanghai World Financial Center is breathtaking, a fitting testament to China's rise. But it was the unexpected sense that we might be experiencing history at DeTao Group's summit in Shanghai, "Future New Economy: Sustainable Model Toward an Ecological Economy," that left an indelible mark on me.

2　I had the honor to address the DeTao Group summit on the topic of regenerative investing in natural capital. Inspired by the vision and leadership of DeTao Chairman George Lee, it was an extraordinary experience. The warm hospitality and genuine appreciation and respect extended to all the visiting "experts" was quite exceptional. As George told me, "in Chinese culture, we honor our teachers."

3　The context of the summit was of course China's unprecedented quarter century boom that has seen China emerge the second largest economy in the world, lifted two hundred million people out of poverty (so I'm told), and created middle class lives for many and immense wealth for more than a few. But this newfound wealth and power has come at a significant cost.

4　China is now the world's largest carbon emitter, the result of the west's outsourcing manufacturing production to a location where environmental standards are lower, and cheap, plentiful coal is the power source of choice. The now infamous air pollution is making people sick and reducing life expectancies. The environmental crisis is not a special interest issue; it is omnipresent.

5　It was quite significant, therefore, when the 18th National Congress of the Communist Party wrote the construction of an "Ecological Civilization" into the Constitution in 2012, requiring a shift away from the industrial civilization modern China had become. Of course a change like this gets translated directly into policy, albeit slowly and unevenly. Note how clear China's President Xi is with respect to the real source of wealth:

6　"We value both natural landscape and resource as well as material wealth. The former overrides and promises the latter."—Chinese President Xi Jinping

7　I can't pretend to know how serious China's leaders are with respect to their stated goal of achieving an "ecological civilization," and one certainly can't help but notice the irony when looking at the pollution belching out of smoke stacks as you travel to and from the airport. But I was impressed with what I saw at this summit. Here are a few highlights:

8   The conference highlighted the work being led by ecological economist Dr. Robert Costanza in Sanya City ("the Miami of China") to create the first natural capital balance sheet for one of the world's major municipal governments. In his speech, Sanya City Vice Mayor Li Baiqing stated that "it is difficult for an entire society to think in a different paradigm," and "this [management of natural capital] project is our destiny."

9   Mr. Long Yongtu, who negotiated China's entrance into the World Trade Organization and is now Secretary General of the Boao Forum for Asia, gave a remarkably honest assessment, stating that, "China is at a crossroads. After thirty years of development, people are getting wealthier but are not feeling happier."

10   And Chairman George Lee closed the conference with a notable speech, calling for a "new economic system" in which investing in natural capital will be the doorway to the new economy. He has a vision for private capital working in collaboration with the public sector, enhancing the efficiency and speed of capital deployment for the shared benefits of healthy ecosystems, and the pathway to a "green mountain" to complement the "gold mountain" that has been built.

11   Now of course the devil is in the details. (For more on that, see my thought piece Limits to Investment.) Unleashing huge surpluses of investment capital in the name of "natural capital investment" can do as much damage as good, and much more is needed than unlocking investment capital. Indeed, Long Yongtu himself cautioned that investment had become "the bad guy" but felt it didn't need to be. I understood what he meant when I peered from atop the Shanghai World Financial Center across endless nondescript concrete blocks of apartment buildings that stretch as far as the eye can see.

12   But what struck me most as I listened to the presentations and even more in the private conversations was that I was experiencing history in the making. Unlike so many conferences in the West where there is a lot of talk, and then everyone knows little will change, in Shanghai, I felt the tide shifting under our feet. I felt that a force was being unleashed, that began, no doubt, with the amendment to the constitution in 2012, in response to profound ecological and human crises.

13   China has pointed to a spot on a distant horizon and set change in motion. Five-year plans were affected, and transitioning the economic system will require an ability to plan (take note, America!). Reward systems have been adjusted. Experts are called in for their ideas. Old

paradigms that brought great success in the past are put on the table and critiqued in light of the new context. No ideological debate casts a shadow, only debate about how to engineer solutions. We may not like all the answers (200 nuclear power plants are in the pipeline). No doubt there will be ups and downs, and likely crisis. Success is far from certain.

14   Yet powerful mainstream Chinese interests appeared interested to learn, not defend. Successful and practical business leaders like George Lee, now a practicing Buddhist, have taken up the reins and are initiating action. The mayor of a major city is establishing a natural capital balance sheet and will begin monitoring its rise or fall as "destiny." Others will follow. We all signed a bold joint declaration, despite an imperfect translation. The media was present in full force doing interviews and reporting on the substance of the event. History was unfolding.

Classroom activities
Class competition: Timed text analysis

(For this part, you are not allowed to make preparations in advance. The following questions can only be read in class following the teacher's instruction. With all study groups beginning their preparations at the same time, whichever group first shows a signal wins the opportunity to answer and score in the class competition. Other groups may also gain points by challenging the first group's answers.)

1.   What are the two major types of smog? How do they differ?

2.   What is the chief culprit of photochemical smog? What are the other causes?

3.   What are the precursor pollutants leading to the formation of smog? And what are the secondary pollutants?

4.   How are the secondary pollutants formed?

5.   Where is the starting point in the diagram "The formation of photochemical smog"? Match each step in the diagram with major chemical reactions explained in the section "Simplified chemistry of photochemical smog formation".

6.   It is stated in Text 1 that smog is more likely to occur when the upper air is warm enough to inhibit vertical circulation. Why? Can you elaborate on this meteorological phenomenon?

7.   What is the major damage that smog can do to human health?

8.   What do areas having been (or having had been) affected by smog have in common?

1. In what way does the pollution problem in China resemble that in western countries? And what is unique to the pollution problem in China?

2. What is the dominant tone of the text?

3. Can you clarify the information flow in Text 2? Do you have any doubt about this arrangement?

Task 3

1. What makes the author's trip to China this time both inspiring and terrifying?

2. In paragraph 11, the author said he understood what Long Yongtu meant by peering at apartments buildings outside the window. How do those buildings explain Long's meaning?

3. What does the first sentence in paragraph 13 mean?

4. The author mentioned that he was "experiencing history" several times in the text. What is the history in the making?

5. Why does the title of Text 3 end with a question mark?

Class discussion

1. Which type of smog does Beijing Smog most possibly fall into? Why?

2. What are the major culprits of China's pollution (or smog) shown in or inferable from the three texts?

3. Who should shoulder primary responsibility for the problem according to the three authors?

Critical thinking

Compare statistics in Text 2 and those in the following text. Although they both are about pollution in China in 2017, statistics in the former create an optimistic atmosphere, while those in the latter darken readers' mood. How do the authors influence readers' responses in opposite ways by using the same data? How do you understand the so-called objectivity in news reports?

The Beijing-Tianjin-Hebei province region saw air pollution worsen in the first three quarters of the year, with concentrations of major pollutants rising and fewer days with blue skies, according to data from the Ministry of Environmental Protection released on Saturday. From January to September, residents in the 13 major cities in the northern region on average saw 52.6 percent of days with good air quality, a year-on-year decrease of 8.7 percentage points, said Liu Zhiquan, head of environmental monitoring at the ministry. Concentrations of PM2.5 and PM10 both increased by about 10 percent in the first three quarters, the figures showed. Beijing saw a significant decline in air quality in September. PM10 levels increased by 53.8 percent year-on-year, and days with blue skies accounted for about half the total, at 53.8 percent of the days—a 13.4

percentage point drop year-on-year—the ministry said in the statement. "From March to August, the strict controls on emissions in Beijing and the neighboring region have worked to push PM2.5 levels down, hitting a record low," the capital's Environmental Protection Bureau said on Sunday. "But the typical air pollution, which occurs in winter, hit the capital earlier in September, creating a severe challenge." Beijing has experienced challenges in meeting the reduction target set by the central government-an average PM2.5 concentration in 2017 of 60 micrograms per cubic meter. Data show that in the first nine months, the average level was 60, and the winter season is unlikely to help maintain that.

(Zheng Jinran, 2017, *China Daily*)

Group discussion and presentation

What on earth is the culprit of smog/pollution in China? What or whom should be blamed for it? Each group needs to prepare a presentation showing their insights into this issue. (Mere echoing of the authors' ideas is not welcomed and may be graded C-.)

Unit 9

China in western people's eyes

Pre-class reading tasks

In this unit, you will read two articles on China from western media. Some westerners who have never been to China may view China through tainted glasses with preconceived notions. Therefore, misunderstandings, strong bias and rudeness are sometimes found in their writings due to their ignorance about the nation. Different from those distorted western reports and one-sided haughty comments, the articles selected in this unit, growing out of the authors' personal experiences in China, are relatively sensible, presenting thought-provoking analyses on China from an outsider's perspective. It is hoped that the reading of them will inspire you to inspect the Chinese (including yourselves) from a different perspective. The following pre-class tasks are designed to guide your group preparation for the unit.

Examine closely the titles and leads of the two texts below. Can you predict the subject matter of the two texts? What other pre-reading expectations can be triggered by the titles & leads?

What social phenomena are addressed in the two texts? What are their respective main themes? Are there some sub-themes around the central themes? What are they?

The two articles are written in the same way to convince readers of their insights into those social phenomena. Can you tell what the method is?

✍ **Text 1** Gilded age, gilded cage

By Leslie T. Chang

China's middle class: China's sudden prosperity brings undreamed-of freedoms and new anxieties.

At the age of four, Zhou Jiaying was enrolled in two classes—Spoken American English and English Conversation—and given the English name Bella. Her parents hoped she might go abroad for college. The next year they signed her up for acting class. When she turned eight, she started on the piano, which taught discipline and developed the cerebrum. In the summers she went to the pool for lessons; swimming, her parents said, would make her taller. Bella wanted to be a lawyer, and to be a lawyer you had to be tall. By the time she was ten, Bella lived a life that was rich with possibility and as regimented as a drill sergeant's. After school she did homework unsupervised until her parents got home. Then came dinner, bath, piano practice. Sometimes she was permitted television, but only the news. On Saturdays she took a private essay class followed by Math Olympics, and on Sundays a piano lesson and a prep class for her entrance exam to a Shanghai middle school. The best moment of the week was Friday afternoon, when school let out early. Bella might take a deep breath and look around, like a man who discovers a glimpse of blue sky from the confines of the prison yard.

For China's emerging middle class, this is an age of aspiration—but also a time of anxiety. Opportunities have multiplied, but each one brings pressure to take part and not lose out, and every acquisition seems to come ready-wrapped in disappointment that it isn't something newer and better. An apartment that was renovated a few years ago looks dated; a mobile phone without a video camera and color screen is an embarrassment. Classes in colloquial English are fashionable among Shanghai schoolchildren, but everything costs money.

Freedom is not always liberating for people who grew up in a stable society; sometimes it feels more like a never ending struggle not to fall behind. A study has shown that 45 percent of Chinese urban residents are at health risk due to stress, with the highest rates among high school students.

Fifth grade was Bella's toughest year yet. At its end she would take entrance exams for middle school. Every student knew where he or she ranked: When teachers handed back tests, they had the students stand in groups according to their scores. Bella ranked in the middle—12th or 13th in a class of 25, lower if she lost focus. She hated America, because she thought it always meddled in the affairs of other countries. She spoke a fair amount of English: "Men like to smoke and drink beer, wine, and whiskey." Her favorite restaurant was Pizza Hut, and she liked the spicy wings at

KFC. Her record on the hula hoop was 2,000 spins.

The best place in the world was the Baodaxiang Children's Department Store on Nanjing Road. In its vast stationery department, Bella would carefully select additions to her eraser collection. She owned 30 erasers—stored in a cookie tin at home—that were shaped like flipflops and hamburgers and cartoon characters; each was not much bigger than a thumbnail, and all remained in their original plastic packaging. When her grandparents took her to the same store, Bella headed for the toy section, but not when she was with her parents. They said she was too old for toys.

If Bella scored well on a test, her parents bought her presents; a bad grade brought a clampdown at home. Her best subject was Chinese, where she had mastered the art of the composition: She could describe a household object in a morally uplifting way.

Last winter Grandmother left her spider plant outdoors and forgot about it.... This spring it actually lived. Some people say this plant is lowly, but the spider plant does not listen to arbitrary orders, it does not fear hardship, and in the face of adversity it continues to struggle. This spirit is worthy of praise.

She did poorly in math. Extra math tutoring was a constant and would remain so until the college entrance examination, which was seven years away. You were only as good as your worst subject. If you didn't get into one of Shanghai's top middle schools, your fate would be mediocre classmates and teachers who taught only what was in the textbook. Your chances of getting into a good high school, not to mention a good college, would diminish.

You had to keep moving, because staying in place meant falling behind. That was how the world worked even if you were only ten years old.

The past decade has seen the rise of a Chinese middle class, now estimated to number between 100 million and 150 million people. Though definitions vary—household income of at least $10,000 a year is one standard—middle-class families tend to own an apartment and a car, to eat out and take vacations, and to be familiar with foreign brands and ideas. They owe their well-being to the government's economic policies, but in private they can be very critical of the society they live in.

The state's retreat from private life has left people free to choose where to live, work, and travel, and material opportunities expand year by year. A decade ago most cars belonged to state enterprises; now many families own one. In 1998, when the government launched reforms to commercialize the housing market, it was the rare person who owned an apartment. Today home ownership is common, and prices have risen beyond what many young couples can afford—as if everything that happened in America over 50 years were collapsed into a single decade.

But pick up a Chinese newspaper, and what comes through is a sense of unease at the pace of social change. Over several months in 2006, these were some of the trends covered in the *Xinmin Evening News*, a popular Shanghai daily: High school girls were suffering from eating disorders. Parents were struggling to choose a suitable English name for their child. Teenage boys were reading novels with homosexual themes. Job seekers were besieging Buddhist temples because the word for "reclining Buddha," wofo, sounds like the English word "offer." Unwed college students were living together.

Parents struggle to teach their children but feel their own knowledge is obsolete; children, more attuned to social trends, guide their parents through the maze of modern life. "Society has completely turned around," says Zhou Xiaohong, a sociologist at Nanjing University who first noticed this phenomenon when his own father, a retired military officer, asked him how to knot a Western tie. "Fathers used to give orders, but now fathers listen to their sons."

Because their parents have such high hopes for them, children are among the most pressured, inhabiting a world that combines old and new and features the most punishing elements of both. The traditional examination system that selects a favored few for higher education remains intact: The number of students entering college in a given year is equal to 11 percent of the college-freshman-age population, compared with 64 percent in the United States. Yet the desire to foster well-rounded students has fed an explosion of activities—music lessons, English, drawing, and martial arts classes—and turned each into an arena of competition.

Such pursuits bring little pleasure. English ability is graded on five levels stretching through college, and parents push children to pass tests years ahead of schedule. Cities assess children's piano playing on a ten-level scale. More than half of preteens take outside classes, a survey found, with the top reason being "to raise the child's future competitiveness."

Parents tend to follow trends blindly and to believe most of what they hear. The past is a foreign country, and the present too. "We are a traditional family" was how Bella's mother, Qi Xiayun, introduced herself when I first met her in 2003. She was 33 years old with the small, pale face of a girl, and she spoke in a nonstop torrent about the difficulty of raising a child. She teaches computer classes at a vocational college; her husband works in quality control at Baosteel, a state-owned company. They were appointed to those jobs after college, as part of the last generation to join the socialist workforce before it started to break apart.

Bella's parents met the old-fashioned way, introduced by their parents. But after they had Bella in 1993, they turned their backs on tradition. They chose not to eat dinner with their in-laws every night and rejected old fashioned child-rearing methods that tend to coddle children.

When Bella was not yet two, her grandmother offered to care for the baby, but her mother worried that the grandparents would spoil her. Bella went to day care instead. When she entered third grade, her mother stopped picking her up after school, forcing her to change buses and cross streets alone. "Sooner or later she must learn independence," her mother said.

So Bella grew up, a chatty girl with Pippi Longstocking pigtails and many opinions—too many for the Chinese schoolroom. In second grade she and several classmates marched to the principal's office to demand more time to play; the protest failed. Her teachers criticized her temper and her tendency to bully other children. "Your ability is strong," read a first-grade report card, "but a person must learn from the strengths of others in order to improve." In second grade: "Hope you can listen to other people's opinions more."

The effort to shape Bella is full of contradictions. Her parents encourage her independence but worry that school and the workplace will punish her for it. They fret over her homework load, then pile more assignments on top of her regular schoolwork. "We don't want to be brutal to her," says Bella's father, Zhou Jiliang. "But in China, the environment doesn't let you do anything else."

Bella teaches her parents the latest slang and shows them cool Internet sites. When they bought a new television, Bella chose the brand. When they go out to eat, Bella picks Pizza Hut. One day soon, her parents worry, her schoolwork will move beyond their ability to help her. When Bella was younger, her parents began unplugging the computer keyboard and mouse so she wouldn't go online when she was home alone, but they knew this wouldn't last.

Recently, Bella's father and his sister and cousins put their grandfather in a nursing home. It was a painful decision; in traditional China, caring for aged parents was an ironclad responsibility, and Bella's parents have extra room in their apartment for their parents to move in some day. But Bella announced that she would one day put her parents in the best nursing home.

"The minute she said that, I thought: It's true, we don't want to be a burden on her," Bella's father says. "When we are old, we'll sell the house, take a trip and see the world, and enter the nursing home and live a quiet life there. This is the education my daughter gives me."

I went to school with Bella one Friday in her fifth-grade year. She sat up in bed at 6:25, pulled on pants and an orange sweatshirt, and tied a Young Pioneers kerchief around her neck. Her parents rushed through the cramped apartment getting ready for work, and breakfast was lost in the shuffle. Bella's mother walked her to the corner, then Bella sighed and headed to the bus stop alone. "This is the most free I am the whole day."

Today there would be elections for class cadres, positions that mirror those in the Communist Party. "My mother says to be a cadre in fifth grade is very important," Bella said.

The bus dropped us off at the elite Yangpu Primary School, which cost $1,200 a year in tuition and fees and rejected 80 percent of its applicants. Her classroom was sunny and loud with the roar of children kept indoors. It had several computers and a bulletin board with student-written movie reviews: *The Birth of New China, Finding Nemo*.

By 8:30 the students were seated at their desks for elections. Their pretty young teacher asked for candidates. Everyone wanted to run.

"This semester I want to change my bad nail-biting habits, so people don't call me the Nail- Biting King," said a boy running for propaganda officer.

"I will not interrupt in class," said a girl in a striped sweater running for children's officer. "Please everyone vote for me."

The speeches followed a set pattern: Name a personal flaw, pledge to fix it, and ask for votes. It was self-criticism as campaign strategy.

Those who strayed from the script were singled out. "My grades are not very good because I write a lot of words wrong," said one girl running for academic officer. "Please everyone vote for me."

"You write words wrong, please vote for me?" the teacher mimicked. "What have you left out?"

The girl tried again. "I want to work to fix this bad habit. Please everyone vote for me."

Bella delivered her pitch for sports officer. "I am very responsible, and my management abilities are pretty good," she said breathlessly. "Sometimes I have conflicts with other students. If you vote for me, it will help me change my bad habits. Please everyone give me your vote."

In a three-way race, Bella squeaked to victory by a single ballot. Election day, like everything in school, ended with a moral. "Don't feel bad if you lost this time," the teacher said. "It just means you must work even harder. You shouldn't let yourself relax just because you lost."

The language of child education is Darwinian-grim. "The elections teach students to toughen themselves," Bella's teacher, Lu Yan, said over lunch in the teachers' cafeteria. "In the future they will face pressure and competition. They need to know how to face defeat."

Some schools link teacher pay to student test performance, and the pressure on teachers is intense. Bella's class had recently seen a drop in grades, and the teacher begged parents to help identify the cause. Lu Yan had just gotten her four-year college degree at night school and planned to study English next. All her colleagues were enrolled in outside classes; even the vice-principal took a weekend class on educational technology. A math teacher was fired three weeks into the school year because parents complained she covered too little material in class.

Life will not always feel like this. The next generation of parents, having grown up with choice and competition, may feel less driven to place all their hopes on their children. "Right now is the hardest time," says Wang Jie, a sociologist who is herself the mother of an only child. "In my generation we have both traditional and new ideas. Inside us the two worlds are at war."

In math class later that day, the fifth graders whipped through dividing decimals using Math Olympics methods, which train kids to use mental shortcuts. They raced across a field in gym class, with the slowest person in each group punished with an extra lap around the track. School ended at 1:30 on Fridays. The bus let Bella off outside her building, where she bought a Popsicle and headed inside. Her weekend was packed with private tutoring, so Friday was the best time to finish her homework.

I told her that no American ten-year-old did homework on a Friday afternoon.

"They must be very happy," Bella said.

In the five years since I met Bella and her family, their lives have transformed. They moved into a new three-bedroom apartment—it is almost twice the size of their old one, which they now rent out—and furnished it with foreign brand-name appliances. They bought their first car, a Volkswagen Bora, and from taking the bus they went straight to driving everywhere. They eat out a couple of times a week now, and the air-conditioner stays on all summer. At age 12, Bella got her first mobile phone—a $250 Panasonic clamshell in Barbie pink. Her parents' annual income reached $18,000, up 40 percent from when we first met.

As the material circumstances of Bella's family improved, the world became to them a more perilous place. Their cleaning lady stole from them and disappeared. Several friends were in near-fatal car accidents. One day Bella's father saw her holding a letter from a man she'd met online. Bella's parents changed the locks and the phone number of the apartment. Her father drove her to and from school now because he thought the neighborhood around it was unsafe.

Bella's mother took on more administrative responsibilities at work and enrolled in a weekend class to qualify to study for a master's degree. Bella's father talked about trading in their car for a newer model with better acceleration and more legroom. They frequently spoke of themselves as if they were mobile phones on the verge of obsolescence. "If you don't continue to upgrade and recharge," Bella's father said, "you'll be eliminated."

Social mobility ran in both directions. A friend of Bella's mother stopped attending class reunions because he was embarrassed to be a security guard. A company run by a family friend went bankrupt, and his daughter, who was Bella's age, started buying clothes at discount stalls. Society was splintering based on small differences. Family members only a decade younger than Bella's parents inhabited another world. One cousin ate out every night and left her baby in the care of her grandparents so she could focus on her career. Bella's father's younger sister, who was childless, thought nothing of buying a full-fare plane ticket to go somewhere for a weekend. Friends who were private entrepreneurs were having a second child and paying a fine; Bella's parents would probably be fired by their state-owned employers if they did that.

Bella tested into one of Shanghai's top middle schools, where teachers often keep students past five in the evening while their parents wait in cars outside. She is level three in English and level eight in piano. She still ranks in the middle of her class, but she no longer has faith in the world of adults.

She disdains class elections now. "It's a lot of work," she says, "and the teacher is always pointing to you as a role model. If you get in trouble and get demoted, it's a big embarrassment." She loves Hollywood films—especially *Star Wars* and disaster movies—and spends hours online with friends discussing Detective Conan, a character from Japanese comic books.

Her parents no longer help with her homework; in spoken English she has surpassed them. They lecture her to be less wasteful. "When she was little, she agreed with all my opinions. Now she sits there without saying anything, but I know she doesn't agree with me," her mother said one afternoon in the living room of their new apartment, as Bella glared without speaking. "Our child-raising has been a failure." In China, there is no concept of the rebellious teenager.

Across Chinese society, parents appear completely at sea when it comes to raising their children. Newspapers run advice columns, their often rudimentary counsel—"Don't Forcibly Plan Your Child's Life" is a typical headline—suggesting what many parents are up against. Some schools have set up parent schools where mothers, and the occasional father, can share frustrations and child-raising tips.

At times educators go to extremes: At the Zhongguancun No. 2 Primary School in Beijing, vice-principal Lu Suqin recently took two fifth-grade boys into her home. "Their parents couldn't get them to behave, so they asked me to take them," she explains. "After they learn disciplined living, I will send them back."

Bella had one free day during the 2006 weeklong National Day holiday. Some of her extended family—seven adults and two children—took a trip to Tongli, a town of imperial mansions an hour's drive from Shanghai. Bella's father hired a minibus and driver for the trip; a friend had just been in a car accident and broken all the bones on one side of his body. Bella sat alone reading a book.

Developing China zipped past the window, city sprawl giving way to a booming countryside of fish ponds and factories and the three-story houses of prosperous farmers. Bella's mother indulged in the quintessential urban dream of a house in the country. "You have your own little yard in front," she said. "I'd love to live in a place like that when we retire."

She was thinking seriously about Bella's future. If she tested into a good college, she should stay in China; otherwise she would go abroad, and they would sell the old apartment to pay for it. She had decided that Bella could date in college. "If she finds someone suitable in the third or fourth year of college, that's fine. But not in the first or second year."

"And not in high school?" I asked.

"No. Study should be most important."

Tongli was mobbed with holiday visitors. Bella's family walked through its courtyards and gardens like sleepwalkers, admiring whatever the tour guides pointed out. They touched the trunk of the

Health and Long Life Tree. They circled a stone mosaic said to bring career success. They could not stop walking for an instant because crowds pressed in from behind. It was the biggest tourist day of the year.

Bella politely translated for a great-aunt visiting from Australia who didn't speak Chinese, but it was just an act. "This is boring," she told me. "Once you've seen one old building, you've seen them all."

I sat with her on the ride home. She was deep into a Korean romance novel.

"It's about high school students," she said. "Three boys chasing a girl."

"Do people have boyfriends and girlfriends in high school?" I asked.

"Yes."

"What about middle school?"

"Yes. Some."

"Do you have a boyfriend?"

She wrinkled her nose. "There's a boy who likes me. But all the boys in my grade are very low-class."

She wanted to go to Australia for graduate school and to work there afterward.

Some observers of Chinese society look at children like Bella and see the potential change her generation may bring to society. But the reality is complicated. Raised and educated in a half-traditional half-modern way, they are just as likely to find ways to accommodate themselves to it, as they have done all along.

"Just because they're curious to see something doesn't mean they want it for themselves," says Zhang Kai, Bella's middle-school teacher. "Maybe they will try something—dye their hair, or pierce an ear—but in their bones, they are very traditional. In her heart Zhou Jiaying is very traditional," he says, and he uses Bella's Chinese name.

Bella is 15 now, in the ninth grade. She has good friends among her classmates, and she has learned how to get along with others. School is a complicated place. One classmate bullied another boy, and the victim's parents came to school to complain.

The incident divided Bella's class, and now her friends in the Tire Clique won't speak to her friends in the Pirate Clique.

Bella's teacher nominated some students for membership in the Communist Youth League. Bella was not very interested in it, but she fell into line and pulled an application essay off the Internet. She couldn't afford to get on her teacher's bad side, she told me, citing a proverb: "A person who stands under someone else's roof must bow his head."

The high school entrance exam is a month away. In the evenings Bella's father watches television on mute so he won't disturb her studies. A good friend is also an enemy because they vie for the same class rank. Her compositions describe what the pressure feels like:

I sit in my middle-school classroom, and the teacher wants us to say good-bye to childhood. I feel at a loss. Happiness is like the twinkling stars suffusing the night sky of childhood. I want only more and more stars. I don't want to see the dawn.

☑ Text 2 Symphony of millions

(Abridged)

By Alex Ross

Taking Stock of the Chinese Music Boom

In March, Chen Qigang, a Chinese composer who is supervising the music program for the opening ceremony of the 2008 Summer Olympics, received a National Spirit Achievers Award at a press event in Beijing. He was one of ten artists and businesspeople to receive the prize, which came courtesy of the Chinese magazine *Life* and of Mercedes-AMG, the high-performance-vehicle division of Mercedes-Benz. The award ceremony, typical of modern China in its mixture of nationalist bombast, materialist excess, and cultural bizarrerie, took place in the 798 art zone—a cavernous factory complex that has been converted into exhibition space. Four AMG vehicles were on display, surrounded by models clad in silver-lamé outfits, in presumably inadvertent homage to "Goldfinger." Projected on the walls and the ceiling of the factory were the words "Will,"

"Power," and "Dream," with Chinese characters to match. "We believe that Mercedes-AMG will infuse powerful new vigor into China's national car culture," Klaus Maier, the head of Mercedes-Benz China, said. Chen stood to one side, a quizzical expression on his face. Before the ceremony began, he had said to me, "I have no idea what is happening."

While classical musicians around the world fight for a glimmer of media attention, their counterparts in China have no trouble drawing the spotlight. Western classical music is big business, or, at least, official business. Chen Qigang, a mild-mannered fifty-two-year-old whose works elegantly fuse Western-modernist and traditional Chinese elements, was reminded of this last year, when he moved from Paris, where he had resided since 1984, back to Beijing. In Paris, he had grown accustomed to a culture in which the same small cohort of connoisseurs attended new-music concerts night after night. On a visit to Beijing last year, Chen was summoned to meet the film director Zhang Yimou, who made "Hero" and "House of Flying Daggers," and who is in charge of the Olympic ceremonies. Zhang inquired if Chen had any "free time" in 2008. Chen agreed, and accepted an offer to run the music program, not only because he felt official pressure but because he relished the challenge of directing a retinue of fifty composers, from both classical and popular genres, to entertain a global audience. In America, he noted, no classical composer would be given such a task.

"For the past fifteen or twenty years, classical music has been very à la mode in China," Chen told me, in French. "The halls are full. There are many students. There might also be some difficulties. But there is a very powerful phenomenon at work in the education system. When I visited my old primary school, I found that, out of a class of forty students, thirty-six were studying piano. This points to the future."

Western musicians, administrators, and critics who visit China have lately come away murmuring observations along the lines of "classical music is exploding" and "the future of classical music lies in China." Between thirty million and a hundred million children are said to be learning piano, violin, or both, depending on which source you consult. When the New York Philharmonic was in Beijing last February, on the eve of its heralded visit to North Korea, the Associated Press offered this summary of a press conference given by Lorin Maazel: "Facing dwindling popularity in the West, classical music could receive a boost from a large Chinese population that is increasingly interested in other cultures, the music director of the New York Philharmonic said." Chinese virtuosos and composers crowd New York halls. In April, the Philharmonic presented the première of Tan Dun's Piano Concerto, with Lang Lang as the soloist; shortly afterward, the Metropolitan Opera revived Tan's 2006 opera, "The First Emperor," with Plácido Domingo in the title role.

After a recent visit to Beijing, I had some doubts about China's putative lock on the musical future. Concert halls may be full and conservatories mobbed, but classical music is hobbled by commercial pressures. The creative climate, heavily influenced the development of China's musical institutions. At the same time, the wider soundscape of Beijing is as chaotically rich as that of any Western city: nights of experimental music, indie-rock shows soaked in hipster attitude, pop idols cavorting on HD monitors in malls, retirees singing Peking opera in parks. In the "Li Chi," or "Book of Rites," it is written, "The music of a well-ruled state is peaceful and joyous ... that of a country in confusion is full of resentment ... and that of a dying country is mournful and pensive." All three kinds of music, together with others that might well have confounded Confucian scholars, intersect in the People's Republic.

The most outwardly impressive symbol of China's musical ambition is the National Center for the Performing Arts, a colossal, low-slung, titanium-clad dome west of Tiananmen Square. An inscription above the center's entrance bears the signature of Jiang Zemin, who was China's President from 1993 to 2003, and made a show of admiring classical music. (After the death of Deng Xiaoping, Jiang told the press that he had consoled himself by listening to Mozart's Requiem through the night.) The president of the center, which Beijingers call the Egg, is a local potentate named Chen Ping, who has developed deluxe shopping malls in the eastern part of the city. The complex was originally scheduled to open in 2004, but Paul Andreu, the architect, had to reëvaluate the design after another of his projects, a terminal at Charles de Gaulle International Airport, partially collapsed. At the opening, which finally took place at the end of last year, Chen Ping described the building as a "concrete example of China's rising soft power."

As architecture, the building may live up to its pompous billing, but, as a place for music, the Egg is problematic. There are two main halls: the opera house, which seats twenty-four hundred, and the concert hall, which seats two thousand. The concert hall has reasonably clear acoustics but lacks warmth. In the top gallery of the opera house, where the sound should be best, the orchestra comes across as tinny and colorless. There is little evidence that musical considerations played a role in the design. No serious acoustician would have approved the halls' pockets of extra space, where sound bounces around and gets lost.

The performances themselves suffered in comparison with what you hear on even a so-so night in New York. They showed the inevitable limitations of a classical culture that is less than a century old. China's music-education system may yield notable soloists, but it has yet to develop the breadth of talent and the collaborative mentality that engender great orchestras. Strings are generally polished; winds and brass threaten to puncture the ears. On my first visit to the Egg, I saw a production of "Turandot" featuring the orchestra and the chorus of the Shanghai Opera

House. The trumpets let out a piercing flubbed note in the first bar, and many misadventures followed; at times, it sounded as though a civic orchestra had been augmented by members of a high-school marching band. Yet the raucousness was oddly arresting. The idea of the production was to reclaim Puccini's Italianized, Romanticized fantasy of imperial China; Chen Xinyi, the director, emulated the values of traditional Chinese theatre, and the composer Hao Weiya supplied a fluid if somewhat watery ending for the opera, which Puccini left unfinished at his death. In that sense, the rawness of the sound added to the effect, though it wasn't an experience I'd want to repeat.

Near-capacity crowds attended "Turandot" and other events I saw at the Egg. This was impressive, considering the cost of the tickets; for a seat in the uppermost gallery of the opera house, I paid four hundred and eighty yuan—about seventy dollars. That price is considerably higher than for an equivalent seat at the Metropolitan Opera, and vertiginously high when you consider that a low-level white-collar worker at a Chinese firm earns only about four hundred dollars a month. But not everyone has to pay to get in. Large blocks of tickets are set aside for politicians, diplomats, C.E.O.s, and corporate clients; some fail to show up, resulting in rows of empty seats at allegedly sold-out events, and others make an early exit to attend another function or to escape boredom. One Beijing composer told me scornfully that much of the audience was "scouting real estate," and that it would disappear once its curiosity had been satisfied.

It was encouraging, however, to see so many young people in the house—many more than you see on an average night at the Met or the New York Philharmonic. At a performance by the China National Symphony Orchestra, under the direction of Michel Plasson, I watched as a cluster of teen-agers, outfitted with bejewelled BlackBerrys, A.P.C. jeans, and other tokens of new wealth, grew excited by the orchestra's noisily energetic rendition of Berlioz's "Symphonie Fantastique," leaving aside their text-messaging to applaud each movement. In general, listeners behaved more informally than I was used to: some older people, following the looser etiquette of Peking opera, talked among themselves, pointed at the stage, or read newspapers. The hubbub was distracting at times—ushers largely failed to prevent the taking of pictures and videos—but it was refreshing in comparison with the self-conscious solemnity that encroaches on Western concert halls. The music wasn't taken for granted; Berlioz still had shock value.

The youthfulness of the audience at the Egg reflects the real wonder of the Chinese classical scene: the staggering number of people who are currently studying music, whether in schools or with private tutors. The Sichuan Conservatory, in Chengdu, is said to have more than ten thousand students; Juilliard, by contrast, has eight hundred. An American high-school student who practices piano several hours a day is apt to be pegged something of a freak; in China, such a routine is commonplace.

The violist Qi Yue, a young professor at Renmin University, explained to me the various factors that are driving the surge in music lessons. For one thing, students who demonstrate musical gifts can get away with scoring fewer points on the gaokao, China's college-admissions test, not unlike athletes in the United States. Also, the conservatory system has a history of fostering pop stars, who prompt legions of imitators. Cui Jian, the founder of Chinese rock, played trumpet in the Beijing Symphony in the nineteeneighties before embarking on a pop career. The Sichuan Conservatory famously produced the pop singer Li Yuchun, who, in 2005, entered as a contestant on "Super Girl," a Chinese version of "American Idol," and won the competition with a hip-hop-flavored, gender-bending style.

Qi took me on a tour of the Central Conservatory, China's flagship music school, in the company of his former teacher, the violist Wing Ho. Familiar airs wafted out of the practice rooms—Chopin from the pianists, Rossini from the singers, Tchaikovsky from the violinists. When I looked in on a composition class, though, it turned out to be a lesson in pop-music arranging. A shaggy-haired, T-shirt-clad student named Zhang Tianye was leaning over a computer terminal, working on a mix of drums, guitar, piano, and bass. When I asked him what music he likes, he said he listened "mostly to pop, sometimes classical." Another student, Qu Dawei, sat down at the piano to execute a half-Romantic, half-jazzy solo somewhat in the manner of Gershwin. In other words, attending a conservatory in China doesn't automatically equate with interest in classical music. Yet the intermingling of genres may have the healthy effect of integrating European tradition into the wider culture.

Like most serious Chinese musicians, Qi Yue politely rejected the notion of China as a classical paradise, although he predicted that it would become a major market in twenty or thirty years. Long Yu, China's most prominent conductor, felt much the same way. "On the outside, newspapers are saying that China is the largest musical country in the world, or that millions of kids are learning piano," he told me. "I'm not that optimistic. The thing is, I do my best to serve the people who really need fine arts and classical music. I do not have the duty to make everyone like it." A German-trained musician who operates with a kind of bulldozer charm, Long Yu directs the Beijing Music Festival, has built the China Philharmonic into China's finest orchestra, and holds posts in Guangzhou and Shanghai. Also, he serves on the Chinese People's Political Consultative Conference. Nonetheless, he keeps a certain distance from the notion of classical music as "official culture"; he has sought funding from private sources and tried to keep ticket prices down.

Western music formally arrived in China in 1601, when the Jesuit missionary Matteo Ricci presented a clavichord to Wanli, the longest-ruling of the Ming emperors. As Sheila Melvin and Jindong Cai relate, in their absorbing book "Rhapsody in Red: How Western Classical Music Became Chinese," the Emperor's eunuchs experimented with the instrument for a little while and then set it aside. It stayed undisturbed in a box for several decades, until Chongzhen, the last of the Ming rulers, discovered it and sought out a German Jesuit priest to explain its workings. Of succeeding emperors, Kangxi and Qianlong showed the most enthusiasm for Western music; the latter, who ruled China for the better part of the eighteenth century, at one point assembled a full-scale chamber orchestra, with the eunuchs dressed in European suits and wigs.

Only in the nineteenth century did Western music really spread beyond the walls of the imperial palaces, often in the form of military and municipal bands. The first true orchestra was the Shanghai Municipal Orchestra (later the Shanghai Symphony), which began playing in 1919, under the direction of an expatriate Italian virtuoso named Mario Paci. At first, the orchestra had only foreign players and stayed within the bounds of Shanghai's colonial settlements, but Paci eventually reached out to the Chinese population. In 1927, Xiao Youmei, a German-trained pianist and composer, founded the Shanghai Conservatory, the first Western-style music school on Chinese soil. The growth of the Shanghai musical scene profited from a lively community of adventurers, exiles, and, with the rise of Nazism, German-Jewish refugees; on the faculty of the Shanghai Conservatory were associates of Arnold Schoenberg and Alban Berg.

The imported music was initially encouraged after the People's Republic of China was founded in 1949. In the library of the Central Conservatory, I looked at back issues of People's Music, a house journal whose first issue appeared in 1950, the year that the conservatory was founded. There were lyrics for songs called "We Are Busy Producing" and "The Little Song of Handing in Your Grains." Composers made fitful attempts to modernize their art by applying appropriate foreign principles and use foreign musical instruments, especially during the Hundred Flowers period.

The Central Conservatory was effectively shut down in 1966. Western classical music was pushed out, along with most of the native traditions from the imperial era. To replace the extant repertory, a group of eight "model" scores on revolutionary topics was created. The most famous of these was the ballet "Red Detachment of Women," which has a charming score in a light-classical vein, with an array of native-Chinese sounds.

When the Central Conservatory reopened, in 1978, eighteen thousand people applied for a hundred places. Present in that first class was a group of composers who define contemporary Chinese music today: Tan Dun, Chen Yi, Zhou Long, Chen Qigang, and Guo Wenjing. Under the guidance of various visiting mentors, these composers westernized themselves at high speed, consuming serialism, chance procedures, and other novelties. In so doing, they came up with fresh and vital combinations of sounds, especially when they added to the mix the clear-cut melodies and jangling timbres of traditional Chinese music.

A diaspora followed. Chen Qigang went to Paris to study with Olivier Messiaen. Tan Dun, Chen Yi, and Zhou Long travelled to New York to work with Chou Wen-chung; all three took up residence in the city. Tan quickly gravitated to New York's downtown scene, particularly to the world of John Cage. By combining Cage's chance processes and natural noises with plush Romantic melodies, Tan concocted a kind of crowd-pleasing avant-gardism. In March, at the Egg, he demonstrated that sensibility with a concert of "Organic Music," with the China Youth Symphony; in "Paper Concerto" and "Water Concerto," the Japanese percussionist Haruka Fujii crinkled paper and swished water in amplified bowls and other receptacles. In a further feat of packaging, Tan relates this music to shamanistic rituals of Hunan province, where he grew up. With such deft gestures of fusion, Tan has satisfied a Western craving for authentic-seeming, folklore-based music.

Many of the 78 composers have worked to reconcile avant-garde and populist values. "In the West, our situation as composers is very sad," Chen Qigang told me. "In the nineteen-fifties, we lost command of the field, not just because popular composers took over but because we ceded the terrain. We 'developed' to the point where we no longer knew anything about the art of writing melody. We had a kind of nonexistence in musical life." Nodding to his Olympics experience, he added, "Now I understand how hard it is to compose a cheery little song."

After several days in Beijing I received an invitation to brunch at the home of the singer Hao Jiang Tian and his wife, the geneticist and pianist Martha Liao. They also invited Guo Wenjing, who, of the composers of the 1978 generation, is the one least known in the West, principally because he never studied abroad.

Guo makes an unassuming first impression. Although he is fifty-two years old, he looks like a perpetual graduate student, his squarish face set off by heavy-rimmed glasses and a serrated edge of jet-black hair. But a certain wildness in his personality quickly emerges. He comes from Chongqing, in Sichuan province. His conversation has a slightly percussive edge, accentuated with sweeping gestures and abrupt exclamations.

At the core of Guo's work is an encyclopedic sympathy for Chinese traditional music. In the nineteen-eighties, he collected folk songs in the mountains around the upper Yangtze River. His hero was Béla Bartók, who immersed himself in Eastern European folk music in the early twentieth century and adopted its irregular rhythms and harsh effects. Guo was also drawn to Dmitri Shostakovich, master of the Soviet symphony; Guo's mature works, with their martial rhythms, flashes of biting wit, and explosive climaxes, have much in common with Shostakovich's, even if the musical material is drastically different.

For a time, Guo chaired the composition department at the Central Conservatory. He stepped down because, he said curtly, "I'm not good at multitasking." He still teaches, although he is discouraged by the tendency among younger Chinese composers to copy European trends in order to establish their academic bona fides. "Say there is a young composer who writes in the style of one of Jiang Qing's revolutionary operas," he said. "Today, others would criticize him because he does not sound like Luciano Berio. But I would say, 'Look, he had the guts to do something that everyone criticizes him for. There must be something good about him.'"

In fact, Guo is carrying on, with far greater subtlety, a musical idea that dominated the revolutionary years: melding Western technique with Chinese tradition. Theatre pieces such as "Wolf Cub Village" and "Poet Li Bai" and symphonic pieces like "Chou Kong Shan" ("Sorrowful, Desolate Mountain") and "Suspended Ancient Coffins on the Cliffs in Sichuan" confront listeners with gritty, grinding sonorities, battering assaults of percussion, exuberant bashings and roarings of gongs, and, in the operas, extreme vocal techniques representing extreme psychological states. If Guo strays at times on the wrong side of the divide between ritual grandeur and monotony, he invariably has a strong impact. Some lines from "Poet Li Bai," which chronicles one of the great free spirits of Taoism, seem to sum him up: "Wild and free / Like my poetry / Would I stoop before men of power, / And deny myself a pleasant hour?"

At brunch, Guo was in a sunny mood, but at one point I succeeded in annoying him. Speaking of the music of Chen Qigang, I said that its refined, free-floating timbres suggested a strong affinity between modern Chinese composition and the sound-world of Debussy and Messiaen. Guo swept his arms wide, nearly upsetting the tableware, and proclaimed, "This view shows that foreigners don't understand China. Music here has nothing to do with France. Opposite direction. Different taste." Then he smiled, his argument made. He held up two stubby fingers in the air, as if about to give a blessing. "I am anti-fashion. I look down on the trend. I want to escape the whole question of sounding like the West or sounding like the East. Non-European composers always have to have their cultural identity, their symbols."

The curious thing about the Chinese enthusiasm for Western classical music is that the People's Republic, with its far-flung provinces and myriad ethnic groups, possesses a store of musical traditions that rival in intricacy the proudest products of Europe, and go back much deeper in time.

Holding to core principles in the face of change, traditional Chinese music is more "classical" than anything in the West.

In many of Beijing's public spaces, you see amateurs playing native instruments, especially the dizi, or bamboo flute, and the erhu, or two-stringed fiddle. They perform mostly for their own pleasure, not for money. But it's surprisingly difficult to find professional performances in strict classical style. In concert halls, the instruments are often deposited, as a sonic spice, into Western-style arrangements, as in the "Genghis Khan" symphony I heard at the Egg. Institutionalized "Chinese orchestras" imitate the layout of Western ensembles. Music intended for intimate spaces has been fleshed out, amplified, and transformed into spectacles suitable for national television. A colleague reports that an allegedly authentic evening of Chinese music in Shanghai ended, bafflingly, with a chunk of Mahler's Second Symphony. Those who remain devoted to the ancient traditions often struggle to show their relevance in the age of "Super Girl." Some master instrumentalists teach at the conservatories but seldom play in public. Even Peking opera, which attracts sizable crowds, feels the pressure. When, earlier this year, the Ministry of Education introduced a new program to foster interest in Peking opera among the young, a poll found that more than fifty per cent opposed the initiative as a waste of resources.

The project of revitalizing Chinese tradition has fallen to younger artists like Wu Na, who, at the age of thirty, has mastered what some consider the supreme aristocrat of instruments: the guqin, or seven-stringed zither. It is more than three thousand years old, and has a repertory that reaches back to the first millennium. Philosophers and poets from Confucius to Li Bai prided themselves on learning it. In the modern era, the guqin has become somewhat esoteric, though interest is growing again. With the support of an elderly Taiwanese couple, Wu runs a guqin school at a teahouse in Zhongshan Park, in Beijing. When I stopped by, two college students were seated at their instruments, imitating their instructor's moves. Wu herself wasn't there; she was in New York, on a fellowship from the Asian Cultural Council. After I returned home, I visited her at her temporary apartment, in Chelsea. When I walked in, she was listening to a recording of Liu Shaochun. It is music of intimate address and subtle power that is able to suggest immense spaces; skittering figures and arching melodies give way to sustained, slowly decaying tones and long, meditative pauses.

Despite her fastidious attention to guqin technique, Wu also loves avant-garde music and jazz. There is a vague likeness between the art of guqin and Western experimental music: the scores indicate tunings, fingerings, and articulations but fail to specify rhythms, resulting in markedly different interpretations by performers of competing schools. Wu sometimes plays in the "old times" style, as she calls it, and sometimes adopts a kind of cool, modal jazz approach; either way, she shows profound sensitivity to her instrument. She recently gave a concert at Roulette, an experimental space in downtown Manhattan, in collaboration with a vocalist and a dancer. Old and new merged in a mesmerizing whole.

When Wu Na returns to Beijing, later this summer, she hopes to develop a cross-cultural exchange that will bring traditional Chinese masters to New York and jazz and blues musicians to Beijing. She noted that audiences in Beijing have little grasp of African-American music in its classic, early-twentieth-century forms. And I realized that, while I had gone around Beijing looking for "authentic" Chinese music, she had been doing the same in New York, searching, with little success, for old-time jazz and blues.

On a day when the center of Beijing was overrun by Olympic hullabaloo—in front of the Gate of Heavenly Peace, the Olympic torch was lit, to the accompaniment of Hollywoodish fanfares—I went for a walk in the august sprawl of the Temple of Heaven complex, and saw a sign pointing to the "Divine Music Administration." No such place existed in my guidebook, but I followed the arrows nonetheless. After going around in circles for a while, I came upon a series of buildings where court musicians of the Ming dynasty once rehearsed. The buildings had recently been renovated, most of the rooms filled with exhibitions on Chinese musical history. One could bang replicas of ancient bronze bells and strum on a guqin. A young attendant was standing by. When I asked a question, she proceeded to play the guqin with expert grace. She seemed grateful for the attention; in the past hour, I had been the museum's only visitor.

Then I heard music—not recorded music but the real thing, a slow, grand, forbiddingly austere procession of sonorities. It emanated from behind the closed doors of a hall in the center of the complex. I cracked open the door, but an attendant shooed me away. "Not allowed," she said. I walked over to the box office and asked if a public performance was scheduled; the man behind the counter shook his head vigorously and said, "No music." Just when I was preparing to give up, I saw a van approaching. Twenty or so well-dressed Chinese tourists piled out. Guessing that they were headed into the hall, I slipped into their midst, and made it through the doors.

A half-hour performance ensued, with a full complement of Chinese instruments, and players dressed in vividly colored courtly garb. It was a sound at once rigid and brilliant, precise in attack and vibrant in delivery. It was the most remarkable musical experience of my trip. At the time, I didn't quite know what I was hearing, but I later surmised that I had witnessed a re-creation of zhonghe shaoyue, the music that resounded at the temple while the emperor made sacrifices to Heaven. Confucius, in the Analects, calls it yayue—"elegant music"—and laments that the people are discarding it in favor of vernacular tunes. Now it is a ghost in a phantom museum.

I walked for another hour in the temple park, thrilled to have had an aural glimpse of what I took to be the true music of China. A little later, I heard a wistful melody coming from an unseen bamboo flute, and went in search of its source, hoping for another revelation. After making my way through a maze of pine trees, I found a man of great age and haunted visage, playing the theme from "The Godfather."

Classroom activities
Class competition: Timed text analysis

1. The lead indicates that the article is about China's middle class. After reading the first paragraph, do you still think the author's focus is the 1st generation of middle class in China? Or is there another group of people that better attract the author's attention?

2. What does the title "Gilded age, gilded cage" mean?

3. What troubles the first-generation middle class in China most? And what troubles the generation represented by Bella? What caused their anxieties?

4. How does the first-generation middle class differ from the next generation in adapting to the rapid social change?

5. What is western people's common view on the generation represented by Bella? What is the author's view on them and their future?

6. It can be inferred that the author considers the generation represented by Bella both traditional and modern. Do you agree with the author? This view can lead to another interpretation of "Gilded age, Gilded cage". Can you find what it is?

7. How many parts can the article be divided into? Can you summarize the main idea of each part? What is the main theme of the article?

8. The author cites other people from time to time. Locate all quotes from Bella and analyze the author's intention lying behind each quote.

1. The article is taken from *The New Yorker*, a magazine for American upper middle class. Classical music, represented by Symphony, is one of the common hobbies among those people. How do you understand the title "Symphony of millions"?

2. What is the dominant tone of the article hinted in the first paragraph?

3. What is the author's view on the boom of western classical music in China? What are the author's arguments to fortify his viewpoint?

4. What does the author think of the idea of popularizing classical music?

5. The author visited some Chinese musicians during his stay in China. What music do those musicians work on? Why does the author introduce them to readers?

6. What music should be promoted in China according to the author? And why?

7. What message is conveyed by the final image (an old man playing the bamboo flute) in the article?

Group discussion and presentation

The two articles are both observational essays. In this kind of writing, the author presents his ideas through a descriptive account of his personal observation of people or events concerned. His insights are usually hidden behind the telling of other people's stories or experiences and seldom directly shown. This increases reading difficulty. Each group needs to select some typical observational paragraphs or identify some particular observational details in the two texts and analyze the author's implied meaning in each case.

For example, the underlined phrases in Text 1 "with Pippi Longstocking pigtails and many opinions" and "The Birth of New China, Finding Nemo" echo each other to imply that children from China's middle class families are partially traditional and partially modern. "Pigtails" and "The Birth of New China" are images representing the traditional part in those children, while "opinions" and "Finding Nemo" are signs of westernization.

Class discussion

1. The two articles show novel opinions on China's emerging middle class and the western classical music boom in China. Instead of joining other's voices in praise, the authors show discreet worries about social and musical prosperity in China. Do you think their worries or warnings are justified? What is your view on the two social phenomena?

2. Besides the two being addressed in this unit, can you name some other Chinese social phenomena that also excite western media's interest, especially those in recent years? Can you find some commonalities among them? What kind of social events are more likely to draw western people's attention?

Critical thinking

In observational essays, the author's viewpoints are not told, but rather shown to readers. The account of observed experiences makes the essay sound more realistic and opinions derived from it more objective and convincing. But observation does not necessarily grant an essay objectivity. Observational writing can also be subjective, or even biased. Analyze how the author stealthily influences readers' formation of views. How do you prevent your mind from being manipulated in reading observational essays.

Unit 10

Disputes over science

Pre-class reading tasks

In this unit, you will read two articles on popular science. Different from informative writing with the aim of introducing science and technology subjects to the general reader, the articles presented below are more interested in exploring impacts of science development on human life and proper attitudes towards it. So you need to collect both information and opinions while reading. The following tasks are designed to guide you through the reading process and prepare you for class discussion. Please finish them in collaboration with your group members before class.

Make some research on the classification of scientific writing. Which type(s) do the two articles below belong to? What are their features in terms of content, language, purpose, structure, etc.?

What do you expect to learn from the two articles after reading titles and lead-ins?

Write a reading outline for each article below.

Research the debate on raising the retirement age in China. Does Text 1 reshape your view on this issue? Prepare to present your group view in class.

☑ Text 1 What happens when we all live to 100?

By Gregg Easterbrook

If life-expectancy trends continue, that future may be near, transforming society in surprising and far-reaching ways.

For millennia, if not for eons—anthropology continuously pushes backward the time of human origin—life expectancy was short. The few people who grew old were assumed, because of their years, to have won the favor of the gods. The typical person was fortunate to reach 40.

Beginning in the 19th century, that slowly changed. Since 1840, life expectancy at birth has risen about three months with each passing year. In 1840, life expectancy at birth in Sweden, a much-studied nation owing to its record-keeping, was 45 years for women; today it's 83 years. The United States displays roughly the same trend. When the 20th century began, life expectancy at birth in America was 47 years; now newborns are expected to live 79 years. If about three months continue to be added with each passing year, by the middle of this century, American life expectancy at birth will be 88 years. By the end of the century, it will be 100 years.

Viewed globally, the lengthening of life spans seems independent of any single, specific event. It didn't accelerate much as antibiotics and vaccines became common. Nor did it retreat much during wars or disease outbreaks. A graph of global life expectancy over time looks like an escalator rising smoothly. The trend holds, in most years, in individual nations rich and poor; the whole world is riding the escalator.

Projections of ever-longer life spans assume no incredible medical discoveries—rather, that the escalator ride simply continues. If anti-aging drugs or genetic therapies are found, the climb could accelerate. Centenarians may become the norm, rather than rarities who generate a headline in the local newspaper.

Pie in the sky? On a verdant hillside in Marin County, California—home to hipsters and towering redwoods, the place to which the Golden Gate Bridge leads—sits the Buck Institute, the first private, independent research facility dedicated to extending the human life span. Since 1999, scientists and postdocs there have studied ways to make organisms live much longer, and with better health, than they naturally would. Already, the institute's researchers have quintupled the life span of laboratory worms. Most Americans have never heard of the Buck Institute, but someday this place may be very well known.

Buck is not alone in its pursuit. The University of Michigan, the University of Texas, and the University of California at San Francisco are studying ways to slow aging, as is the Mayo Clinic. Late in 2013, Google brought its trove of cash into the game, founding a spin-off called the California Life Company (known as Calico) to specialize in longevity research. Six months after Calico's charter was announced, Craig Venter, the biotech entrepreneur who in the 1990s conducted a dramatic race against government laboratories to sequence the human genome, also founded a start-up that seeks ways to slow aging.

Should research find a life-span breakthrough, the proportion of the U.S. population that is elderly—fated to rise anyway, considering declining fertility rates, the retirement of the Baby Boomers, and the continuing uplift of the escalator—may climb even more. Longer life has obvious appeal, but it entails societal risks. Politics may come to be dominated by the old, who might vote themselves ever more generous benefits for which the young must pay. Social Security and private pensions could be burdened well beyond what current actuarial tables suggest. If longer life expectancy simply leads to more years in which pensioners are disabled and demand expensive services, health-care costs may balloon as never before, while other social needs go unmet.

But the story might have a happy ending. If medical interventions to slow aging result in added years of reasonable fitness, life might extend in a sanguine manner, with most men and women living longer in good vigor, and also working longer, keeping pension and health-care subsidies under control. Indeed, the most-exciting work being done in longevity science concerns making the later years vibrant, as opposed to simply adding time at the end.

Postwar medical research has focused on specific conditions: there are heart-disease laboratories, cancer institutes, and so on. Traditional research assumes the chronic later-life diseases that are among the nation's leading killers—cardiovascular blockage, stroke, Alzheimer's—arise individually and should be treated individually. What if, instead, aging is the root cause of many chronic diseases, and aging can be slowed? Not just life span but "health span" might increase.

Drugs that lengthen health span are becoming to medical researchers what vaccines and antibiotics were to previous generations in the lab: their grail. If health-span research is successful, pharmaceuticals as remarkable as those earlier generations of drugs may result. In the process, society might learn the answer to an ancient mystery: Given that every cell in a mammal's body contains the DNA blueprint of a healthy young version of itself, why do we age at all?

"Here in our freezers we have 100 or so compounds that extend life in invertebrates," says Gordon Lithgow, a geneticist at the Buck Institute. He walks with me through labs situated on a campus of modernistic buildings that command a dreamlike view of San Pablo Bay, and encourage dreamlike thoughts. The 100 compounds in the freezer? "What we don't know is if they work in people."

The Buck Institute bustles with young researchers. Jeans and San Francisco 49ers caps are common sights—this could be a Silicon Valley software start-up were not microscopes, cages, and biological-isolation chambers ubiquitous. The institute is named for Leonard and Beryl Buck, a Marin County couple who left oil stocks to a foundation charged with studying why people age, among other issues. When the institute opened, medical research aimed at slowing aging was viewed as quixotic—the sort of thing washed-up hippies talk about while sipping wine and watching the sunset. A mere 15 years into its existence, the Buck Institute is at the bow wave of biology.

In one lab, researchers laboriously tamper with yeast chromosomes. Yeast is expedient as a research subject because it lives out a lifetime before an analyst's eyes, and because a third of yeast genes are similar to human genes. Deleting some genes kills yeast; deleting others causes yeast to live longer. Why deleting some genes extends life isn't known—Buck researchers are trying to figure this out, in the hope that they might then carry the effect over to mammals. The work is painstaking, with four microscopes in use at least 50 hours a week.

Buck employs Lilliputian electrocardiogram machines and toy-size CT scanners to examine the internal organs of mice, since the goal is not just to make them live longer but to keep them healthy longer, with less cancer or heart disease. Researchers curious about aging mainly work with mice, worms, flies, and yeast, because they are small and easily housed, and because they don't live long, so improvements to life expectancy are quickly observable. "Twenty years ago it was a really big deal to extend the life span of worms. Now any postdoc can do that," says Simon Melov, a Buck geneticist. Experiments funded by the National Institute on Aging have shown that drugs can extend a mouse's life span by about a quarter, and Buck researchers have been able to reverse age-related heart dysfunction in the same animal. Think how the world would be upended if human longevity quickly jumped another 25 percent.

The rubber will meet the road with human trials. "We hope to find five to 10 small molecules that extend healthy life span in mice, then stage a human trial," says Brian Kennedy, the Buck Institute's CEO. A drug called rapamycin—being tested at the institute and elsewhere—seems closest to trial stage and has revolutionary potential. But in addition to being ethically fraught, human trials of a life-extension substance will be costly, and might take decades. The entry of Google's billions into the field makes human trials more likely. Calico is tight-lipped about its plans—the company agreed to let me visit, then backed out.

Anti-aging research is not without antecedents, some of which offer notes of caution. A generation ago, Linus Pauling, a winner of the Nobel Prize in chemistry, proposed that megadoses of vitamin C would retard aging. It turned out that at megadoses, vitamins can become toxic. If you take vitamins, swallow the amounts recommended by the Food and Drug Administration.

A decade ago, a biotech start-up called Sirtris sought to devise drugs that mimic the supposed health-giving properties of red wine. GlaxoSmithKline bought Sirtris for $790 million in today's dollars, money the company may wish it had back: Sirtris experiments have yet to lead to any practical product.

About 15 years ago, Bruce Ames, an accomplished scientist at the University of California at Berkeley, proposed that acetylcarnitine, which regulates the mitochondria of cells, combined with an antioxidant, might retard aging while treating mild Alzheimer's. Antioxidant has become a buzzword of supplement marketing and Dr. Oz–style quackery. Too much antioxidant would be unhealthy, since oxidation is essential to the body's respiration. Ames thought he had found a compound that safely moderates the pace at which cells use themselves up. He began dosing himself with acetylcarnitine, and continues to work at Berkeley, at age 85; whether he would have enjoyed such longevity anyway is unknowable. Pharmaceutical companies have shown little interest in Ames's idea—because it occurs naturally, acetylcarnitine cannot be patented, and, worse from Big Pharma's standpoint, the substance is inexpensive.

Today, lab results show a clear relationship between a restricted-calorie diet and longevity in mice. That eating less extends the life spans of small mammals is the strongest finding of anti-aging research to this point. A restrictive diet seems to put mouse cells into a state vaguely similar to hibernation; whether caloric restriction would work in people isn't known. A campaign against calories might seem to possess broad practical appeal, since what's recommended—eating less—costs nothing. But if the mice are any indication, one would need to eat a lot less, dropping caloric intake to the level at which a person feels hunger pangs throughout the day. "Caloric restriction is a fad diet in Northern California," Melov told me. "We had a caloric-restriction group come in to visit the institute. They did not look at all healthy."

Recently, separate teams at Harvard, Stanford, and UC San Francisco reported that transferring the blood of adolescent mice into old, declining mice had a rejuvenating effect on the latter. The thought of the old rich purchasing blood from the young poor is ghoulish on numerous levels. The research goal is to determine what chemical aspect of youthful blood benefits mature tissue. Perhaps compounds in adolescent blood excite dormant stem cells, and a drug could be developed that triggers the effect without transfusion.

The Buck Institute and other labs have been looking for health-span DNA that may exist in other mammals. Whales are a lot less likely than people are to get cancer. Polar bears consume an extremely high-fat diet yet don't develop arterial plaque. If the biological pathways for such qualities were understood, a drug might be designed to trigger the effect in people. Mimicking what nature has already developed seems more promising than trying to devise novel DNA.

In worms, genes called daf-2 and daf-16 can change in a way that causes the invertebrates to live twice as long as is natural, and in good vigor. A molecular biologist named Cynthia Kenyon, among the first hires at Calico, made that discovery more than two decades ago, when she was a researcher at UC San Francisco. By manipulating the same genes in mice, Kenyon has been able to cause them to live longer, with less cancer than mice in a control group: that is, with a better health span. The daf-16 gene is similar to a human gene called foxo3, a variant of which is linked to exceptional longevity. A drug that mimics this foxo3 variant is rumored to be among Calico's initial projects.

A long time has passed since Kenyon's eureka moment about worm genes, and she's still far from proving that this insight can help people. But the tempo of the kind of work she does is accelerating. Twenty years ago, genetic sequencing and similar forms of DNA research were excruciatingly time-consuming. New techniques and equipment have altered that: for instance, one Silicon Valley lab-services firm, Sequetech, advertises, "Go from [cell] colony to sequence" in a day. The accelerating pace of genetic-information gathering may come in handy for health-span research.

The Buck Institute became cautiously optimistic about rapamycin when its life-extension properties were noticed in yeast. Lab mice dosed with rapamycin are dying off more slowly than they would naturally, and many of the old mice appear energetic and youthful. Devised to prevent rejection of transplanted organs, rapamycin seems to alter some chemistry associated with cellular senescence. (More on that later.) If the drug turns out to delay aging in people, it would be the greatest off-label pharmaceutical use ever. But don't ask your doctor for a prescription—health-span therapy based on rapamycin is years away, if it ever happens. Kennedy, the Buck Institute CEO, does not dose himself with rapamycin, whose side effects are not understood.

Researchers at the Buck Institute are lean: society's obesity problems are not in evidence there. Everyone takes the stairs; elevators are viewed as strictly for visitors. If there is a candy machine on the 488-acre grounds, it is well hidden. I met some researchers for lunch in a glass-and-chrome conference room (Buck's buildings were designed by I. M. Pei and fairly shout "Give me an architecture award!"). Lunch was an ascetic affair: water and a small sandwich with greens; no sides, soda, or cookies. Kennedy says he seldom eats lunch, and runs up to 20 miles weekly. Yet, even doing everything right by the lights of current assumptions about how to stave off aging, at age 47, Kennedy has wrinkle lines around his eyes.

Except with regard to infectious diseases, medical cause and effect is notoriously hard to pin down. Coffee, salt, butter: good, bad, or neither? Studies are inconclusive. Why do some people develop heart disease while others with the same habits don't? The Framingham Heart Study, in its 66th year and following a third generation of subjects, still struggles with such questions. You should watch your weight, eat more greens and less sugar, exercise regularly, and get ample sleep. But you should do these things because they are common sense—not because there is any definitive proof that they will help you live longer.

The uncertainty inherent in the practice of medicine is amplified when the subject is longevity, because decades might pass before anyone knows whether a particular drug or lifestyle modification does any good. Scrutinizing the very old has not been the gold mine some researchers hoped it would be. "Lifestyle studies of centenarians can be really puzzling," Kennedy says. "They smoke more and drink less than we might guess. Few are vegetarians. Nothing jumps out as a definitive cause of their long lives."

Among the first wide-scale efforts to understand gerontology was the Baltimore Longitudinal Study of Aging, begun by federal researchers in 1958 and ongoing. Its current director, Luigi Ferrucci, says, "The study has determined that disabilities among the elderly often have warning signs that can be detected in youth, and this insight might lead to early-life interventions that decrease late-life chronic disease. But on some of the big questions, such as whether longevity is caused mainly by genes or mainly by lifestyle and environment, we just have no idea at all."

Studies of twins suggest that about 30 percent of longevity is inherited. This is one of the factors that make researchers optimistic—if 30 percent of longevity is inherited, perhaps laboratories can design a compound that causes anyone's blood chemistry to mimic what happens in the bodies of those who were born with the DNA for long life. "But when we sequence the genome, only 1 percent seems linked to longevity," Ferrucci told me. "The other 99 percent of the presumed genetic effect is unexplained."

At medical conferences, Ferrucci likes to show physicians and researchers an elaborate medical profile of an anonymous patient, then ask them to guess her age. "Guesses are off by as much as 20 years too high or low," he says. "This is because medically, we do not know what 'age' is. The sole means to determine age is by asking for date of birth. That's what a basic level this research still is at."

Aging brings with it, of course, senescence. Cellular senescence, a subset of the overall phenomenon, is a subject of fascination in longevity research.

The tissues and organs that make up our bodies are prone to injury, and the cells are prone to malfunctions, cancer being the most prominent. When an injury must be healed, or cancerous tissue that is dividing must be stopped, nearby cells transmit chemical signals that trigger the repair of injured cells or the death of malignant ones. (Obviously this is a simplification.) In the young, the system works pretty well. But as cells turn senescent, they begin to send out false positives. The body's healing ability falters as excess production of the repair signal leads to persistent inflammation, which is the foundation of heart disease, Alzheimer's, arthritis, and other chronic maladies associated with the passage of time. Cars wear out because they cannot repair themselves; our bodies wear out because they lose the ability to repair themselves. If the loss of our ability to self-repair were slowed down, health during our later years would improve: a longer warranty, in the auto analogy.

"If we can figure out how to eliminate senescent cells or switch off their secretions," says Judith Campisi, who runs the Buck Institute's research on this topic, "then we could prevent or lessen the impact of many chronic diseases of aging. It's not a coincidence that incidence of these chronic diseases increases sharply after the age of 50, a time when senescent cells also increase in number. If you believe, as many scientists do, that aging is a prime cause of many chronic diseases, it is essential that we understand the accumulation of senescent cells." Rapamycin excites longevity researchers because it seems to switch off the repair signal mistakenly sent by senescent cells. Mayo Clinic researchers are studying other substances that dampen the effects of cellular senescence; some have proved to keep mice fit longer than normal, extending their health span. Many elderly people decline into years of progressive disability, then become invalids. If instead most people enjoyed reasonable vigor right up to the end, that would be just as exciting for society as adding years to life expectancy.

Big medical efforts tend to be structured as assaults on specific conditions—the "war on cancer" and so on. One reason is psychological: a wealthy person who survived a heart attack, or lost a parent to one, endows a foundation to study the problem. Another reason is symbolic: we tend to view diseases as challenges thrown at us by nature, to be overcome one by one. If the passage of time itself turns out to be the challenge, interdisciplinary study of aging might overtake the disease-by-disease approach. As recently as a generation ago, it would have seemed totally crazy to suppose that aging could be "cured." Now curing aging seems, well, only somewhat crazy.

The escalator debate

The life-expectancy escalator has for nearly two centuries risen about three months a year, despite two world wars, the 1918 influenza pandemic, the AIDS epidemic, and the global population's growing sevenfold—the latter deceptively important, because crowded conditions are assumed to more readily communicate disease. Will life-span increases continue regardless of what may happen in biotech? The yea position is represented by James Vaupel, the founder of Germany's Max Planck Institute for Demographic Research; the nay by Jay Olshansky, a professor of public health at the University of Illinois at Chicago.

In 2002, Vaupel published an influential article in Science documenting the eerily linear rise in life expectancy since 1840. Controversially, Vaupel concluded that "reductions in mortality should not be seen as a disconnected sequence of unrepeatable revolutions but rather as a regular stream of continuing progress." No specific development or discovery has caused the rise: improvements in nutrition, public health, sanitation, and medical knowledge all have helped, but the operative impetus has been the "stream of continuing progress."

Vaupel called it a "reasonable scenario" that increases will continue at least until life expectancy at birth surpasses 100. His views haven't changed. "The data still support the conclusions of the 2002 paper. Linear rise in life expectancy has continued," Vaupel told me earlier this year. In a recent report, the Centers for Disease Control and Prevention found that the age-adjusted U.S. death rate declined to a record low in 2011. Today the first four causes of death in the United States are chronic, age-related conditions: heart disease, cancer, chronic lower-respiratory diseases, and stroke. As long as living standards continue to improve, Vaupel thinks, life expectancy will continue to increase.

On the opposite side of this coin, Olshansky told me the rise in life expectancy will "hit a wall soon, if it hasn't already." He noted, "Most of the 20th-century gains in longevity came from reduced infant mortality, and those were onetime gains." Infant mortality in the United States trails some other nations', but has dropped so much—down to one in 170—that little room for improvement remains. "There's tremendous statistical impact on life expectancy when the young are saved," Olshansky says. "A reduction in infant mortality saves the entire span of a person's life. Avoiding mortality in a young person—say, by vaccine—saves most of the person's life. Changes in medicine or lifestyle that extend the lives of the old don't add much to the numbers." Olshansky calculates that if cancer were eliminated, American life expectancy would rise by only three years, because a host of other chronic fatal diseases are waiting to take its place. He thinks the 21st century will see the average life span extend "another 10 years or so," with a bonus of more health span. Then the increase will slow noticeably, or stop.

Whether human age may have a biological limit does not factor into this debate. A French woman who lived from 1875 to 1997, Jeanne Calment, had the longest confirmed life span, at 122. She's obviously an outlier, and while outliers don't tell us much, they do hint at what's possible. Her age at death was well beyond the average life span that either Vaupel or Olshansky are contemplating in their analyses. And in any case, various experts, at various times across the past century, have argued that life span was nearing a ceiling, only to be proved wrong.

Diminishing smoking and drunk driving have obviously contributed to declining mortality. Homicide has fallen so much—shootings aren't necessarily down, but improved trauma response saves more victims—that murder is no longer among the top 15 causes of death in the United States. Other health indicators seem positive as well. All forms of harmful air and water emissions except greenhouse gases are in long-term decline. Less smog, acid rain, and airborne soot foster longevity—the old are sensitive to respiratory disease—while declining levels of industrial toxins may contribute to declining cancer rates. Life expectancy can be as much as 18 years shorter in low-income U.S. counties than in high-income counties, but Obamacare should correct some of that imbalance: Romneycare, enacted in 2006 and in many ways Obamacare's precursor, reduced mortality in low-income Massachusetts counties. These and many other elements of Vaupel's "stream of continuing progress" seem to favor longevity. So does climate change: people live longer in warm climates than cold, and the world is warming.

Popular attention tends to focus on whether what we gulp down determines how long we live: Should people take fish oil and shop for organic probiotic kefir? The way our homes, families, and friendships are organized may matter just as much. Thomas Perls, a professor at Boston Medical Center who analyzes the genomes of centenarians, notes that Seventh-Day Adventists enjoy about a decade more life expectancy than peers of their birth years: "They don't drink or smoke, most are vegetarians, they exercise regularly even when old, and take a true weekly day of rest." But what really strikes Perls about Seventh-Day Adventists is that they maintain large social groups. "Constant interaction with other people can be annoying, but overall seems to keep us engaged with life."

For years, the American social trend has been away from "constant interaction with other people"—fewer two-parent homes, fewer children per home, declining participation in religious and community activities, grandparents living on their own, electronic interaction replacing the face-to-face in everything from work to dating. Prosperity is associated with smaller households, yet the large multigeneration home may be best for long life. There are some indications that the

Great Recession increased multigeneration living. This may turn out to boost longevity, at least for a time.

The single best yardstick for measuring a person's likely life span is education. John Rowe, a health-policy professor at Columbia University and a former CEO of Aetna, says, "If someone walked into my office and asked me to predict how long he would live, I would ask two things: What is your age, and how many years of education did you receive?"

Jay Olshansky's latest research suggests that American women with no high-school diploma have experienced relatively small life-span increases since the 1950s, while the life expectancy of highly educated women has soared since then. Today the best-educated Americans live 10 to 14 years longer than the least educated, on average. "Nothing pops out of the data like the link between education and life expectancy," Olshansky says. "The good news is that the share of the American population that is less educated is in gradual decline. The bad news is that lack of education seems even more lethal than it was in the past."

Education does not sync with life expectancy because reading Dostoyevsky lowers blood pressure; college is a proxy for other aspects of a person's life. Compared with the less educated, people with a bachelor's degree have a higher income, smoke less, are less likely to be overweight, and are more likely to follow doctors' instructions. College graduates are more likely to marry and stay married, and marriage is good for your health: the wedded suffer fewer heart attacks and strokes than the single or divorced.

Many of the social developments that improve longevity—better sanitation, less pollution, improved emergency rooms—are provided to all on an egalitarian basis. But today's public high schools are dreadful in many inner-city areas, and broadly across states including California. Legislatures are cutting support for public universities, while the cost of higher education rises faster than inflation. These issues are discussed in terms of fairness; perhaps health should be added as a concern in the debate. If education is the trump card of longevity, the top quintile may pull away from the rest.

Aging and politics

Society is dominated by the old—old political leaders, old judges. With each passing year, as longevity increases, the intergenerational imbalance worsens. The old demand benefits for which the young must pay, while people in their 20s become disenchanted, feeling that the deck is stacked against them. National debt increases at an alarming rate. Innovation and fresh thinking disappear as energies are devoted to defending current pie-slicing arrangements.

This isn't a prediction about the future of the United States, but rather a description of Japan right now. The Land of the Rising Sun is the world's grayest nation. Already the median age is 45 (in the U.S., by comparison, it is 37), and it will jump to 55 by 2040. As Nicholas Eberstadt, a demographer at the American Enterprise Institute, has noted, median age in the retirement haven of Palm Springs, California, is currently 52 years. Japan is on its way to becoming an entire nation of Palm Springs residents.

Japan's grayness stems from a very low fertility rate—not enough babies to bring down the average age—and strict barriers against immigration. The United States remains a nation of immigrants, and because of the continual inflow of young people, the U.S. median age won't go haywire even as life expectancy rises: the United Nations' "World Population Prospects" estimates that the U.S. median age will rise to 41 by mid-century.

Nonetheless, that Japan is the first major nation to turn gray, and is also the deepest in debt, is not encouraging. Once, Japan was feared as the Godzilla of global trade, but as it grayed, its economy entered a long cycle of soft growth. In 2012 the centrist Democratic Party of Japan, then holding the Diet, backed a tax whose goal was not to pay down what the country owes but merely to slow the rate of borrowing. The party promptly got the heave-ho from voters. Last year Japan's public debt hit $10 trillion, twice the nation's GDP.

Sheila Smith, a Japan specialist at the Council on Foreign Relations, told me, "Young people in Japan have some of the world's worst voter-participation rates. They think the old have the system so rigged in their favor, there's no point in political activity. The young don't seem excited by the future." News accounts of young Japanese becoming so apathetic that they've lost interest in having sex sound hard to believe, but may bear some truth.

Young urban Japanese surely are aware that their elders are ringing up bills to be handed to them, but they're also aware that if funding for the retired is cut, Grandma may want to move into their very small apartment. As life expectancy rises, a Japanese person entering the happy-go-lucky phase of early adulthood may find that parents and grandparents both expect to be looked after. Because the only child is common in Japan's newest generation, a big cast of aging people may turn to one young person for financial support or caregiving or both. Acceding to public borrowing may have become, to young Japanese, a way to keep older generations out of the apartment—even if it means crushing national debt down the road.

That America may become more like Japan—steadily older, with rising debt and declining economic growth—is unsettling. From the second half of the George W. Bush administration until

2013, U.S. national debt more than doubled. The federal government borrowed like there was no tomorrow. The debt binge, for which leaders of both political parties bear blame, was a prelude to the retirement of the Baby Boomers. Tomorrow has a way of coming.

Suppose the escalator slows, and conservative assumptions about life expectancy prevail. In a 2009 study, Olshansky projected future demographics under the "hit a wall" scenario. The number of Americans 65 or older, 43 million today, could reach 108 million in 2050—that would be like adding three more Floridas, inhabited entirely by seniors. The "oldest old" cohort, those 85 and older, may increase at least fivefold, to more than 6 percent of the U.S. citizenry. Olshansky projected that by 2050, life expectancy will extend three to eight years past the age used by the Social Security Administration to assess the solvency of its system, while forecasting that by 2050, Medicare and Social Security will rack up between $3.2 trillion and $8.3 trillion in unfunded obligations. (State and local governments have at least another $1 trillion in unfunded pension liabilities.) These disconcerting numbers flow from the leading analyst who thinks that the life-span increase is slowing down.

When President Obama took office, Social Security's trustees said the current benefits structure was funded until 2037. Now the Congressional Budget Office says the year of reckoning may come as soon as 2031. States may be "funding" their pension obligations using fuzzy math: New York issues promissory notes; Illinois and New Jersey sell debt instruments distressingly similar to junk bonds. Many private pension plans are underfunded, and the Pension Benefit Guaranty Corporation, which on paper appears to insure them, is an accident looking for a place to happen. Twice in the past three years, Congress has voted to allow corporations to delay contributions to pension plans. This causes them to pay more taxes in the present year, giving Congress more to spend, while amplifying problems down the road. Social Security's disability fund may fail as soon as late 2016. Medicare spending is rising faster than Social Security spending, and is harder to predict. Projections show the main component of Medicare, its hospital fund, failing by 2030.

The Congressional Budget Office estimates that over the next decade, all federal spending growth will come from entitlements—mainly Social Security and Medicare—and from interest on the national debt. The nonpartisan think tank Third Way has calculated that at the beginning of the Kennedy presidency, the federal government spent $2.50 on public investments—infrastructure, education, and research—for every $1 it spent on entitlements. By 2022, Third Way predicts, the government will spend $5 on entitlements for every $1 on public investments. Infrastructure, education, and research lead to economic growth; entitlement subsidies merely allow the nation to tread water.

If health span can be improved, the costs of aging-related disability may be manageable. Not that long ago, vast sums were spent on iron lungs and sanitariums for treatment of polio: preventing the disease has proved much less expensive than treating it. If chronic ailments related to aging can be prevented or significantly delayed, big-ticket line items in Medicare might not go off the rails.

But if health span does not improve, longer life could make disability in aging an economic crisis. Today, Medicare and Medicaid spend about $150 billion annually on Alzheimer's patients. Absent progress against aging, the number of people with Alzheimer's could treble by 2050, with society paying as much for Alzheimer's care as for the current defense budget.

Many disabilities associated with advanced years cannot be addressed with pharmaceuticals or high-tech procedures; caregivers are required. Providing personal care for an aged invalid is a task few wish to undertake. Already many lists of careers with the most job openings are headed by "caregiver" or "nurse's aide," professions in which turnover is high.

As longevity increases, so too does the number of living grandparents. Families that once might have had one "oldest old" relative find themselves with three or four, all expecting care or money. At the same time, traditional family trees are being replaced with diagrams that resemble maps of the London Underground. Will children of blended families feel the same obligation to care for aging stepparents as they feel for biological parents? Just the entry of the phrase birth parent into the national lexicon suggests the magnitude of the change.

With Japan at the leading edge of lengthening life expectancy, its interest in robotics can be eerie. Foxconn, the Asian electronics giant, is manufacturing for the Japanese market a creepy mechanized thing named Pepper that is intended to provide company for the elderly. More-sophisticated devices may be in store. A future in which large numbers of very old, incapacitated people stare into the distance as robot attendants click and hum would be a bad science-fiction movie if it didn't stand a serious chance of happening.

The problem of aging leadership

As the population ages, so do the political powers that be—and they're aging in place. Computerized block-by-block voting analysis and shameless gerrymandering—Maryland's new sixth congressional district is such a strange shape, it would have embarrassed Elbridge Gerry—lock incumbents into power as never before. Campaign-finance laws appear to promote reform, but in fact have been rigged to discourage challengers. Between rising life expectancy and the mounting power of incumbency, both houses of Congress are the oldest they've ever been: the average senator is 62 years old; the average representative, 57.

A graying Congress would be expected to be concerned foremost with protection of the status quo. Government may grow sclerotic at the very time the aging of the populace demands new ideas. "There's already a tremendous advantage to incumbency," one experienced political operative told me. "As people live longer, incumbents will become more entrenched. Strom Thurmond might not be unusual anymore. Many from both parties could cling to power too long, freezing out fresh thinking. It won't be good for democracy." The speaker was no starry-eyed radical: he was Karl Rove.

Now think of the Supreme Court as life expectancy increases. The nine justices on the first Court sat an average of nine years; the last nine to depart, an average of 27 years. John Paul Stevens, the most recent to retire, was a justice for 35 years. If Clarence Thomas lives to the actuarial life expectancy of a male his current age, he could be a Supreme Court justice for 40 years.

The Framers would be aghast at the idea of a small cadre of unelected potentates lording it over the body politic for decades. When the Constitution was written, no one could have anticipated how much life span would increase, nor how much power the Supreme Court would accrue. If democracy is to remain vibrant as society ages, campaign laws must change to help challengers stand a chance versus incumbents, and the Constitution must be amended to impose a term limit on the Supreme Court, so confirmation as a justice stops being a lifetime appointment to royalty.

A new view of retirement

In 1940, the typical American who reached age 65 would ultimately spend about 17 percent of his or her life retired. Now the figure is 22 percent, and still rising. Yet Social Security remains structured as if longevity were stuck in a previous century. The early-retirement option, added by Congress in 1961—start drawing at age 62, though with lower benefits—is appealing if life is short, but backfires as life span extends. People who opt for early Social Security may reach their 80s having burned through savings, and face years of living on a small amount rather than the full benefit they might have received. Polls show that Americans consistently underestimate how long they will live—a convenient assumption that justifies retiring early and spending now, while causing dependency over the long run.

James Vaupel has warned that refusing to acknowledge longevity's steady march "distorts people's decisions about how much to save and when to retire" and gives "license to politicians to postpone painful adjustments to Social Security." Ronald Reagan was the last president to push through legislation to account for life-span changes. His administration increased the future eligible age of full Social Security benefits from 65 to 66 or 67, depending on one's birth year. Perhaps 99 percent of members of Congress would agree in private that retirement economics must change; none will touch this third rail. Generating more Social Security revenue by lifting the payroll-tax cap, currently $117,000, is the sole politically attractive option, because only the well-to-do would be impacted. But the Congressional Budget Office recently concluded that even this soak-the-rich option is insufficient to prevent insolvency for Social Security. At least one other change, such as later retirement or revised cost-of-living formulas, is required. A fair guess is that the government will do nothing about Social Security reform until a crisis strikes—and then make panicked, ill-considered moves that foresight might have avoided.

Americans may decry government gridlock, but they can't blame anyone else for their own decisions. People's retirement savings simply must increase, though this means financial self-discipline, which Americans are not known for. Beyond that, most individuals will likely need to take a new view of what retirement should be: not a toggle switch—no work at all, after years of full-time labor—but a continuum on which a person gradually downshifts to half-time, then to working now and then. Let's call it the "retirement track" rather than retirement: a phase of continuing to earn and save as full-time work winds down.

Widespread adoption of a retirement track would necessitate changes in public policy and in employers' attitudes. Banks don't think in terms of smallish loans to help a person in the second half of life start a home-based business, but such lending might be vital to a graying population. Many employers are required to continue offering health insurance to those who stay on the job past 65, even though they are eligible for Medicare. Employers' premiums for these workers are much higher than for young workers, which means employers may have a logical reason to want anyone past 65 off the payroll. Ending this requirement would make seniors more attractive to employers.

Many people may find continuing to work but under the lower-stress circumstances of part-time employment to be preferable to a gold watch, then idleness. Gradual downshifting could help ease aging people into volunteer service roles, where there's never any end of things to do. The retirement track could be more appealing than traditional retirement. A longer health span will be essential to making it possible.

Longer life as directed evolution

Understanding the evolutionary biology of aging might help the quest for improved health span. Each cell of the body contains DNA code for a fresh, healthy cell, yet that blueprint is not called on as we grow old. Evolutionists including Alfred Russel Wallace have toyed with the idea of programmed death—the notion that natural selection "wants" old animals to die in order to free up resources for younger animals, which may carry evolved genetic structures. Current thinking tends to hold that rather than trying to make older animals die, natural selection simply has no mechanism to reward longevity.

Felipe Sierra, a researcher at the National Institute on Aging, says, "Evolution doesn't care about you past your reproductive age. It doesn't want you either to live longer or to die, it just doesn't care. From the standpoint of natural selection, an animal that has finished reproducing and performed the initial stage of raising young might as well be eaten by something, since any favorable genetic quality that expresses later in life cannot be passed along." Because a mutation that favors long life cannot make an animal more likely to succeed at reproducing, selection pressure works only on the young.

A generation ago, theorists suspected that menopause was an evolutionary adaptation exclusive to the Homo genus—women stop expending energy to bear children so they can care longer for those already born, as mothers and grandmothers. This, the theory goes, increases children's chances of survival, allowing them to pass along family genes. Yet recent research has shown that animals including lions and baboons also go through menopause, which increasingly looks more like a malfunction of aging cells than a quality brought about by selection pressure. As for the idea that grandparents help their grandchildren prosper, favoring longevity—the "grandmother effect"—this notion, too, has fared poorly in research.

The key point is: if nothing that happens after a person reproduces bears on which genes flourish, then nature has never selected for qualities that extend longevity. Evolution favors strength, intelligence, reflexes, sexual appeal; it does not favor keeping an organism running a long time. For example, a growing body needs calcium, so nature selected for the ability to metabolize this element. In later life, calcium causes stiffening of the arteries, a problem that evolution has no mechanism to correct, since hardened arteries do not occur until it's too late for natural selection to side with any beneficial mutation. Testosterone is essential to a youthful man; in an aging man, it can be a factor in prostate cancer. Evolution never selected for a defense against that.

Similar examples abound; the most important may be senescent cells. Natural selection probably favors traits that reduce the risk of cancer, because cancer can strike the young before reproductive age is reached. Senescence doesn't occur until evolution is no longer in play, so natural selection has left all mammal bodies with a defect that leads to aging and death.

If senescence could be slowed, men and women hardly would become immortal. Violence, accidents, and contagious disease still would kill. Even if freed of chronic conditions, eventually our bodies would fail.

But it is not credulous futurism to suppose that drugs or even genetic therapy may alter the human body in ways that extend longevity. Brian Kennedy, of the Buck Institute, notes, "Because natural selection did not improve us for aging, there's a chance for rapid gains. The latest BMWs are close to perfect. How can an engineer improve on them? But the Model T would be easy to improve on now. When young, genetically we are BMWs. In aging, we become Model Ts. The evolutionary improvements haven't started yet."

A grayer, quieter, better future

In the wild, young animals outnumber the old; humanity is moving toward a society where the elderly outnumber the recently arrived. Such a world will differ from today's in many outward aspects. Warm-weather locations are likely to grow even more popular, though with climate change, warm-weather locations may come to include Buffalo, New York. Ratings for football, which is loud and aggressive, may wane, while baseball and theatergoing enjoy a renaissance. The shift back toward cities, initiated by the educated young, may give way to another car-centric suburban and exurban growth phase.

The university, a significant aspect of the contemporary economy, centuries ago was a place where the fresh-faced would be prepared for a short life; today the university is a place where adults watch children and grandchildren walk to Pomp and Circumstance. The university of the future may be one that serves all ages. Colleges will reposition themselves economically as offering just as much to the aging as to the adolescent: courses priced individually for later-life knowledge seekers; lots of campus events of interest to students, parents, and the community as a whole; a pleasant college-town atmosphere to retire near. In decades to come, college professors may address students ranging from age 18 to 80.

Products marketed to senior citizens are already a major presence on television, especially during newscasts and weathercasts. Advertising pitched to the elderly may come to dominate the airwaves, assuming there still is television. But consumerism might decline. Neurological studies of healthy aging people show that the parts of the brain associated with reward-seeking light up less as time goes on. Whether it's hot new fashions or hot-fudge sundaes, older people on the whole don't desire acquisitions as much as the young and middle-aged do. Denounced for generations by writers and clergy, wretched excess has repelled all assaults. Longer life spans may at last be the counterweight to materialism.

Deeper changes may be in store as well. People in their late teens to late 20s are far more likely to commit crimes than people of other ages; as society grays, the decline of crime should continue. Violence in all guises should continue downward, too. Horrible headlines from Afghanistan or Syria are exceptions to an overall trend toward less warfare and less low-intensity conflict. As Steven Pinker showed in the 2011 book Better Angels of Our Nature, total casualties of combat, including indirect casualties from the economic harm associated with fighting, have been declining, even as the global population has risen. In 1950, one person in 5,000 worldwide died owing to combat; by 2010, this measure was down to one person in 300,000. In recent years, far more people have been killed by car crashes than by battle. Simultaneously, per capita military expenditure has shrunk. My favorite statistic about the world: the Stockholm International Peace Research Institute reports that, adjusting to today's dollars, global per capita military spending has declined by one-third in the past quarter century.

The end of the Cold War, and the proxy conflicts it spawned, is an obvious influence on the subsiding of warfare, as is economic interconnectedness. But aging may also be a factor. Counterculture optics notwithstanding, polls showed that the young were more likely to support the Vietnam War than the old were; the young were more likely to support the 2003 invasion of Iraq, too. Research by John Mueller, a political scientist at Ohio State University, suggests that as people age, they become less enthusiastic about war. Perhaps this is because older people tend to be wiser than the young—and couldn't the world use more wisdom?

Older people also report, to pollsters and psychologists, a greater sense of well-being than the young and middle-aged do. By the latter phases of life, material and romantic desires have been attained or given up on; passions have cooled; and for most, a rich store of memories has been compiled. Among the core contentions of the well-being research of the Princeton University psychologist Daniel Kahneman is that "in the end, memories are all you keep"—what's in the mind matters more than what you own. Regardless of net worth, the old are well off in this sense.

Should large numbers of people enjoy longer lives in decent health, the overall well-being of the human family may rise substantially. In As You Like It, Jaques declares, "Man in his time plays many parts, his acts being seven ages." The first five embody promise and power—infant, schoolboy, lover, soldier, and success. The late phases are entirely negative—pantaloon, a period as the butt of jokes for looking old and becoming impotent; then second childishness, a descent into senile dependency. As life expectancy and health span increase, the seven ages may demand revision, with the late phases of life seen as a positive experience of culmination and contentment.

Further along may be a rethinking of life as better structured around friendship than around family, the basic unit of human society since the mists of prehistory. In the brief life of previous centuries, all a man or woman could hope to accomplish was to bear and raise children; enervation followed. Today, life is longer, but an education-based economy requires greater investments in children—contemporary parents are still assisting offspring well into a child's 20s. As before, when the child-rearing finally is done, decline commences.

But if health span extends, the nuclear family might be seen as less central. For most people, bearing and raising children would no longer be the all-consuming life event. After child-rearing, a phase of decades of friendships could await—potentially more fulfilling than the emotionally charged but fast-burning bonds of youth. A change such as this might have greater ramifications for society than changes in work schedules or health-care economics.

Regardless of where increasing life expectancy leads, the direction will be into the unknown—for society and for the natural world. Felipe Sierra, the researcher at the National Institute on Aging, puts it this way: "The human ethical belief that death should be postponed as long as possible does not exist in nature—from which we are now, in any case, diverging."

☑ Text 2 The illusion of 'natural'

By Eula Biss

Misunderstandings of purity fuel fears of toxins and vaccines, but the lines between humans, technology, and the environment are far blurrier than those who avoid the artificial realize.

It is difficult to read any historical account of smallpox without encountering the word *filth*. In the 19th century, smallpox was widely considered a disease of filth, which meant that it was largely understood to be a disease of the poor. According to filth theory, any number of contagious diseases were caused by bad air that had been made foul by excrement or rot. The sanitary conditions of the urban poor threatened the middle class, who shuttered their windows against the air blowing off the slums. Filth, it was thought, was responsible not just for disease, but also for immorality. "Unclean! Unclean!" the heroine of *Dracula* laments when she discovers she has been bitten by the vampire, and her despair is for the fate of her soul as much as the fate of her body.

Filth theory was eventually replaced by germ theory, a superior understanding of the nature of contagion, but filth theory was not entirely wrong or useless. Raw sewage running in the streets can certainly spread diseases, although smallpox is not one of them, and the sanitation reforms inspired by filth theory dramatically reduced the incidence of cholera, typhus, and plague. Clean drinking water was among the most significant of those reforms. The reversal of the Chicago River, for instance, so that the sewage dumped in the river was not delivered directly to Lake Michigan, the city's drinking-water supply, had some obvious benefits for the citizens of Chicago.

Long after the reversal of that river, the mothers I meet on the beaches of Lake Michigan do not worry much over filth. Most of us believe that dirt is good for our kids, but some of us are wary of the grass in the parks, which may or may not have been treated with toxic chemicals. The idea that "toxins," rather than filth or germs, are the root cause of most maladies is a popular theory of disease among people like me. The toxins that concern us range from particle residue to high-fructose corn syrup, and particularly suspect substances include the bisphenol A lining our tin cans, the phthalates in our shampoos, and the chlorinated Tris in our couches and mattresses.

I already practiced some intuitive toxicology before my pregnancy, but I became thoroughly immersed in it after my son was born. As long as a child takes only breast milk, I discovered, one can enjoy the illusion of a closed system, a body that is not yet in dialogue with the impurities of farm and factory. Caught up in the romance of the untainted body, I remember feeling agony when my son drank water for the first time. "Unclean! Unclean!" my mind screamed.

"He was too pure," a Baltimore mother said of her son, who developed leukemia as an infant. His mother blamed the pollutants in vaccines for his illness, and herself for allowing him to be vaccinated. Fears that formaldehyde from vaccines may cause cancer are similar to fears of mercury and aluminum, in that they coalesce around miniscule amounts of the substance in question, amounts considerably smaller than amounts from other common sources of exposure to the same substance. Formaldehyde is in automobile exhaust and cigarette smoke, as well as paper bags and paper towels, and it is released by gas stoves and open fireplaces. Many vaccines contain traces of the formaldehyde used to inactivate viruses, and this can be alarming to those of us who associate formaldehyde with dead frogs in glass jars. Large concentrations are indeed toxic, but formaldehyde is a product of our bodies, essential to our metabolism, and the amount of formaldehyde already circulating in our systems is considerably greater than the amount we receive through vaccination.

As for mercury, a child will almost certainly get more mercury exposure from her immediate environment than from vaccination. This is true, too, of the aluminum that is often used as an adjuvant in vaccines to intensify the immune response. Aluminum is in a lot of things, including fruits and cereals as well as, again, breast milk. Our breast milk, it turns out, is as polluted as our environment at large. Laboratory analysis of breast milk has detected paint thinners, dry-cleaning fluids, flame retardants, pesticides, and rocket fuel. "Most of these chemicals are found in microscopic amounts," the journalist Florence Williams notes, "but if human milk were sold at the local Piggly Wiggly, some stock would exceed federal food-safety levels for DDT residues and PCBs."

The definition of *toxin* can be somewhat surprising if you have grown accustomed to hearing the word in the context of flame retardants and parabens. Though *toxin* is now often used to refer to man-made chemicals, the most precise meaning of the term is still reserved for biologically produced poisons. The pertussis toxin, for example, is responsible for damage to the lungs that can cause whooping cough to linger for months after the bacteria that produce it have been killed by antibiotics. The diphtheria toxin is a poison potent enough to cause massive organ failure, and tetanus produces a deadly neurotoxin. Vaccination now protects us against all these toxins.

Toxoid is the term for a toxin that has been rendered no longer toxic, but the existence of a class of vaccines called toxoids probably does not help quell widespread concerns that vaccination is a source of toxicity. The consumer advocate Barbara Loe Fisher routinely supports these fears, referring to vaccines as "biologicals of unknown toxicity" and calling for nontoxic preservatives and more studies on the "toxicity of all other vaccine additives" and their potential "cumulative toxic effects." The toxicity she speaks of is elusive, shirting from the biological components of the vaccines to their preservatives, then to an issue of accumulation that implicates not just vaccines, but also toxicity from the environment at large.

In this context, fear of toxicity strikes me as an old anxiety with a new name. Where the word *filth* once suggested, with its moralist air, the evils of the flesh, the word *toxic* now condemns the chemical evils of our industrial world. This is not to say that concerns over environmental pollution are not justified—like filth theory, toxicity theory is anchored in legitimate dangers—but that the way we think about toxicity bears some resemblance to the way we once thought about filth. Both theories allow their subscribers to maintain a sense of control over their own health by pursuing personal purity. For the filth theorist, this means a retreat into the home, where heavy curtains and shutters might seal out the smell of the poor and their problems. Our version of this shuttering is now achieved through the purchase of purified water, air purifiers, and food produced with the promise of purity.

Purity, especially bodily purity, is the seemingly innocent concept behind a number of the most sinister social actions of the past century. A passion for bodily purity drove the eugenics movement that led to the sterilization of women who were blind, black, or poor. Concerns for bodily purity were behind miscegenation laws that persisted for more than a century after the abolition of slavery. Quite a bit of human solidarity has been sacrificed in pursuit of preserving some kind of imagined purity.

If we do not yet know exactly what the presence of a vast range of chemicals in umbilical cord blood and breast milk might mean for the future of our children's health, we do at least know that we are no cleaner, even at birth, than our environment at large. We are all already polluted. We have more microorganisms in our guts than we have cells in our bodies—we are crawling with bacteria and we are full of chemicals. We are, in other words, continuous with everything here on Earth. Including, and especially, each other.

One of the appeals of alternative medicine is that it offers not just an alternative philosophy or an alternative treatment but also an alternative language. If we feel polluted, we are offered a "cleanse." If we feel inadequate, lacking, we are offered a "supplement." If we fear toxins, we are offered "detoxification." If we fear that we are rusting with age, physically oxidizing, we are reassured with "antioxidants." These are metaphors that address our base anxieties. And what the language of alternative medicine understands is that when we feel bad we want something unambiguously good.

Most of the pharmaceuticals available to us are at least as bad as they are good. My father has a habit of saying, "There are very few perfect therapies in medicine." True as it may be, the idea that our medicine is as flawed as we are is not comforting. And when comfort is what we want, one of the most powerful tonics alternative medicine offers is the word *natural*. This word implies a medicine untroubled by human limitations, contrived wholly by nature or God or perhaps intelligent design. What *natural* has come to mean to us in the context of medicine is *pure* and *safe* and *benign*. But the use of *natural* as a synonym for *good* is almost certainly a product of our profound alienation from the natural world.

"Obviously," the naturalist Wendell Berry writes, "the more artificial a human environment becomes, the more the word 'natural' becomes a term of value." If, he argues, "we see the human and the natural economies as necessarily opposite or opposed, we subscribe to the very opposition that threatens to destroy them both. The wild and the domestic now often seem isolated values, estranged from one another. And yet these are not exclusive polarities like good and evil. There can be continuity between them, and there must be."

Allowing children to develop immunity to contagious diseases "naturally," without vaccination, is appealing to some of us. Much of that appeal depends on the belief that vaccines are inherently unnatural. But vaccines are of that liminal place between humans and nature—a mowed field,

Berry might suggest, edged by woods. Vaccination is a kind of domestication of a wild thing, in that it involves our ability to harness a virus and break it like a horse, but its action depends on the natural response of the body to the effects of that once-wild thing.

The antibodies that generate immunity following vaccination are manufactured in the human body, not in factories. "In the pharmaceutical world," the writer Jane Smith observes, "the great division is between biologicals and chemicals—drugs that are made from living substances and drugs that are made from chemical compounds." Using ingredients from organisms, once living or still alive, vaccines invite the immune system to produce its own protection. The live viruses in vaccines are weakened, sometimes by having been passed through the bodies of animals, so that they cannot infect a healthy person. The most unnatural part of vaccination is that it does not, when all goes well, introduce disease or produce illness.

Infectious disease is one of the primary mechanisms of natural immunity. Whether we are sick or healthy, disease is always passing through our bodies. "Probably we're diseased all the time," as one biologist puts it, "but we're hardly ever ill." It is only when disease manifests itself as illness that we see it as unnatural, in the "contrary to the ordinary course of nature" sense of the word. When a child's fingers blacken on his hand from Hib disease, when tetanus locks a child's jaw and stiffens her body, when a baby barks for breath from pertussis, when a child's legs are twisted and shrunken with polio—then disease does not seem natural.

"I know you're on my side," an immunologist once remarked to me as we discussed the politics of vaccination. I did not agree with him, but only because I was uncomfortable with both sides, as I had seen them delineated. The debate over vaccination tends to be described with what the philosopher of science Donna Haraway would call "troubling dualisms." These dualisms pit science against nature, public against private, truth against imagination, self against another, thought against emotion, and man against woman.

The metaphor of a "war" between mothers and doctors is sometimes used for conflicts over vaccination. Depending on who is employing the metaphor, the warring parties may be characterized as ignorant mothers and educated doctors, or intuitive mothers and intellectual doctors, or caring mothers and heartless doctors, or irrational mothers and rational doctors—sexist stereotypes abound.

Rather than imagine a war in which we are ultimately fighting against ourselves, perhaps we can accept a world in which we are all irrational rationalists. We are bound, in this world, to both nature and technology. We are all "cyborgs, hybrids, mosaics, chimeras," as Haraway suggests in her feminist provocation *A Cyborg Manifesto*. She envisions a cyborg world "in which people are not afraid of their joint kinship with animals and machines, not afraid of permanently partial identities and contradictory standpoints."

All of us who have been vaccinated are cyborgs, the cyborg scholar Chris Hables Gray suggests. Our bodies have been programmed to respond to disease, and modified by technologically altered viruses. As a cyborg and a nursing mother, I join my modified body to a breast pump, a modern mechanism to provide my child with the most primitive food. On my bicycle, I am part human and part machine, a collaboration that exposes me to injury. Our technology both extends and endangers us. Good or bad, it is part of us, and this is no more unnatural than it is natural.

When a friend asked, years ago, if my son's birth was a "natural" birth, I was tempted to say that it was an animal birth. While his head was crowning, I was trying to use my own hands to pull apart my flesh and bring him out of my body. Or so I have been told, but I do not remember any intention to tear myself open—all I remember is the urgency of the moment. I was both human and animal then. Or I was neither, as I am now. "We have never been human," Haraway suggests. And perhaps we have never been modern, either.

Classroom activities
Text analysis

1. What is the respective subject matter in the texts? What subtopics centering round the subject matter are addressed?

2. What are the main themes in the two texts?

3. Both authors in this unit express their attitudes towards the impact of science advancement. With different technologies being concerned, their attitudes diverge in a certain sense. Can you explain the divergence of their attitudes?

4. In each of the two texts, a quote can be found in the ending paragraph. What messages do the quotes convey respectively?

5. In Text 1, the author distinguishes the life span from another kind of span. What is the span being compared with the life span? What is the importance of making this distinction?

6. Guess the meaning of the following words from Text 2, and name the context clues you use to do the guess work:

   Para. 1: smallpox, filth

   Para. 2: cholera, typhus, plague

Para. 3: toxin, particle residue, high-fructose corn syrup, bisphenol A, phthalate, chlorinated Tris

Para. 4: toxicology, impurity, agony

7. What are the respective main ideas of paragraphs 1 to 4 in Text 2? What is the main idea of the four paragraphs as a whole? Can you now tell the difference between reading a paragraph alone and reading it as part of a piece of writing?

Group discussion and presentation

Although the topics are quite different, the two texts share a lot in terms of writing techniques. Have a group discussion on the commonalities and the purposes of adopting them. Then present your findings in class.

For example, you may notice that both articles end with a quote from a certain authority. Through another person's voice, the author reiterates his own opinion and leaves readers with the impression that he is not alone in thinking this way. Thus he makes good use of the last opportunity to convince readers.

Class discussion

Compare the two titles to see how the articles are named respectively. Which way of naming do you like? Why? Which title do you like better? Why? Can you propose a title to replace the one you think unfavorable? Exchange your opinions with others in class.

Hint 1: What language structures are shown in the titles? What are the pros and cons of using these language structures in writing a title?

Hint 2: What reading expectations do the titles invite? What topics are actually addressed in the texts? Are your reading expectations consistent with the topics?

Critical thinking

Comment on the authors' ways of elaborating their points. Can you detect any weakness in the development of authors' ideas?

Hint: You may consider the overall organization of the texts. Don't you think that the logical flow in one of the texts is a bit bumpy? What information rearrangement could be made if you were the author?

Class debate

After studying Text 1, you may get a better understanding of our government's decision to reform the retirement policy. Does this convince you of the necessity to raise the retirement age? Take for the inter-group debate in class.

Proposition: The retirement age should be raised in China?

Opposition: The retirement age should not be raised in China.

Note again: Debating must be interactive. You should engage with your opponents by rebutting their arguments, instead of merely stating your own. Don't stick rigidly to what you have prepared.

Group Presentation

Nowadays people tend to take the development of science and technology for granted and the more advanced human technologies are, the happier and better our life can be. It is time that we reconsidered the impact of science advancement on society and the people. Is the invention of smart phone entirely good to people? Is the prolongation of a dying patient's suffering and undignified life really merciful? Prepare a presentation to share your group reflection on this topic.

Unit 11

Detective stories

Pre-class reading tasks

In this unit, you will read two detective stories, featuring respectively the first hard-boiled detective and the first consulting detective in the history of literature. Please fulfill the following reading tasks in collaboration with your group members before class.

Do some research on the two authors, with special attention to the information related to the creation of the two detective prototypes.

Divide up the stories into sections, and summarize each section in one sentence.

Task 3

Choose and adapt a section in "The False Burton Combs" for performance, and prepare to stage it in class. Talk with other groups before making your choice so as to prevent identical choices.

Prepare to retell the story of *The Adventure of the Six Napoleons*.

Task 5

Compare the two stories from various aspects that strike you as worthy of discussion, such as the theme, writing method, protagonist's personality, and etc.

☑ Text 1 The False Burton Combs

By Carroll John Daly

I had an outside stateroom on the upper deck of the Fall River boat and ten minutes after I parked my bag there I knew that I was being watched. The boat had already cleared and was slowly making its way toward the Battery.

I didn't take the shadowing too seriously. There was nothing to be nervous about—my little trip was purely a pleasure one this time. But then a dick getting your smoke is not pleasant under the best of circumstances. And yet I was sure I had come aboard unobserved.

This chap was a new one on me and I thought he must have just picked me up on suspicion— trailed along in the hope of getting something. But I checked up my past offences and there was really nothing they could hold me on.

I ain't a crook; just a gentleman adventurer and make my living working against the law breakers. Not that I work with the police—no, not me. I'm no knight errant, either. It just came to me that the simplest people in the world are crooks. They are so set on their own plans to fleece others that they never imagine that they are the simplest sort to do. Why, the best safe cracker in the country— the dread of the police of seven States—will drop all his hard-earned money in three weeks on the race track and many a well-thought-of stick-up man will turn out his wad in one evening's crap game. Get the game? I guess I'm just one of the few that see how soft the lay is.

There's a lot of little stunts to tell about if I wanted to give away professional secrets but the game's too good to spread broadcast. It's enough to say that I've been in card games with four sharpers and did the quartet. At that I don't know a thing about cards and couldn't stack a deck if I was given half the night.

But as I say, I'm an adventurer. Not the kind the name generally means; those that sit around waiting for a sucker or spend their time helping governments out of trouble. Not that I ain't willing to help governments at a certain price but none have asked me. Those kind of chaps are found between the pages of a book, I guess. I know. I tried the game just once and nearly starved to death. There ain't nothing in governments unless you're a politician. And as I said before, I ain't a crook.

I've done a lot of business in blackmail cases. I find out a lad that's being blackmailed and then I visit him. He pays me for my services and like as not we do the blackmailers every time. You see I'm a kind of a fellow in the centre—not a crook and not a policeman. Both of them look on me with suspicion, though the crooks don't often know I'm out after their hides. And the police—well, they run me pretty close at times but I got to take the chances.

But it ain't a nice feeling to be trailed when you're out for pleasure so I trot about the deck a few times whistling just to be sure there wasn't any mistake. And that bird come a-tramping after me as innocent as if it was his first job.

Then I had dinner and he sits at the next table and eyes me with a wistful longing like he hadn't made a pinch in a long time and is just dying to lock somebody up. But I study him, too, and he strikes me queer. He ain't got none of the earmarks of a dick. He acts like a lad with money and orders without even looking at the prices and it comes to me that I may have him wrong and that he might be one of these fellows that wanted to sell me oil stock. I always fall hard for the oil stock game. There ain't much in it but it passes the time and lets you eat well without paying for it.

Along about nine o'clock I am leaning over the rail just thinking and figuring how far the swim to shore is if a fellow had to do it. Not that I had any thought of taking to the water—no, not me—but I always like to figure what the chances are. You never can tell.

Well, that bird with the longing eyes cuddles right up and leans over the rail alongside of me.

"It's a nice night," he says.

"A first rate night for a swim."

I looked him over carefully out of the corner of my eyes.

He sort of straightens up and looks out toward the flickering shore lights.

"It is a long swim," he says, just like he had the idea in mind.

Then he asks me to have a cigar and it's a quarter one and I take it.

"I wonder would you do me a favour," he says, after a bit.

This was about what I expected. Con men are full of that kind of gush.

"Hmmm," is all I get off. My game is a waiting one.

"I came aboard a bit late," he goes right on. "I couldn't get a room—now I wonder would you let me take the upper berth in yours. I have been kind of watching you and saw that you were all alone."

Kind of watching me was right. And now he wanted to share my room. Well, that don't exactly appeal to me, for I'm banking on a good night's sleep. Besides, I know that the story is fishy, for I bought my room aboard and got an outsider. But I don't tell him that right off. I think I'll work him out a bit first.

"I'm a friend of the purser," I tell him. "I'll get you a room."

And I make to pass him.

"No—don't do that," he takes me by the arm. "It isn't that."

"Isn't what?"

I look him straight in the eyes and there's a look there that I have seen before and comes in my line of business. As he half turned and I caught the reflection of his eyes under the tiny deck light I read fear in his face—a real fear—almost a terror.

Then I give it to him straight.

"Out with what you want," I says. "Maybe I can help you but let me tell you first that there are plenty of rooms aboard the boat. Now, you don't look like a crook—you don't look sharp enough. What's the big idea of wanting to bunk with me?"

He thought a moment and then leaned far over the rail and started to talk, keeping his eyes on the water.

"I'm in some kind of trouble. I don't know if I have been followed aboard this boat or not. I don't think so but I can't chance it. I haven't had any sleep in two nights and while I don't expect to sleep tonight I'm afraid I may drop off. I don't want to be alone and—and you struck me as an easy-going fellow who might—might—"

"Like to take a chance on getting bumped off," I cut in.

He kind of drew away when I said this but I let him see right away that perhaps he didn't have me wrong. "And you would like me to sit up and protect you, eh?"

"I didn't exactly mean that but I—I don't want to be alone. Now, if you were a man I could offer money to—"

He paused and waited. I give him credit for putting the thing delicately and leaving the next move to me.

I didn't want to scare him off by putting him wise that he had come within my line of business. It might look suspicious to him. And I didn't want him to get the impression that I was a novice. There might be some future money in a job like this and it wouldn't do to be underrated.

"I'll tell you what I'll do," I says. "I've been all over the world and done some odd jobs for different South American governments"—that always has its appeal—"and I'll sit up and keep an eye on you for a hundred bucks."

Crude? —maybe—but then I know my game and you don't.

"And I can sleep?" he chirps, and his eyes sort of brighten up.

"Like a baby," I tells him.

"Good," he says, and "Come to my cabin."

So I take the number of his cabin and tell him that I'll meet him there as soon as I get my bag. Then leave him and fetch my bag and put what money I have in the purser's office, for, although I can size up a game right away, a fellow can't afford to take chances. I have run across queerer ducks than this in my time.

Twenty minutes later he's in bed and we've turned the sign about smoking to the wall and are puffing away on a couple of good cigars. All content—he's paid me the hundred like a man; two nice new fifties.

He just lay there and smoked and didn't talk much and didn't seem as sleepy as I had thought he was. But I guess he was too tired to sleep, which is a queer thing but I've had it lots of times myself.

He seemed to be thinking, too. Like he was planning something and I was concerned in it. But I didn't bother him none. I saw what was on his chest and he didn't seem in a condition to keep things to himself. I thought he'd out with some proposition for me. But I didn't know. I wasn't anxious to travel about and be a nurse to him. That's more of a job for a private detective but they ain't used over much because they want to know all about your business and then you're worse off than you were before.

At last he opens up.

"What's your business?" he says.

And seeing I got his hundred there ain't no reason to dodge the question. I up and tells him.

"I'm a soldier of fortune."

He kind of blinks at this and then asks.

"That means a chap who takes chances for—for a consideration."

"Certain kind of chances." I qualify his statement.

"Like this for instance?"

"Sometimes; but I don't reckon to travel around as a body guard if that's what you're thinking."

He laughs like he was more at ease. But I often see them laugh when they are getting ready to send me into the danger that they fear. It's not downright meanness like I used to think when I was younger. It's relief, I guess.

"I think I can use you," he said slowly. "And pay you well and you won't need to see me again."

"Oh, I ain't got any particular dislike to you," I tell him. "It's only that I like to work alone. Let me hear what you have to offer and then—well, you can get some sleep tonight anyways."

He thought a moment.

"How much do I have to tell you?" he asked.

"As much or as little as you like. The less the better—but all I ought to know to make things go right for you."

"Well, then, there isn't much to tell. In the first place I want you to impersonate me for the summer or a greater part of it."

"That's not so easy." I shook my head.

"It's easy enough," he went on eagerly. "I am supposed to go to my father's hotel on Nantucket Island—"

Then he leaned out of the bed and talked quickly. He spoke very low and was very much in earnest. They could not possibly know me there. His father was abroad and he had not been to Nantucket since he was ten.

"How old are you?" he asked me suddenly.

"Thirty," I told him.

"You don't look more than I do. We are much alike—about the same size—the same features. And you won't meet anyone I know. If things should go wrong I'll be in touch with you."

"And your trouble?" I questioned. "What should I know about that?"

"That my life is threatened. I have been mixed up with some people whom I am not proud of."

"And they threaten to kill you."

I stroked my chin. Not that I minded taking the chances but somewhere I had learned that a labourer is worthy of his hire. It looked like he was hiring me to get bumped off in his place. Which was all right if I was paid enough. I had taken such chances before and nothing had come of it. That is nothing to me.

"Yes, they threaten my life—but I think it's all bluff."

I nodded. I could plainly see it was that, so I handed out a little talk.

"And that's why you paid me a hundred to sit up with you all night. Mind you, I don't mind the risk, but I must be paid accordingly."

When he saw that it was only a question of money he opens up considerable. He didn't exactly give me the facts in the case but he tells me enough and I learned that he had never seen the parties.

The end of it was that he draws up a paper which asks me to impersonate him and lets me out of all trouble. Of course, the paper wouldn't be much good in a bad jam but it would help if his old man should return suddenly from Europe. But I don't aim to produce that paper. I play the game fair and the figure he names was a good one—not what I would have liked perhaps but all he could afford to pay without bringing his old man into the case, which could not be done.

Somehow, when we finished talking, I got the idea that he had been mixed up in a shady deal—bootlegging or something—and a couple of friends had gone to jail on his evidence. There were three others from Canada who were coming on to get him—the three he had never seen. But it didn't matter much to me. I was just to show them that he wasn't afraid and then when they called things off or got me all was over.

Personally I did think that there was a lot of bluff in the whole business but he didn't and it wasn't my game to wise him up.

It was a big hotel I was going to for the summer and if things got melodramatic, why, I guess I could shoot as good as any bootlegger that ever robbed a church. They're hard guys, yes, but then I ain't exactly a cake-eater myself.

An hour or more talk in which I learn all about his family and the hotel and Burton Combs drops off for his first real sleep in months.

The next morning we part company in his stateroom and I taxied over to New Bedford. He thinks that's better than taking the train because there is a change of cars in the open country and he don't want me to drop too soon.

There are only about ten staterooms on the little tub that makes the trip from New Bedford to Nantucket and I have one of them which is already reserved in Burton Combs's name. After taking a walk about the ship I figure that there ain't no Desperate Desmonds aboard, and having earned my hundred the night before I just curl up in that little cabin and hit the hay.

Five hours and not a dream disturbed me and when I come on deck there's Nantucket right under our nose and we are rounding the little lighthouse that stands on the point leading into the bay.

There's a pile of people on the dock and they sure did look innocent enough and I take a stretch and feel mighty good. From some of the outfits I see I know that I'm going to travel in class and I hope that Burton Combs's clothes fit me for I didn't come away prepared for any social gayety. But it's early in the season yet and I'll get a chance to look around before the big rush begins.

There is a bus at the dock which is labelled 'Sea Breeze Inn' and that's my meat. I climb in with about five others and we are off. Up one shady street and down another; up a bit of a hill and a short straightaway and we are at the hotel. It's a peach, too, with a view of the ocean that would knock your eye out.

The manager spots me at once and says that he'd know me among a thousand as a Combs. Which was real sweet of him seeing that he was expecting me, and the others in the bus were an old man, three old women and a young girl about nineteen. But it wasn't my part to enlighten him and tell him that I was on to his flattery. Besides he was an old bird and probably believed what he said.

He was right glad to see me and tried to look like he meant it and wondered why I hadn't come up there again in all these years but guessed it was because it was kind of slow with my father having a hotel at Atlantic City and at Ostend. And he wanted to know if I was going to study the business. Said my father wrote him that he would like to see me interested in the hotel line.

I didn't say much. There wasn't no need. Mr. Rowlands, the manager, was one of those fussy old parties and he talked all the way up in the elevator and right into the room.

There were about fifty people there all told on the first of July but they kept coming in all the time and after I was there about two weeks the place was fairly well crowded. But I didn't make any effort to learn the business, thinking it might hurt young Combs who didn't strike me as a chap who would like any kind of work.

There was one young girl there—the one that came up in the bus with me—Marion St. James, and we had quite some times together. She was young and full of life and wanted to be up and doing all the time and we did a great deal of golf together.

Then there was another who took an interest in me. She was a widow and a fine looker and it was her first season there. I thought that she was more used to playing Atlantic City for she didn't look like the usual run of staunch New England dames. Sort of out of place and she looked to me to trot her around.

But I didn't have the time; there was Marion to be taken about. She was what you'd call a flapper and talked of the moonlight and such rot but she was real and had a big heart and after all a sensible little head on her shoulders. And she couldn't see the widow a mile and looked upon me as her own special property and blew the widow up every chance she got.

But the widow, I guess, was bent on making a match and she was finding the Island pretty dead though the son of John B. Combs, the hotel magnate, looked like a big catch. So you see my time was fairly well taken up and I grabbed many a good laugh. I never took women seriously. My game and women don't go well together.

Yet that widow was persistent and curious and wanted to know every place Marion and me went and used to keep asking me where we drove to nights. For the kid and me did a pile of motoring. Yes, I had a car. A nice little touring car came with the Burton Combs moniker.

Marion was different. She was just a slip of a kid stuck up in a place like that and it was up to me to show her a good time. I kind of felt sorry for her and then she was pretty and a fellow felt proud to be seen with her.

All the time I kept an eye peeled for the bad men. I wondered if they'd come at all and if they did I thought that they would come in the busy season when they wouldn't be noticed much. But that they'd come at all I very much doubted.

And then they came—the three of them. I knew them the very second they entered the door. They were dolled right up to the height of fashion—just what the others were wearing. But I knew them. They just didn't belong. Maybe the others didn't spot them as outsiders but I did.

They were no bluff, either. I have met all kinds of men in my day; bad and worse and these three were the real thing. It came to me that if these gents were bent on murder I had better be up and doing.

And that Island boasted that it had never had a real murder. Yes, it sure did look like all records were going to be broken.

One of them was a tall skinny fellow and he looked more like a real summer visitor than the others. But his mouth gave him away. When he thought he was alone with the others he'd talk through the side of it, a trick which is only found in the underworld or on the track.

One of the others was fat and looked like an ex-bartender and the third I should say was just a common jailbird that could cut a man's throat with a smile.

The tall skinny one was the leader and he was booked as Mr. James Farrow. He made friends with me right off the bat. Didn't overdo it, you know; just gave me the usual amount of attention that most of the guests showed toward the owner's son. He must-a read a book about the Island for he tried to tell me things about the different points of interest like he'd been there before. But he had a bad memory like on dates and things. Marion gave me the dope on that. She knew that Island like a book.

I didn't have much doubt as to who they were but I checked them up, liking to make sure. I didn't know just what their game was and I didn't see the big idea of wanting to bump me off. If they wanted money I could catch their point but they seemed well supplied with the ready. Yes, sir, I looked this Farrow over and he's a tough bird and no mistake. But then I've seen them just as tough before and pulled through it. Besides, I hold a few tricks myself. They don't know I'm on and they don't know that I'm mighty quick with the artillery myself.

And that gun is always with me. It ain't like I only carry it when I think there's trouble coming. I always have it. You see, a chap in my line of work makes a lot of bad friends and he can't tell when one of them is going to bob up and demand an explanation. But they all find out that I ain't a bird to fool with and am just as likely to start the fireworks as they are.

Nearly every night after dinner I'd take the car and Marion and me would go for a little spin about the Island. I don't know when I ever enjoyed anything so much and sometimes I'd forget the game I was playing and think that things were different. I've met a pile of women in my time but none like Marion nor near like her. Not since the days when I went to school—and that's a memory only.

Well, we'd just drive about and talk and she'd ask me about the different places I had been to. And I could hold my own there, for I've been all over the world.

Then one night—about ten days after the troupe arrived—I get a real scare. We've been over 'Scònset way and are driving home along about nine-thirty when—zip—there's a whiz in the air and a hole in the windshield. Then there's another zip and I see Marion jump.

It's nothing new to me. I knew that sound right away. It's a noiseless gun and someone has taken a couple of plugs at us from the distance. Well, it ain't my cue to stop, so I speed up and it's pretty near town before I slow down beneath a lamp and turn to Marion.

There is a little trickle of blood running down her cheek and she's pretty white. But she ain't hurt any. It's just a scratch and I stop in the drug store and get some stuff and bathe it off.

She is a mighty game little kid and don't shake a bit and act nervous. But I'm unsteady for the first time in my life and my hand shook. I wouldn't of been much good on a quick draw then. But later I would, for I was mad—bad mad—if you know what that is. I see that all the danger ain't mine. Not that I think they meant to get Marion. But I had brought that Kid into something, and all because she kind of liked me a bit and I took her around.

On the way back to the hotel I buck up and tell her that it must have been some of the natives hunting the hares and not to say anything about it but that I would speak to the authorities in the morning.

She just looked at me funny and I knew that she did not believe me but she let it go at that.

"If that's all you want to tell me, Burt—why—all right—I shan't say a word to anyone. You can trust me."

That was all. Neither of us spoke again until we reached the hotel and I had parked the car under the shed at the side and we were standing at the bottom of the steps by the little side entrance. Then she turned and put her two tiny hands up on my shoulders and the paleness had gone from her face but just across her cheek where the bullet had passed was the smallest streak of vivid red.

"You can trust me, Burt," she said again and there seemed to be a question in her voice.

"Of course I trust you, Marion," I answered and my voice was husky and seemed to come from a distance.

It all happened very suddenly after that. Her head was very close. I know, for her soft hair brushed my cheek. I think that she leaned forward but I know that she looked up into my eyes and that the next moment I had leaned down and kissed and held her so a moment. So we stood and she did not draw away and I made no movement to release her. We were alone there, very much alone.

Then there was the sudden chug of a motor, a second's flash of light and I had opened my arms and Marion was gone and I stood alone in the blackness.

So the spell of Marion's presence was broken and I stood silently in the shadow as Farrow and his two companions passed and entered the hotel lobby.

Had they seen us? Yes—I knew that they had. For they smiled as they passed. Smiled and never knew that they had passed close to death. For at that moment it was only the press of a trigger that lay between them and eternity.

The curtain had been rung up on the first act and the show was on. Before, I could sleep easy at night for the danger was mine and I had thought little of it. But now I felt that it was another's—and—well, I resolved to bring things to a head that night.

Ten minutes later I went to my room but not to bed. I put my light out and sat in the room until about twelve o'clock. At that time the hotel was as quiet as death.

Then I stepped out of my window and climbed down the fire escape which led to the little terrace which overlooked the ocean. I knew just where Farrow's room was and I walked along the terrace until I was under it and then swung myself up the fire escape and climbed to the third story. His window was open and thirty seconds later I had dropped into the room and was seated on the end of Farrow's bed.

Then I switched on the light and waited till he woke up. Guess he didn't have much fear of me for he slept right on for another five minutes and then he kind of turned over and blinked and—opened his eyes. He was awake fast enough then for he was looking in the mean end of my automatic.

He was quick witted, too, for he rubbed his eyes with one hand while he let the other slip under his pillow. Then I laughed and he drew it out empty and sat bolt upright in bed and faced the gun.

"Farrow," I says. "You were mighty near to going out tonight. And if I hadn't already lifted that gun of yours I'd a popped you then."

And I half wished that I had let his gun stay there for then there would have been an excuse to let him have it. A poor excuse but still an excuse. It's hard to shoot a man when he ain't armed and prepared but it's another thing to shoot when he's reaching for a gun and it's your life or his. Then you can let him have it with your mind easy.

He was a game bird, was Farrow, for he must have had plenty to think about at that moment. You see he couldn't tell just what was coming to him and from his point of view it must have looked mighty bad but he started right in to talk. Told me the chances I was taking and that I couldn't possibly get away with it. He didn't waste any time in bluffing and pretending surprise at seeing me sitting there with the gun. I give him credit—now—for understanding the situation.

But I stopped his wind.

"Shut up," I says.

And he caught the anger in my eyes and in my voice and he shut—which was good for him, for a chap can't tell for sure what he's going to do when he's seeing red and has the drop on a lad that he figures needs killing.

Then I did a bit of talking. I told him what had taken place that night and I knew it was his doing. And he nodded and never tried to deny it.

"You killed my brother," he says, "for he died in trying to break jail a few months ago—the jail where you sent him."

"So—I killed your brother, eh? Well, every man is entitled to his own opinion. Now, I don't know about the killing of your brother but I'll tell you this, my friend, I come mighty near to killing you and I don't miss either and I don't crack windshields and I don't go for to hit innocent parties."

I could see that he was kind of surprised at the way I talked for I wasn't specially careful about my language like I had been about the hotel and like what he would expect from the real Burton Combs. But I could see that he kind of smacked his lips at the mention of the girl and he knew that he had a hold on me there. But I didn't care what was on his chest. I knew that the morning would see the end of the thing one way or the other.

"I am going to give you until the six-thirty boat tomorrow morning to leave the Island," I told him.

And I was not bluffing, either. After a man has had his warning it's good ethics to shoot him down—at least I see it that way. That is, if he needs it bad and you happen to have my code of morals. Also if you want to live to a ripe old age.

"What then?" he sort of sneers.

Seeing as how he wasn't going over the hurdles right away he thinks I'm a bit soft. In the same position his own doubt about shooting me would be the chances of a getaway. And the chances were not good on that Island unless you had made plans in advance. Perhaps he had—I didn't know then for I hadn't seen any boat hanging about the harbour.

"What then?" he sneers again.

"Then—" I says very slowly and thinking of Marion. "Then I'll cop you off at breakfast tomorrow morning. Yes—as soon as that boat leaves the dock I'll be gunning for you, Mr. James Farrow. And as sure as you're not a better shot than you were tonight out on the moors you'll go join your brother."

With that I turned from the bed and, unlocking his door, walked out of his room. The temptation to shoot was too great.

But I didn't go to bed that night. I just put out my light and sat smoking in my room—smoking and thinking. So I spent the second night that summer awake. I knew that the three would meet and talk it over and no doubt—get. But I just sat there; half facing the door and half facing the window with my gun on my knees waiting.

How nice would it be if they would only come by the window? It would be sweet then—and what a lot of credit I'd get as Burton Combs protecting his father's property. They meant real business all right for I see now that there was sentiment behind the whole thing—sentiment and honour. That peculiar honour of the underworld which goes and gets a squealer. Combs had evidently squealed and Farrow's brother had paid the price. And Combs went free. Position and evidence and politics had done the trick, I guess.

I heard the clock strike two and then two-thirty and then there was a footstep in the hall and I turned and faced the door and then there came a light tap on the door. This sure was a surprise.

I didn't turn on the electric light but just went to the door and swung it open suddenly and stepped back. But no one came in.

Then I heard a kind of a gasp—a woman's voice. The first thing I thought of was Marion and then I see the widow in the dim hall light. Her hair was all down and she had thrown a light robe about her and she was excited and her eyes were wide open and she looked frightened.

"It's Marion—little Miss St. James," she sobbed, "and she's in my room now—and it was terrible and I think—I think she fainted."

Then she stopped and kind of choked a bit.

Right away it came to me that this gang had done something to her and I wished that I had settled the whole thing earlier in the evening when I had the chance but—

"Come," I said to the widow and took her by the arm and led her down the hall to her room. The door was open and gun in hand I rushed into the room ahead of her.

"There on the bed," she gasped behind me.

I turned to the bed—and it was empty and then I knew. But it was too late, for I was trapped. There was a muzzle of a gun shoved into the middle of my back and a hard laugh. Then Farrow spoke.

"Throw that gun on the bed and throw it quick."

And—and I threw it and threw it quick. I was done. I should have suspected the widow from the first day I laid eyes on her, for she didn't belong. Yes, she was this gang's come on. And me, who had never fallen for women, was now caught by women. A good one and a bad one. One whom I wanted to protect and one who knew it. Now you see how the game is played. Neither a good nor a bad woman can help you in my sort of life. And yet I would take any chance for that little Marion who used to stand out on the moor at the—but Farrow was talking.

"And now, Mr. Combs, we meet again—and you're the one to do the listening. We are going to take you for a little motor ride—that is, you are going out with me to meet my friends. We don't intend to kill you. That is, if you have proved yourself a man and come along quietly. There is some information I want from you. And thanks for the return of my gun," he finished as he picked the gun off the bed.

Yes, it was his gun and mine was still in my pocket and I'd-a shot him then only I saw that the widow was covering me.

"Come."

Farrow turned and, poking the gun close to my ribs, he induced me to leave the room with him.

"If you make a noise you go," he told me as we walked down the long narrow hall to the servants' stairs. But I didn't intend to cry out. If he would just move that gun of his the least little bit I could draw and shoot. I almost laughed, the thing was so easy.

"The Elsie is lying right off the point," he went on, as we approached the little shed where my car was kept. "You remember the Elsie—it used to be your boat. The government remembers it, too. But they don't know it now nor would you. But enough of that. Climb into your car—we'll use that for our little jaunt."

We had reached the little shed now and I climbed into the car, always waiting for a chance to use my gun, but he watched me like a hawk. Then he laughed—a queer, weird laugh which had the ring of death in it.

I drove as he said and we turned from the hotel and out onto the moors—that long stretch of desolate road that leads across the Island. And then he made me stop the car and stand up.

"I'll take your gun," he said and he lifted it from my hip. "We won't need more than one gun between us tonight. For if it comes to shooting I'll take care of that end of it."

He threw the gun into the back of the car where I heard it strike the cushion of the rear seat and bounce to the floor.

We drove on in silence. He never said a word but I felt as clearly as if he had told me so that he was driving me to my death. The gun, he had let me carry until we were safe away. Perhaps he had thought that without it I might have cried out in the hotel but this I shall never know. That he knew all along I had it I have no doubt.

More than once I was on the edge of telling him that I was not the man he thought I was, for it looked as though the game was up. But he would not have believed me and besides my little agreement with Combs was back in my hotel room.

Not a soul did we pass as we sped over the deserted road. No light but the dulled rays of the moon broke the darkness all around us. Half hour or more and then suddenly I see a car in the road as the moon pops out from behind the clouds.

Then Farrow spoke and there was the snarl of an animal in his voice.

"Here's where you stop," he growled, "and here's where you get yours. They'll find you out here in the morning and they can think what they want; we'll be gone. And the killing of a rat like you is the only business I've got on the moors this night."

I had pulled up short in the centre of the road now for a big touring car which I recognised as Farrow's was stretched across our path blocking the passage. In it I clearly saw his two friends.

It was death now sure but I made up my mind to go out as gracefully as possible and when he ordered me to open the door I leaned over and placed my hand upon the seat. And it fell on the cool muzzle of a revolver. Yes, my fingers closed over a gun and I knew that that gun was mine.

Thrills in life—yes—there are many but I guess that that moment was my biggest. I didn't stop to think how that gun got there. I didn't care. I just tightened on it and felt the blood of life pass quickly through my body—if you know what I mean.

I couldn't turn and shoot him for he had his pistol pressed close against my side. What he feared I don't know but I guess he was just one of these over-careful fellows who didn't take any chances.

"Open that door and get out," he ordered again as he gave me a dig in the ribs.

I leaned over again and placed my hand upon the handle of the door and then I got a happy thought.

"I can't open it," I said and I let my voice tremble and my hand shake. But in my left hand I now held my gun and thanked my lucky stars that I was left-handed, for I knew if I got the one chance that I hoped for it would have to be a perfect shot.

"White livered after all," he muttered and he stooped over and placed his left hand upon the handle of the door.

His right hand still held the gun close to my side and his eyes were watching my every movement.

I never seen a man so careful before. I couldn't pull the gun up and shoot for he would get me at the very first movement—and although I was tempted I waited. The other two sat in the car ahead and were smoking and laughing. Of course I knew that if I once stepped out in the moonlight with the gun in my hand that it was all up but I waited and then—

The door really stuck a bit, for the nights are mighty damp on that island and it was that dampness which saved my life. For just the fraction of a second he took his eyes off me—just a glance down at the door with a curse on his lips.

And with that curse on his lips he died.

For as he turned the handle I give it to him right through the heart. I don't miss at that range—no—not me. The door flew open and he tumbled out on the road—dead.

I don't offer no apologies, for it was his life or mine and—as I said—he tumbled out on the road—dead.

Another fellow writing might say that things weren't clear after that. But they were clear enough to me because I never lose my head. That's why I have lived to be thirty and expect to die in bed. Yes, things are always clear when clearness means a little matter of life or death.

Those other chaps were so surprised at the turn things had taken that I had jumped to the road and winged one of them before they knew what had happened. But the other fellow was quick and had started shooting and I felt a sharp pain in my right shoulder. But one shot was all that he fired and then I had him—one good shot was all I needed and—he went out. I don't go for to miss.

I didn't take the time to examine them to see if they were dead. I'm not an undertaker and it wasn't my business. I guessed they were but if they wasn't I didn't intend to finish the job. I'm not a murderer, either. Then there were a couple of houses not so far off and I could see lights—lights that weren't there before—in both of them. Even on a quiet island like that you can't start a gun party without disturbing some of the people.

I just turned my car around and started back to the hotel. Twenty minutes later I had parked it in the shed and gone to my room. As far as I knew no one could know what had taken place on the lonely moor that night. I played doctor to my shoulder. It wasn't so very bad, either, though it pained a lot, but the bullet had gone through the flesh and passed out. I guess a little home treatment was as good as any doctor could do.

Then the morning came and my arm was not so good but I dressed and went down to breakfast and saw the manager and he told me that the widow had gone on the early boat. I don't think that she was a real widow but that she was the wife of one of those chaps. Farrow, I guess. But that didn't bother me none. She was a widow now all right.

And then about nine o'clock news of the three dead men being found away off on the road came in. And I know I got all three of them.

There was a lot of talk and newspaper men from the city came over and detectives and one thing and another. The morning papers of the following day had it all in and wild guesses as to how it happened. The three were recognised by the police as notorious characters and then it got about that a rum-runner had been seen off the east shore that very morning. The general opinion seemed to be that there had been a fight among the pirates and that these three men got theirs—which suited me to a T.

I would-a beat it only that would have looked mighty queer and honestly I didn't see where they had a thing on me. I thought the best thing to do was to sit tight and for nearly a week I sat.

And then the unexpected—unexpected by me at least—happened.

The widow sent a telegram to the Boston police and they came down and nailed me. You see the writing on the wall? Keep clear of the women.

A dick from Boston dropped in one morning and I knew him the minute he stepped foot in the hotel. And I also knew that he was after me though at the time I didn't wise up as to how he was on. But he wasn't sure of himself and he had the manager introduce him to me. Then he talked about everything but the killing and of course he was the only one at the hotel that left that topic out of his conversation. And that was his idea of hiding his identity!

But he was sharp enough at that and hadn't gone about the Island more than a couple of days before he stuck this and that together and had enough on me to make the charge. But he was a decent sort of chap and came up to my room late at night with the manager and put the whole thing straight up to me and told me about the widow's telegram and that I was under arrest and that I had better get a hold of the best lawyer that money could buy for I was in for a tough time.

He was right and I knew that I was in a mighty bad hole. But I also knew that there would be plenty of money behind me when the whole thing came out and money is a mighty good thing to get out of a hole with.

So I played the game and never let on that I wasn't the real Burton Combs. They locked me up and notified my adopted father and the next morning the news was shouted all over the world, for John B. Combs cut a big figure and his son's arrest made some music.

And then the Combs lawyer, Harvey Benton, came up to see me and the minute he set eyes on me the cat was out of the bag and I up and tells him the whole story though I didn't give him the reason for Combs being frightened but just said that he was threatened by these three rum-runners. I felt that my playing the game fair would give me a better standing with the Combses and help loosen up the old purse strings.

Young Combs wasn't such a bad fellow either, for the next day he was down to see me and ready to tell the whole story and stand up for me.

The we moved over to the mainland and I couldn't get out on bail and the prosecuting attorney started to have my record looked up and I can tell you that after that things didn't look so rosy. It all goes to prove that a clean sheet helps a man though mine wasn't nothing to be ashamed of. But I will admit that it looked pretty sick on the front pages of the newspapers.

Then John B. Combs himself arrives and comes up to see me. He listens to my story at first with a hard, cold face but when I come to the part where I have to shoot quick or die his eyes kind of fill and I see he's thinking of his son and the chances he would of had in the same place—and how if I hadn't got them they would-a got Burton.

Then he stretches forth his hand and grasps mine and I see it would have been better if Burton had taken his father into his confidence in the first place.

Yes, the old boy was a good scout and he told me that he loved his son and that I had saved his son's life and he didn't care what my past had been. And he would see me through this thing that his son had gotten me into if it cost a fortune.

It was a funny thing all around. Here was me, the sufferer, comforting the old boy and telling him that it was nothing. Just like the chair looking me in the face was an everyday affair. But I didn't much like the idea of his being so sad, for it gives me the impression that my chances are not so good and that I am going to pay the price for his son. Which ain't nothing to sing about. But it was my word against the word of the gang, and they being dead wouldn't have much to say.

Yes, I was indicted all right and held for the grand jury—first degree murder was the charge. Then come a wait with my lawyers trying to get a hold of some farmer who might of seen something of the shooting and would corroborate my story.

Then comes the trial and you would-a thought that the District Attorney had a personal grudge against me all his life and that all the politicians and one-horse newspapers were after his job. He paints up those three crooks like they were innocent young country girls that had been trapped by a couple of designing men. And he tells how Burton Combs done them in a shady deal and when he feared they was going to tell the authorities he up and hires a professional murderer to kill them.

I tell you it made a mighty good story and he told it well. One could almost see those three cherubs going forth in child-like innocence to be slaughtered by the butcher—which is me.

And he punched holes in my story. Especially that part about how I put down my hand and found the gun on the seat. And he said that I took them out on some pretence and shot them down in cold blood—quick shooting being my business and shady deals my living.

When he got through with my story it was as full of holes as a sieve and I had a funny feeling around the chest because I thought anyone could see what a rotten gang this was and what a clean-living young fellow I was. For my lawyer painted me up as a young gentleman what went around the world trying to help others.

Just when I think that things are all up and the jury are eyeing me with hard, stern faces comes the surprise. You see, I had never told a soul about Marion being in the car with me when that gang first started the gun play out on the 'Scònset road. You see, I didn't see the need of it and—and—well, somehow I just couldn't drag her into it. Weakness, I'll admit, for a fellow facing death should fight with every weapon he can grab. And there's that thing about women cropping up again.

But somehow there in that stuffy courtroom her innocent face and those soft, child-like eyes come up before me and I see she might of helped me a lot with the simple truth about the bullet that crossed her cheek. And while I was thinking about Marion and telling myself that my goose was cooked comes that big surprise.

My lawyer calls a witness, and it's Marion St. James. Gad! my heart just stops beating for the moment.

She was very quiet and very calm but her voice was low and the jury had to lean forward to catch what she said. She told about the ride that night and how the bullet broke the windshield and scratched her cheek.

And then came the shock. I was just dreaming there and thinking of the trouble I had caused her when I heard what she was saying and I woke up—quick.

"—after I left Mr. Combs—I called him Burton," and she pointed down at me. "I went upstairs but I couldn't sleep. I was thinking about what had happened out on the moor that night. Of course, I didn't believe what Burton had told me—about the hares. And then I remembered the look on his face as he bathed off my cheek—and it was terrible to see and—"

Then she paused a moment and wiped her eyes and went on.

"After a bit I looked out the window and I could see the little shed, where Burt kept his car, and I just caught the glimpse of a man going into it. I thought it was Burt and that he was going to drive out on the moor and—Oh, I don't know what I thought, but I was frightened and didn't want him to go and I just rushed out of my room and down the back stairs and out toward the shed.

"I was just in time to see a big touring car pull out and two men were in it. And then I waited a minute and went and looked into the shed and Burt's car was still there. I don't know why but I was frightened and I climbed into the little touring car and sat down in the back and kind of rested.

"Then I heard someone coming and I hid down in the back of the car and pulled some rugs up over me and waited."

"And why did you wait?" my lawyer asked her kindly.

"I just thought that I would be able to help Mr.—Burt—and I wanted to help him."

"Was there any other reason?"

"Yes—I thought that he was going into trouble for me and—and—" she paused a moment.

"Yes," the lawyer encouraged.

"And I wanted to help him."

She said the words so low that you could hardly catch them. But the lawyer didn't ask her to repeat them. I guess he thought it went over better that way and it sure did—at least with me. For I knew what she meant.

Then she went on.

"Pretty soon Mr. Combs came along" (for she kept calling me Burton Combs) "and that big man was with him. The one they called Mr. Farrow. I looked carefully up over the door, for it was very dark where I was, and I saw that Mr. Farrow had a gun in his hand and that he held it close up against Mr. Combs's back. And he talked rough but too low to understand and then they both climbed into the front of the machine. I did not know just what I could do, but I thought—oh—I don't know what I thought, but I did so want to help him and I was just too scared to cry out.

"And then they started off and after they were a little way out in the country Mr. Farrow made Burton stop the car and stand up while he searched him. And he found his revolver and took it from him and threw it into the back of the car. It landed on the seat and bounced off and I stretched out my hand and took hold of it and held it there under the rugs. I didn't know what to do with it at first for I had never fired a gun.

"Then I heard Mr. Farrow say that he was going to kill Mr. Combs and I was terribly frightened but I leaned up and stretched my hand over the seat and tried to give the pistol to Mr. Combs. But Mr. Farrow turned suddenly and I became frightened and dropped the pistol. Then I dropped back in the car again but I was half out of the covers and afraid to pull them over me for the car had stopped again and I had a feeling that someone was looking down at me. Then I heard them moving in front of the car and I looked up and I saw that Mr. Farrow had his gun pressed close against Mr. Combs's side and that Mr. Combs was trying to open the door.

"Then came the sudden report and I think that I cried out, for I thought that Burt was shot. Then came several more shots, one right after another, and I looked out and saw Mr. Combs standing in the moonlight and a man beside another big car firing at him—and then the man fell and—"

She broke off suddenly and started to cry.

"And after that?" my lawyer smiled at her.

"I climbed back under the robes and—Mr. Combs drove me back to the hotel—but he never knew I was there."

Well, that just about settled it, I guess. The room was in more or less of an uproar. And you ought to have heard my lawyer! Now I know why good lawyers get so much money. He started in and he sure did paint that gang up mighty black, and now I was the innocent boy led into danger by these hardened criminals. And he showed how the gun was held close to my side when I fired.

"And if that isn't self-defence and good American pluck I'd like to ask you what in heaven's name is?"

And that's the whole show. One hour later I was a free man. Everybody was shaking hands with me, and from a desperate criminal I had suddenly become a hero. And I guess that Marion had done it.

Then Old Combs came up to me and shook me by the hand and told me how glad he was that I was free and what a plucky little thing Marion was, and how I owed my life twice over to her.

Then he offered me a job. Imagine! Another job for the Combs family. But this was different.

"There is too much good in you to lead the life you have been leading. You may think that it is all right, but there will be others that won't. I can offer you something that will be mighty good."

But I shook my head.

"I guess I'll stick to my trade," I said. "I've had good offers before, and in my line—this little notoriety won't hurt none."

"It's a good position," he says, not paying much attention to what I was getting off. "The right people will be glad to know you—and there will be enough money in it to get married."

I started to shake my head again when he handed me a note.

"Read this note and then let me know. Not another word until you have read it."

He smiles.

I took the little blue envelope and tore it open, and it was from Marion:

I would like to see you again when you take that position of Mr. Combs.

I guess I read that simple sentence over a couple of dozen times before I again turned to Mr. Combs.

"I guess I'll take that job—if it pays enough to get married on," was all that I said.

There ain't no explanation unless—unless I wanted to see Marion again myself.

That's all, unless to warn you that it would be kind of foolish to take too seriously anything I said about keeping clear of the women.

Text 2 The Adventure of the Six Napoleons

By Sir Arthur Conan Doyle

It was no very unusual thing for Mr. Lestrade, of Scotland Yard, to look in upon us of an evening, and his visits were welcome to Sherlock Holmes, for they enabled him to keep in touch with all that was going on at the police headquarters. In return for the news which Lestrade would bring, Holmes was always ready to listen with attention to the details of any case upon which the detective was engaged, and was able occasionally, without any active interference, to give some hint or suggestion drawn from his own vast knowledge and experience.

On this particular evening, Lestrade had spoken of the weather and the newspapers. Then he had fallen silent, puffing thoughtfully at his cigar. Holmes looked keenly at him.

"Anything remarkable on hand?" he asked.

"Oh, no, Mr. Holmes—nothing very particular."

"Then tell me about it."

Lestrade laughed.

"Well, Mr. Holmes, there is no use denying that there IS something on my mind. And yet it is such an absurd business, that I hesitated to bother you about it. On the other hand, although it is trivial, it is undoubtedly queer, and I know that you have a taste for all that is out of the common. But, in my opinion, it comes more in Dr. Watson's line than ours."

"Disease?" said I.

"Madness, anyhow. And a queer madness, too. You wouldn't think there was anyone living at this time of day who had such a hatred of Napoleon the First that he would break any image of him that he could see."

Holmes sank back in his chair.

"That's no business of mine," said he.

"Exactly. That's what I said. But then, when the man commits burglary in order to break images which are not his own, that brings it away from the doctor and on to the policeman."

Holmes sat up again.

"Burglary! This is more interesting. Let me hear the details."

Lestrade took out his official notebook and refreshed his memory from its pages.

"The first case reported was four days ago," said he. "It was at the shop of Morse Hudson, who has a place for the sale of pictures and statues in the Kennington Road. The assistant had left the front shop for an instant, when he heard a crash, and hurrying in he found a plaster bust of Napoleon, which stood with several other works of art upon the counter, lying shivered into fragments. He rushed out into the road, but, although several passers-by declared that they had noticed a man run out of the shop, he could neither see anyone nor could he find any means of identifying the rascal. It seemed to be one of those senseless acts of Hooliganism which occur from time to time, and it was reported to the constable on the beat as such. The plaster cast was not worth more than a few shillings, and the whole affair appeared to be too childish for any particular investigation.

"The second case, however, was more serious, and also more singular. It occurred only last night.

"In Kennington Road, and within a few hundred yards of Morse Hudson's shop, there lives a well-known medical practitioner, named Dr. Barnicot, who has one of the largest practices upon the south side of the Thames. His residence and principal consulting-room is at Kennington Road, but he has a branch surgery and dispensary at Lower Brixton Road, two miles away. This Dr. Barnicot is an enthusiastic admirer of Napoleon, and his house is full of books, pictures, and relics of the French Emperor. Some little time ago he purchased from Morse Hudson two duplicate plaster casts of the famous head of Napoleon by the French sculptor, Devine. One of these he placed in his hall in the house at Kennington Road, and the other on the mantelpiece of the surgery at Lower Brixton. Well, when Dr. Barnicot came down this morning he was astonished to find that his house had been burgled during the night, but that nothing had been taken save the plaster head from the hall. It had been carried out and had been dashed savagely against the garden wall, under which its splintered fragments were discovered."

Holmes rubbed his hands.

"This is certainly very novel," said he.

"I thought it would please you. But I have not got to the end yet. Dr. Barnicot was due at his surgery at twelve o'clock, and you can imagine his amazement when, on arriving there, he found that the window had been opened in the night and that the broken pieces of his second bust were strewn all over the room. It had been smashed to atoms where it stood. In neither case were there any signs which could give us a clue as to the criminal or lunatic who had done the mischief. Now, Mr. Holmes, you have got the facts."

"They are singular, not to say grotesque," said Holmes. "May I ask whether the two busts smashed in Dr. Barnicot's rooms were the exact duplicates of the one which was destroyed in Morse Hudson's shop?"

"They were taken from the same mould."

"Such a fact must tell against the theory that the man who breaks them is influenced by any general hatred of Napoleon. Considering how many hundreds of statues of the great Emperor must exist in London, it is too much to suppose such a coincidence as that a promiscuous iconoclast should chance to begin upon three specimens of the same bust."

"Well, I thought as you do," said Lestrade. "On the other hand, this Morse Hudson is the purveyor of busts in that part of London, and these three were the only ones which had been in his shop for years. So, although, as you say, there are many hundreds of statues in London, it is very probable that these three were the only ones in that district. Therefore, a local fanatic would begin with them. What do you think, Dr. Watson?"

"There are no limits to the possibilities of monomania," I answered. "There is the condition which the modern French psychologists have called the 'IDEE FIXE,' which may be trifling in character, and accompanied by complete sanity in every other way. A man who had read deeply about Napoleon, or who had possibly received some hereditary family injury through the great war, might conceivably form such an IDEE FIXE and under its influence be capable of any fantastic outrage."

"That won't do, my dear Watson," said Holmes, shaking his head, "for no amount of IDEE FIXE would enable your interesting monomaniac to find out where these busts were situated."

"Well, how do YOU explain it?"

"I don't attempt to do so. I would only observe that there is a certain method in the gentleman's eccentric proceedings. For example, in Dr. Barnicot's hall, where a sound might arouse the family, the bust was taken outside before being broken, whereas in the surgery, where there was less danger of an alarm, it was smashed where it stood. The affair seems absurdly trifling, and yet I dare call nothing trivial when I reflect that some of my most classic cases have had the least promising commencement. You will remember, Watson, how the dreadful business of the Abernetty family was first brought to my notice by the depth which the parsley had sunk into the butter upon a hot day. I can't afford, therefore, to smile at your three broken busts, Lestrade, and I shall be very much obliged to you if you will let me hear of any fresh development of so singular a chain of events."

The development for which my friend had asked came in a quicker and an infinitely more tragic form than he could have imagined. I was still dressing in my bedroom next morning, when there was a tap at the door and Holmes entered, a telegram in his hand. He read it aloud:

"Come instantly, 131 Pitt Street, Kensington.

"LESTRADE."

"What is it, then?" I asked.

"Don't know—may be anything. But I suspect it is the sequel of the story of the statues. In that case our friend the image-breaker has begun operations in another quarter of London. There's coffee on the table, Watson, and I have a cab at the door."

In half an hour we had reached Pitt Street, a quiet little backwater just beside one of the briskest currents of London life. No. 131 was one of a row, all flat-chested, respectable, and most unromantic dwellings. As we drove up, we found the railings in front of the house lined by a curious crowd. Holmes whistled.

"By George! It's attempted murder at the least. Nothing less will hold the London message-boy. There's a deed of violence indicated in that fellow's round shoulders and outstretched neck. What's this, Watson? The top steps swilled down and the other ones dry. Footsteps enough, anyhow! Well, well, there's Lestrade at the front window, and we shall soon know all about it."

The official received us with a very grave face and showed us into a sitting-room, where an exceedingly unkempt and agitated elderly man, clad in a flannel dressing-gown, was pacing up and down. He was introduced to us as the owner of the house—Mr. Horace Harker, of the Central Press Syndicate.

"It's the Napoleon bust business again," said Lestrade. "You seemed interested last night, Mr. Holmes, so I thought perhaps you would be glad to be present now that the affair has taken a very much graver turn."

"What has it turned to, then?"

"To murder. Mr. Harker, will you tell these gentlemen exactly what has occurred?"

The man in the dressing-gown turned upon us with a most melancholy face.

"It's an extraordinary thing," said he, "that all my life I have been collecting other people's news, and now that a real piece of news has come my own way I am so confused and bothered that I can't put two words together. If I had come in here as a journalist, I should have interviewed myself and had two columns in every evening paper. As it is, I am giving away valuable copy by telling my story over and over to a string of different people, and I can make no use of it myself. However, I've heard your name, Mr. Sherlock Holmes, and if you'll only explain this queer business, I shall be paid for my trouble in telling you the story."

Holmes sat down and listened.

"It all seems to centre round that bust of Napoleon which I bought for this very room about four months ago. I picked it up cheap from Harding Brothers, two doors from the High Street Station. A great deal of my journalistic work is done at night, and I often write until the early morning. So it was to-day. I was sitting in my den, which is at the back of the top of the house, about three o'clock, when I was convinced that I heard some sounds downstairs. I listened, but they were not repeated, and I concluded that they came from outside. Then suddenly, about five minutes later, there came a most horrible yell—the most dreadful sound, Mr. Holmes, that ever I heard. It will ring in my ears as long as I live. I sat frozen with horror for a minute or two. Then I seized the poker and went downstairs. When I entered this room I found the window wide open, and I at once observed that the bust was gone from the mantelpiece. Why any burglar should take such a thing passes my understanding, for it was only a plaster cast and of no real value whatever.

"You can see for yourself that anyone going out through that open window could reach the front doorstep by taking a long stride. This was clearly what the burglar had done, so I went round and opened the door. Stepping out into the dark, I nearly fell over a dead man, who was lying there. I ran back for a light and there was the poor fellow, a great gash in his throat and the whole place swimming in blood. He lay on his back, his knees drawn up, and his mouth horribly open. I shall see him in my dreams. I had just time to blow on my police-whistle, and then I must have fainted, for I knew nothing more until I found the policeman standing over me in the hall."

"Well, who was the murdered man?" asked Holmes.

"There's nothing to show who he was," said Lestrade. "You shall see the body at the mortuary, but we have made nothing of it up to now. He is a tall man, sunburned, very powerful, not more than thirty. He is poorly dressed, and yet does not appear to be a labourer. A horn-handled clasp knife was lying in a pool of blood beside him. Whether it was the weapon which did the deed, or whether it belonged to the dead man, I do not know. There was no name on his clothing, and nothing in his pockets save an apple, some string, a shilling map of London, and a photograph. Here it is."

It was evidently taken by a snapshot from a small camera. It represented an alert, sharp-featured simian man, with thick eyebrows and a very peculiar projection of the lower part of the face, like the muzzle of a baboon.

"And what became of the bust?" asked Holmes, after a careful study of this picture.

"We had news of it just before you came. It has been found in the front garden of an empty house in Campden House Road. It was broken into fragments. I am going round now to see it. Will you come?"

"Certainly. I must just take one look round." He examined the carpet and the window. "The fellow had either very long legs or was a most active man," said he. "With an area beneath, it was no mean feat to reach that window ledge and open that window. Getting back was comparatively simple. Are you coming with us to see the remains of your bust, Mr. Harker?"

The disconsolate journalist had seated himself at a writing-table.

"I must try and make something of it," said he, "though I have no doubt that the first editions of the evening papers are out already with full details. It's like my luck! You remember when the stand fell at Doncaster? Well, I was the only journalist in the stand, and my journal the only one that had no account of it, for I was too shaken to write it. And now I'll be too late with a murder done on my own doorstep."

As we left the room, we heard his pen travelling shrilly over the foolscap.

The spot where the fragments of the bust had been found was only a few hundred yards away. For the first time our eyes rested upon this presentment of the great emperor, which seemed to raise such frantic and destructive hatred in the mind of the unknown. It lay scattered, in splintered shards, upon the grass. Holmes picked up several of them and examined them carefully. I was convinced, from his intent face and his purposeful manner, that at last he was upon a clue.

"Well?" asked Lestrade.

Holmes shrugged his shoulders.

"We have a long way to go yet," said he. "And yet—and yet—well, we have some suggestive facts to act upon. The possession of this trifling bust was worth more, in the eyes of this strange criminal, than a human life. That is one point. Then there is the singular fact that he did not break it in the house, or immediately outside the house, if to break it was his sole object."

"He was rattled and bustled by meeting this other fellow. He hardly knew what he was doing."

"Well, that's likely enough. But I wish to call your attention very particularly to the position of this house, in the garden of which the bust was destroyed."

Lestrade looked about him.

"It was an empty house, and so he knew that he would not be disturbed in the garden."

"Yes, but there is another empty house farther up the street which he must have passed before he came to this one. Why did he not break it there, since it is evident that every yard that he carried it increased the risk of someone meeting him?"

"I give it up," said Lestrade.

Holmes pointed to the street lamp above our heads.

"He could see what he was doing here, and he could not there. That was his reason."

"By Jove! that's true," said the detective. "Now that I come to think of it, Dr. Barnicot's bust was broken not far from his red lamp. Well, Mr. Holmes, what are we to do with that fact?"

"To remember it—to docket it. We may come on something later which will bear upon it. What steps do you propose to take now, Lestrade?"

"The most practical way of getting at it, in my opinion, is to identify the dead man. There should be no difficulty about that. When we have found who he is and who his associates are, we should have a good start in learning what he was doing in Pitt Street last night, and who it was who met him and killed him on the doorstep of Mr. Horace Harker. Don't you think so?"

"No doubt; and yet it is not quite the way in which I should approach the case."

"What would you do then?"

"Oh, you must not let me influence you in any way. I suggest that you go on your line and I on mine. We can compare notes afterwards, and each will supplement the other."

"Very good," said Lestrade.

"If you are going back to Pitt Street, you might see Mr. Horace Harker. Tell him for me that I have quite made up my mind, and that it is certain that a dangerous homicidal lunatic, with Napoleonic delusions, was in his house last night. It will be useful for his article."

Lestrade stared.

"You don't seriously believe that?"

Holmes smiled.

"Don't I? Well, perhaps I don't. But I am sure that it will interest Mr. Horace Harker and the subscribers of the Central Press Syndicate. Now, Watson, I think that we shall find that we have a long and rather complex day's work before us. I should be glad, Lestrade, if you could make it convenient to meet us at Baker Street at six o'clock this evening. Until then I should like to keep this photograph, found in the dead man's pocket. It is possible that I may have to ask your company and assistance upon a small expedition which will have be undertaken to-night, if my chain of reasoning should prove to be correct. Until then good-bye and good luck!"

Sherlock Holmes and I walked together to the High Street, where we stopped at the shop of Harding Brothers, whence the bust had been purchased. A young assistant informed us that Mr. Harding would be absent until afternoon, and that he was himself a newcomer, who could give us no information. Holmes's face showed his disappointment and annoyance.

"Well, well, we can't expect to have it all our own way, Watson," he said, at last. "We must come back in the afternoon, if Mr. Harding will not be here until then. I am, as you have no doubt surmised, endeavouring to trace these busts to their source, in order to find if there is not something peculiar which may account for their remarkable fate. Let us make for Mr. Morse Hudson, of the Kennington Road, and see if he can throw any light upon the problem."

A drive of an hour brought us to the picture-dealer's establishment. He was a small, stout man with a red face and a peppery manner.

"Yes, sir. On my very counter, sir," said he. "What we pay rates and taxes for I don't know, when any ruffian can come in and break one's goods. Yes, sir, it was I who sold Dr. Barnicot his two statues. Disgraceful, sir! A Nihilist plot—that's what I make it. No one but an anarchist would go about breaking statues. Red republicans—that's what I call 'em. Who did I get the statues from? I don't see what that has to do with it. Well, if you really want to know, I got them from Gelder & Co., in Church Street, Stepney. They are a well-known house in the trade, and have been this twenty years. How many had I? Three—two and one are three—two of Dr. Barnicot's, and one smashed in broad daylight on my own counter. Do I know that photograph? No, I don't. Yes, I do, though. Why, it's Beppo. He was a kind of Italian piece-work man, who made himself useful in the shop. He could carve a bit, and gild and frame, and do odd jobs. The fellow left me last week, and I've heard nothing of him since. No, I don't know where he came from nor where he went to. I had nothing against him while he was here. He was gone two days before the bust was smashed."

"Well, that's all we could reasonably expect from Morse Hudson," said Holmes, as we emerged from the shop. "We have this Beppo as a common factor, both in Kennington and in Kensington, so that is worth a ten-mile drive. Now, Watson, let us make for Gelder & Co., of Stepney, the source and origin of the busts. I shall be surprised if we don't get some help down there."

In rapid succession we passed through the fringe of fashionable London, hotel London, theatrical London, literary London, commercial London, and, finally, maritime London, till we came to a riverside city of a hundred thousand souls, where the tenement houses swelter and reek with the outcasts of Europe. Here, in a broad thoroughfare, once the abode of wealthy City merchants, we found the sculpture works for which we searched. Outside was a considerable yard full of monumental masonry. Inside was a large room in which fifty workers were carving or moulding. The manager, a big blond German, received us civilly and gave a clear answer to all Holmes's questions. A reference to his books showed that hundreds of casts had been taken from a marble copy of Devine's head of Napoleon, but that the three which had been sent to Morse Hudson a year or so before had been half of a batch of six, the other three being sent to Harding Brothers, of Kensington. There was no reason why those six should be different from any of the other casts. He could suggest no possible cause why anyone should wish to destroy them—in fact, he laughed at the idea. Their wholesale price was six shillings, but the retailer would get twelve or more. The cast was taken in two moulds from each side of the face, and then these two profiles of plaster of Paris were joined together to make the complete bust. The work was usually done by Italians, in the room we were in. When finished, the busts were put on a table in the passage to dry, and afterwards stored. That was all he could tell us.

But the production of the photograph had a remarkable effect upon the manager. His face flushed with anger, and his brows knotted over his blue Teutonic eyes.

"Ah, the rascal!" he cried. "Yes, indeed, I know him very well. This has always been a respectable establishment, and the only time that we have ever had the police in it was over this very fellow. It was more than a year ago now. He knifed another Italian in the street, and then he came to the works with the police on his heels, and he was taken here. Beppo was his name—his second name I never knew. Serve me right for engaging a man with such a face. But he was a good workman—one of the best."

"What did he get?"

"The man lived and he got off with a year. I have no doubt he is out now, but he has not dared to show his nose here. We have a cousin of his here, and I daresay he could tell you where he is."

"No, no," cried Holmes, "not a word to the cousin—not a word, I beg of you. The matter is very important, and the farther I go with it, the more important it seems to grow. When you referred in your ledger to the sale of those casts I observed that the date was June 3rd of last year. Could you give me the date when Beppo was arrested?"

"I could tell you roughly by the pay-list," the manager answered. "Yes," he continued, after some turning over of pages, "he was paid last on May 20th."

"Thank you," said Holmes. "I don't think that I need intrude upon your time and patience any more." With a last word of caution that he should say nothing as to our researches, we turned our faces westward once more.

The afternoon was far advanced before we were able to snatch a hasty luncheon at a restaurant. A news-bill at the entrance announced "Kensington Outrage. Murder by a Madman," and the contents of the paper showed that Mr. Horace Harker had got his account into print after all. Two columns were occupied with a highly sensational and flowery rendering of the whole incident. Holmes propped it against the cruet-stand and read it while he ate. Once or twice he chuckled.

"This is all right, Watson," said he. Listen to this:

"It is satisfactory to know that there can be no difference of opinion upon this case, since Mr. Lestrade, one of the most experienced members of the official force, and Mr. Sherlock Holmes, the well known consulting expert, have each come to the conclusion that the grotesque series of incidents, which have ended in so tragic a fashion, arise from lunacy rather than from deliberate crime. No explanation save mental aberration can cover the facts.

"The Press, Watson, is a most valuable institution, if you only know how to use it. And now, if you have quite finished, we will hark back to Kensington and see what the manager of Harding Brothers has to say on the matter."

The founder of that great emporium proved to be a brisk, crisp little person, very dapper and quick, with a clear head and a ready tongue.

"Yes, sir, I have already read the account in the evening papers. Mr. Horace Harker is a customer of ours. We supplied him with the bust some months ago. We ordered three busts of that sort from Gelder & Co., of Stepney. They are all sold now. To whom? Oh, I daresay by consulting our sales book we could very easily tell you. Yes, we have the entries here. One to Mr. Harker you see, and one to Mr. Josiah Brown, of Laburnum Lodge, Laburnum Vale, Chiswick, and one to Mr. Sandeford, of Lower Grove Road, Reading. No, I have never seen this face which you show me in the photograph. You would hardly forget it, would you, sir, for I've seldom seen an uglier. Have we any Italians on the staff? Yes, sir, we have several among our workpeople and cleaners. I daresay they might get a peep at that sales book if they wanted to. There is no particular reason for keeping a watch upon that book. Well, well, it's a very strange business, and I hope that you will let me know if anything comes of your inquiries."

Holmes had taken several notes during Mr. Harding's evidence, and I could see that he was thoroughly satisfied by the turn which affairs were taking. He made no remark, however, save that, unless we hurried, we should be late for our appointment with Lestrade. Sure enough, when we reached Baker Street the detective was already there, and we found him pacing up and down in a fever of impatience. His look of importance showed that his day's work had not been in vain.

"Well?" he asked. "What luck, Mr. Holmes?"

"We have had a very busy day, and not entirely a wasted one," my friend explained. "We have seen both the retailers and also the wholesale manufacturers. I can trace each of the busts now from the beginning."

"The busts," cried Lestrade. "Well, well, you have your own methods, Mr. Sherlock Holmes, and it is not for me to say a word against them, but I think I have done a better day's work than you. I have identified the dead man."

"You don't say so?"

"And found a cause for the crime."

"Splendid!"

"We have an inspector who makes a specialty of Saffron Hill and the Italian Quarter. Well, this dead man had some Catholic emblem round his neck, and that, along with his colour, made me think he was from the South. Inspector Hill knew him the moment he caught sight of him. His name is Pietro Venucci, from Naples, and he is one of the greatest cut-throats in London. He is connected with the Mafia, which, as you know, is a secret political society, enforcing its decrees by murder. Now, you see how the affair begins to clear up. The other fellow is probably an Italian also, and a member of the Mafia. He has broken the rules in some fashion. Pietro is set upon his track. Probably the photograph we found in his pocket is the man himself, so that he may not knife the wrong person. He dogs the fellow, he sees him enter a house, he waits outside for him, and in the scuffle he receives his own death-wound. How is that, Mr. Sherlock Holmes?"

Holmes clapped his hands approvingly.

"Excellent, Lestrade, excellent!" he cried. "But I didn't quite follow your explanation of the destruction of the busts."

"The busts! You never can get those busts out of your head. After all, that is nothing; petty larceny, six months at the most. It is the murder that we are really investigating, and I tell you that I am gathering all the threads into my hands."

"And the next stage?"

"Is a very simple one. I shall go down with Hill to the Italian Quarter, find the man whose photograph we have got, and arrest him on the charge of murder. Will you come with us?"

"I think not. I fancy we can attain our end in a simpler way. I can't say for certain, because it all depends—well, it all depends upon a factor which is completely outside our control. But I have great hopes—in fact, the betting is exactly two to one—that if you will come with us to-night I shall be able to help you to lay him by the heels."

"In the Italian Quarter?"

"No, I fancy Chiswick is an address which is more likely to find him. If you will come with me to Chiswick to-night, Lestrade, I'll promise to go to the Italian Quarter with you to-morrow, and no harm will be done by the delay. And now I think that a few hours' sleep would do us all good, for I do not propose to leave before eleven o'clock, and it is unlikely that we shall be back before morning. You'll dine with us, Lestrade, and then you are welcome to the sofa until it is time for us to start. In the meantime, Watson, I should be glad if you would ring for an express messenger, for I have a letter to send and it is important that it should go at once."

Holmes spent the evening in rummaging among the files of the old daily papers with which one of our lumber-rooms was packed. When at last he descended, it was with triumph in his eyes, but he said nothing to either of us as to the result of his researches. For my own part, I had followed step by step the methods by which he had traced the various windings of this complex case, and, though I could not yet perceive the goal which we would reach, I understood clearly that Holmes expected this grotesque criminal to make an attempt upon the two remaining busts, one of which, I remembered, was at Chiswick. No doubt the object of our journey was to catch him in the very act, and I could not but admire the cunning with which my friend had inserted a wrong clue in the evening paper, so as to give the fellow the idea that he could continue his scheme with impunity. I was not surprised when Holmes suggested that I should take my revolver with me. He had himself picked up the loaded hunting-crop, which was his favourite weapon.

A four-wheeler was at the door at eleven, and in it we drove to a spot at the other side of Hammersmith Bridge. Here the cabman was directed to wait. A short walk brought us to a secluded road fringed with pleasant houses, each standing in its own grounds. In the light of a street lamp we read "Laburnum Villa" upon the gate-post of one of them. The occupants had evidently retired to rest, for all was dark save for a fanlight over the hall door, which shed a single blurred circle on to the garden path. The wooden fence which separated the grounds from the road threw a dense black shadow upon the inner side, and here it was that we crouched.

"I fear that you'll have a long wait," Holmes whispered. "We may thank our stars that it is not raining. I don't think we can even venture to smoke to pass the time. However, it's a two to one chance that we get something to pay us for our trouble."

It proved, however, that our vigil was not to be so long as Holmes had led us to fear, and it ended in a very sudden and singular fashion. In an instant, without the least sound to warn us of his coming, the garden gate swung open, and a lithe, dark figure, as swift and active as an ape, rushed up the garden path. We saw it whisk past the light thrown from over the door and disappear against the black shadow of the house. There was a long pause, during which we held our breath, and then a very gentle creaking sound came to our ears. The window was being opened. The noise ceased, and again there was a long silence. The fellow was making his way into the house. We saw the sudden flash of a dark lantern inside the room. What he sought was evidently not there, for again we saw the flash through another blind, and then through another.

"Let us get to the open window. We will nab him as he climbs out," Lestrade whispered.

But before we could move, the man had emerged again. As he came out into the glimmering patch of light, we saw that he carried something white under his arm. He looked stealthily all round him. The silence of the deserted street reassured him. Turning his back upon us he laid down his burden, and the next instant there was the sound of a sharp tap, followed by a clatter and rattle. The man was so intent upon what he was doing that he never heard our steps as we stole across the grass plot. With the bound of a tiger Holmes was on his back, and an instant later Lestrade and I had him by either wrist, and the handcuffs had been fastened. As we turned him over I saw a hideous, sallow face, with writhing, furious features, glaring up at us, and I knew that it was indeed the man of the photograph whom we had secured.

But it was not our prisoner to whom Holmes was giving his attention. Squatted on the doorstep, he was engaged in most carefully examining that which the man had brought from the house. It was a bust of Napoleon, like the one which we had seen that morning, and it had been broken into similar fragments. Carefully Holmes held each separate shard to the light, but in no way did it differ from any other shattered piece of plaster. He had just completed his examination when the hall lights flew up, the door opened, and the owner of the house, a jovial, rotund figure in shirt and trousers, presented himself.

"Mr. Josiah Brown, I suppose?" said Holmes.

"Yes, sir; and you, no doubt, are Mr. Sherlock Holmes? I had the note which you sent by the express messenger, and I did exactly what you told me. We locked every door on the inside and awaited developments. Well, I'm very glad to see that you have got the rascal. I hope, gentlemen, that you will come in and have some refreshment."

However, Lestrade was anxious to get his man into safe quarters, so within a few minutes our cab had been summoned and we were all four upon our way to London. Not a word would our captive say, but he glared at us from the shadow of his matted hair, and once, when my hand seemed within his reach, he snapped at it like a hungry wolf. We stayed long enough at the police-station to learn that a search of his clothing revealed nothing save a few shillings and a long sheath knife, the handle of which bore copious traces of recent blood.

"That's all right," said Lestrade, as we parted. "Hill knows all these gentry, and he will give a name to him. You'll find that my theory of the Mafia will work out all right. But I'm sure I am exceedingly obliged to you, Mr. Holmes, for the workmanlike way in which you laid hands upon him. I don't quite understand it all yet."

"I fear it is rather too late an hour for explanations," said Holmes. "Besides, there are one or two details which are not finished off, and it is one of those cases which are worth working out to the very end. If you will come round once more to my rooms at six o'clock to-morrow, I think I shall be able to show you that even now you have not grasped the entire meaning of this business, which presents some features which make it absolutely original in the history of crime. If ever I permit you to chronicle any more of my little problems, Watson, I foresee that you will enliven your pages by an account of the singular adventure of the Napoleonic busts."

When we met again next evening, Lestrade was furnished with much information concerning our prisoner. His name, it appeared, was Beppo, second name unknown. He was a well-known ne'er-do-well among the Italian colony. He had once been a skilful sculptor and had earned an honest living, but he had taken to evil courses and had twice already been in jail—once for a petty theft, and once, as we had already heard, for stabbing a fellow-countryman. He could talk English perfectly well. His reasons for destroying the busts were still unknown, and he refused to answer any questions upon the subject, but the police had discovered that these same busts might very well have been made by his own hands, since he was engaged in this class of work at the establishment of Gelder & Co. To all this information, much of which we already knew, Holmes listened with polite attention, but I, who knew him so well, could clearly see that his thoughts were elsewhere, and I detected a mixture of mingled uneasiness and expectation beneath that mask which he was wont to assume. At last he started in his chair, and his eyes brightened. There had been a ring at the bell. A minute later we heard steps upon the stairs, and an elderly red-faced man with grizzled side-whiskers was ushered in. In his right hand he carried an old-fashioned carpet-bag, which he placed upon the table.

"Is Mr. Sherlock Holmes here?"

My friend bowed and smiled. "Mr. Sandeford, of Reading, I suppose?" said he.

"Yes, sir, I fear that I am a little late, but the trains were awkward. You wrote to me about a bust that is in my possession."

"Exactly."

"I have your letter here. You said, 'I desire to possess a copy of Devine's Napoleon, and am prepared to pay you ten pounds for the one which is in your possession.' Is that right?"

"Certainly."

"I was very much surprised at your letter, for I could not imagine how you knew that I owned such a thing."

"Of course you must have been surprised, but the explanation is very simple. Mr. Harding, of Harding Brothers, said that they had sold you their last copy, and he gave me your address."

"Oh, that was it, was it? Did he tell you what I paid for it?"

"No, he did not."

"Well, I am an honest man, though not a very rich one. I only gave fifteen shillings for the bust, and I think you ought to know that before I take ten pounds from you.

"I am sure the scruple does you honour, Mr. Sandeford. But I have named that price, so I intend to stick to it."

"Well, it is very handsome of you, Mr. Holmes. I brought the bust up with me, as you asked me to do. Here it is!" He opened his bag, and at last we saw placed upon our table a complete specimen of that bust which we had already seen more than once in fragments.

Holmes took a paper from his pocket and laid a ten-pound note upon the table.

"You will kindly sign that paper, Mr. Sandeford, in the presence of these witnesses. It is simply to say that you transfer every possible right that you ever had in the bust to me. I am a methodical man, you see, and you never know what turn events might take afterwards. Thank you, Mr. Sandeford; here is your money, and I wish you a very good evening."

When our visitor had disappeared, Sherlock Holmes's movements were such as to rivet our attention. He began by taking a clean white cloth from a drawer and laying it over the table. Then he placed his newly acquired bust in the centre of the cloth. Finally, he picked up his hunting-crop and struck Napoleon a sharp blow on the top of the head. The figure broke into fragments, and Holmes bent eagerly over the shattered remains. Next instant, with a loud shout of triumph he held up one splinter, in which a round, dark object was fixed like a plum in a pudding.

"Gentlemen," he cried, "let me introduce you to the famous black pearl of the Borgias."

Lestrade and I sat silent for a moment, and then, with a spontaneous impulse, we both broke at clapping, as at the well-wrought crisis of a play. A flush of colour sprang to Holmes's pale cheeks, and he bowed to us like the master dramatist who receives the homage of his audience. It was at such moments that for an instant he ceased to be a reasoning machine, and betrayed his human love for admiration and applause. The same singularly proud and reserved nature which turned away with disdain from popular notoriety was capable of being moved to its depths by spontaneous wonder and praise from a friend.

"Yes, gentlemen," said he, "it is the most famous pearl now existing in the world, and it has been my good fortune, by a connected chain of inductive reasoning, to trace it from the Prince of Colonna's bedroom at the Dacre Hotel, where it was lost, to the interior of this, the last of the six busts of Napoleon which were manufactured by Gelder & Co., of Stepney. You will remember, Lestrade, the sensation caused by the disappearance of this valuable jewel and the vain efforts of the London police to recover it. I was myself consulted upon the case, but I was unable to throw any light upon it. Suspicion fell upon the maid of the Princess, who was an Italian, and it was proved that she had a brother in London, but we failed to trace any connection between them. The maid's name was Lucretia Venucci, and there is no doubt in my mind that this Pietro who was murdered two nights ago was the brother. I have been looking up the dates in the old files of the paper, and I find that the disappearance of the pearl was exactly two days before the arrest of Beppo, for some crime of violence—an event which took place in the factory of Gelder & Co., at the very moment when these busts were being made. Now you clearly see the sequence of events, though you see them, of course, in the inverse order to the way in which they presented themselves to me. Beppo had the pearl in his possession. He may have stolen it from Pietro, he may have been Pietro's confederate, he may have been the go-between of Pietro and his sister. It is of no consequence to us which is the correct solution.

"The main fact is that he HAD the pearl, and at that moment, when it was on his person, he was pursued by the police. He made for the factory in which he worked, and he knew that he had only a few minutes in which to conceal this enormously valuable prize, which would otherwise be found on him when he was searched. Six plaster casts of Napoleon were drying in the passage. One of them was still soft. In an instant Beppo, a skilful workman, made a small hole in the wet plaster, dropped in the pearl, and with a few touches covered over the aperture once more. It was an admirable hiding-place. No one could possibly find it. But Beppo was condemned to a year's imprisonment, and in the meanwhile his six busts were scattered over London. He could not tell which contained his treasure. Only by breaking them could he see. Even shaking would tell him nothing, for as the plaster was wet it was probable that the pearl would adhere to it—as, in fact, it has done. Beppo did not despair, and he conducted his search with considerable ingenuity and perseverance. Through a cousin who works with Gelder, he found out the retail firms who had bought the busts. He managed to find employment with Morse Hudson, and in that way tracked down three of them. The pearl was not there. Then, with the help of some Italian employee, he succeeded in finding out where the other three busts had gone. The first was at Harker's. There he was dogged by his confederate, who held Beppo responsible for the loss of the pearl, and he stabbed him in the scuffle which followed."

"If he was his confederate, why should he carry his photograph?" I asked.

"As a means of tracing him, if he wished to inquire about him from any third person. That was the obvious reason. Well, after the murder I calculated that Beppo would probably hurry rather than delay his movements. He would fear that the police would read his secret, and so he hastened on before they should get ahead of him. Of course, I could not say that he had not found the pearl in Harker's bust. I had not even concluded for certain that it was the pearl, but it was evident to me that he was looking for something, since he carried the bust past the other houses in order to break it in the garden which had a lamp overlooking it. Since Harker's bust was one in three, the chances were exactly as I told you—two to one against the pearl being inside it. There remained two busts, and it was obvious that he would go for the London one first. I warned the inmates of the house, so as to avoid a second tragedy, and we went down, with the happiest results. By that time, of course, I knew for certain that it was the Borgia pearl that we were after. The name of the murdered man linked the one event with the other. There only remained a single bust—the Reading one—and the pearl must be there. I bought it in your presence from the owner—and there it lies."

We sat in silence for a moment.

"Well," said Lestrade, "I've seen you handle a good many cases, Mr. Holmes, but I don't know that I ever knew a more workmanlike one than that. We're not jealous of you at Scotland Yard. No, sir, we are very proud of you, and if you come down to-morrow, there's not a man, from the oldest inspector to the youngest constable, who wouldn't be glad to shake you by the hand."

"Thank you!" said Holmes. "Thank you!" and as he turned away, it seemed to me that he was more nearly moved by the softer human emotions than I had ever seen him. A moment later he was the cold and practical thinker once more. "Put the pearl in the safe, Watson," said he, "and get out the papers of the Conk-Singleton forgery case. Good-bye, Lestrade. If any little problem comes your way, I shall be happy, if I can, to give you a hint or two as to its solution."

Classroom activities

Group presentation

1. How much do you know about Carroll John Daly? Where and when was *The False Burton Combs* first published? What social background leads to Daly's creation of the very first hard-boiled detective in the literary history?

2. What do you know about Arthur Conan Doyle? Who are the respective real-life prototypes for Dr. Waston and Sherlock Holmes? How many stories of Sherlock Holmes did Doyle write? Which collection is this story from? Why is the collection entitled the way it is?

Performance

Now all the groups are ready to act out the story *The False Burton Combs*. Each group should be followed closely by another based on the story line. The performance of each group will be graded based on the acting skills and the appropriateness of lines you write for the roles.

Story-telling

Students from different study groups will be chosen to retell the story *The Adventure of the Six Napoleons* in a row. The first chosen student begins the story, and stops at the teacher's signal, and the second student continues where the first student leaves off, and stops when the third student is required to come in.

Text analysis

1. Who are the narrators in the two stories? In what ways may the choice of narrator affect story-telling?

2. The two stories are developed in different orders. What are their respective order of development? Why do they differ in this aspect?

3. The employment of dialogues also diverges in the two stories. What is their difference from this aspect? What does the difference serve?

4. The two stories are told in very different language style. What are their respective language features? What do these features imply about the detectives' backgrounds?

5. Language learners sometimes prefer reading simplified literature for ease of understanding. After doing the above analysis, how do you think of reading literature in this way? Why is it highly recommended to read an original literary work instead of a simplified or adapted version?

Class discussion

1. What are the design features of hard-boiled crime stories? Name some action movies featuring tough guys, and check whether they can be labelled as the hard-boiled type.

2. What qualities can make a good consulting detective like Sherlock Holmes?

3. In what ways is the hard-boiled detective distinct from the consulting one? List as many differences as you can. (You may start with the ways they solve the criminal cases, their personalities, and so on.)

4. The two writers take quite different measures to tell stories and impress readers. As a result, the stories diverge in how they appeal to readers. Which story do you like better? Why?

Unit 12

Adolescent stories

Pre-class reading tasks

This unit presents two stories featuring "growing pains". One is a short story and the other an excerpt from *The Catcher in the Rye*, one of the top 100 best literary works in the world. Despite the different life experiences, the two protagonists are troubled by the same problem in the process of growing up. Please finish the following reading tasks before class.

Have a group discussion on the theme of "Peter Two". The story begins with a description of violence on TV and ends with the young boy's change of views on gangster programs. Does this mean that the story focuses on the influence of violent TV programs on children?

Prepare in your group to retell the first story in no more than ten sentences.

Once being banned for its profane and sexual themes, the novel *The Catcher in the Rye* is listed among the top 100 best literary works and popular among generations of young people. Read Text 2 if possible, the whole novel. Discuss themes shown in Text 2. You may find it helpful to google some reviews on the novel. A very helpful resource can be traced in the following way:

SparkNotes Editors. (2007). SparkNote on The Catcher in the Rye. From http://www.sparknotes.com/lit/catcher/

Analyze the personalities of the main characters shown in the excerpt of the novel *The Catcher in the Rye*: the young boy, his sister and his former English teacher.

☑ Text 1 Peter Two

By Irwin Shaw

It was Saturday night and people were killing each other by the hour on the small screen. Policemen were shot in the line of duty, gangsters were thrown off roofs, and an elderly lady was slowly poisoned for her pearls, and her murderer brought to justice by a cigarette company after a long series of discussions in the office of a private detective. Brave, unarmed actors leaped at villains holding forty-fives, and ingénues were saved from death by the knife by the quick thinking of various handsome and intrepid young men.

Peter sat in the big chair in front of the screen, his feet up over the arm, eating grapes. His mother wasn't home, so he ate the seeds and all as he stared critically at the violence before him. When his mother was around, the fear of appendicitis hung in the air and she watched carefully to see that each seed was neatly extracted and placed in an ashtray. Too, if she were home, there would be irritated little lectures on the quality of television entertainment for the young, and quick-tempered fiddling with the dials to find something that was vaguely defined as educational. Alone, daringly awake at eleven o'clock, Peter ground the seeds between his teeth, enjoying the impolite noise and the solitude and freedom of the empty house. During the television commercials Peter closed his eyes and imagined himself hurling bottles at large unshaven men with pistols and walking slowly up dark stairways toward the door behind which everyone knew the Boss was waiting, the bulge of his shoulder holster unmistakable under the cloth of his pencil-striped flannel jacket.

Peter was thirteen years old. In his class there were three other boys with the same given name, and the history teacher, who thought he was a funny man, called them Peter One, Peter Two (now eating grapes, seeds and all), Peter Three, and Peter the Great. Peter the Great was, of course, the smallest boy in the class. He weighed only sixty-two pounds, and he wore glasses, and in games he was always the last one to be chosen. The class always laughed when the history teacher called out "Peter the Great," and Peter Two laughed with them, but he didn't think it was so awfully funny.

He had done something pretty good for Peter the Great two weeks ago, and now they were what you might call friends. All the Peters were what you might call friends, on account of that comedian of a history teacher. They weren't real friends, but they had something together, something the other boys didn't have. They didn't like it, but they had it, and it made them responsible for each other. So two weeks ago, when Charley Blaisdell, who weighed a hundred and twenty, took Peter the Great's cap at recess and started horsing around with it, and Peter the Great looked as if he was going to cry, he, Peter Two, grabbed the cap and gave it back and faced Blaisdell. Of course, there was a fight, and Peter thought it was going to be his third defeat of the term, but a wonderful thing happened. In the middle of the fight, just when Peter was hoping one of the teachers would show up (they sure showed up plenty of times when you didn't need them), Blaisdell let a hard one go. Peter ducked and Blaisdell hit him on the top of the head and broke his arm. You could tell right off he broke his arm, because he fell to the ground yelling, and his arm just hung like a piece of string. Walters, the gym teacher, finally showed up and carried Blaisdell off, yelling all the time, and Peter the Great came up and said admiringly, "Boy, one thing you have to admit, you sure have a hard head."

Blaisdell was out of class two days, and he still had his arm in the sling, and every time he was excused from writing on the blackboard because he had a broken arm, Peter got a nice warm feeling all over. Peter the Great hung around him all the time, doing things for him and buying him sodas, because Peter the Great's parents were divorced and gave him all the money he wanted, to make up to him. And that was O.K.

But the best thing was the feeling he'd had since the fight. It was like what the people on the television must feel after they'd gone into a room full of enemies and come out with the girl or with the papers or with the suspect, leaving corpses and desolation behind them. Blaisdell weighed a hundred and twenty pounds but that hadn't stopped Peter any more than the fact that the spies all had two guns apiece ever stopped the F.B.I. men on the screen. They saw what they had to do and they went in and did it, that was all. Peter couldn't phrase it for himself, but for the first time in his life he had a conscious feeling of confidence and pride in himself.

"Let them come," he muttered obscurely, munching grape seeds and watching the television set through narrowed eyes, "just let them come."

He was going to be a dangerous man, he felt, when he grew up, but one to whom the weak and the unjustly hunted could safely turn. He was sure he was going to be six feet tall, because his father was six feet tall, and all his uncles, and that would help. But he would have to develop his arms. They were just too thin. After all, you couldn't depend on people breaking their bones on your head every time. He had been doing pushups each morning and night for the past month. He could only do five and a half at a time so far, but he was going to keep at it until he had arms like steel bars. Arms like that really could mean the difference between life and death later on, when you had to dive under the gun and disarm somebody. You had to have quick reflexes, too, of course, and be able to feint to one side with your eyes before the crucial moment. And, most important of all, no matter what the odds, you had to be fearless. One moment of hesitation and it was a case for the morgue. But now, after the battle of Peter the Great's cap, he didn't worry about that part of it, the fearless part. From now on, it would just be a question of technique.

Comedians began to appear all over the dial, laughing with a lot of teeth, and Peter went into the kitchen and got another bunch of grapes and two tangerines from the refrigerator. He didn't put on the light in the kitchen and it was funny how mysterious a kitchen could be near midnight when nobody else was home, and there was only the beam of the light from the open refrigerator, casting shadows from the milk bottles onto the linoleum. Until recently he hadn't liked the dark too much and he always turned on lights wherever he went, but you had to practice being fearless, just like anything else.

He ate the two tangerines standing in the dark in the kitchen, just for practice. He ate the seeds, too, to show his mother. Then he went back into the living room, carrying the grapes.

The comedians were still on and still laughing. He fiddled with the dial, but they were wearing funny hats and laughing and telling jokes about the income tax on all the channels. If his mother hadn't made him promise to go to sleep by ten o'clock, he'd have turned off the set and gone to bed. He decided not to waste his time and got down on the floor and began to do pushups, trying to be sure to keep his knees straight. He was up to four and slowing down when he heard the scream. He stopped in the middle of a pushup and waited, just to make sure. The scream came again. It was a woman and it was real loud. He looked up at the television set. There was a man there talking about floor wax, a man with a mustache and a lot of teeth, and it was a cinch he wasn't doing any screaming.

The next time the scream came there was moaning and talking at the end of it, and the sound of fists beating on the front door. Peter got up and turned off the television, just to be sure the sounds he was hearing weren't somehow being broadcast.

The beating on the door began again and a woman's voice cried "Please, please, please." and there was no doubt about it any more.

Peter looked around him at the empty room. Three lamps were lit and the room was nice and bright and the light was reflected off the grapes and off the glass of the picture of the boats on Cape Cod that his Aunt Martha painted the year she was up there. The television set stood in the corner, like a big blind eye now that the light was out. The cushions of the soft chair he had been sitting in to watch the programs were pushed in and he knew his mother would come and plump them out before she went to sleep, and the whole room looked like a place in which it was impossible to hear a woman screaming at midnight and beating on the door with her fists and yelling, "Please, please, please."

The woman at the door yelled "Murder, murder, he's killing me!" and for the first time Peter was sorry his parents had gone out that night.

"Open the door!" the woman yelled. "Please, please open the door!" You could tell she wasn't saying please just to be polite by now.

Peter looked nervously around him. The room, with all its lights, seemed strange, and there were shadows behind everything. Then the woman yelled again, just noise this time. Either a person is fearless, Peter thought coldly, or he isn't fearless. He started walking slowly toward the front door. There was a long mirror in the foyer and he got a good look at himself. His arms looked very thin.

The woman began hammering once more on the front door and Peter looked at it closely. It was a big steel door, but it was shaking minutely, as though somebody with a machine was working on it. For the first time he heard another voice. It was a man's voice, only it didn't sound quite like a man's voice. It sounded like an animal in a cave, growling and deciding to do something unreasonable. In all the scenes of threat and violence on the television set, Peter had never heard anything at all like it. He moved slowly toward the door, feeling the way he had felt when he had the flu, remembering how thin his arms looked in the mirror, regretting that he had decided to be fearless.

"Oh, God!" the woman yelled, "Oh, God, don't do it!"

Then there was some more hammering and the low, animal sound of the beast in the cave that you never heard over the air, and he threw the door open.

Mrs. Chalmers was there in the vestibule, on her knees, facing him, and behind her Mr. Chalmers was standing, leaning against the wall, with the door to his own apartment open behind him. Mr. Chalmers was making that funny sound and he had a gun in his hand and he was pointing it at Mrs. Chalmers.

The vestibule was small and it had what Peter's mother called Early American wallpaper and a brass light fixture. There were only the two doors opening on the vestibule, and the Chalmers had a mat in front of theirs with "Welcome" written on it. The Chalmers were in their mid-thirties, and Peter's mother always said about them, "One thing about our neighbors, they are quiet." She also said that Mrs. Chalmers put a lot of money on her back.

Mrs. Chalmers was kind of fat and her hair was pretty blond and her complexion was soft and pink and she always looked as though she had been in the beauty parlor all afternoon. She always said "My, you're getting to be a big boy" to Peter when she met him in the elevator, in a soft voice, as though she was just about to laugh. She must have said that fifty times by now. She had a good, strong smell of perfume on her all the time, too.

Mr. Chalmers wore pince-nez glasses most of the time and he was getting bald and he worked late at his office a good many evenings of the week. When he met Peter in the elevator he would say, "It's getting colder," or "It's getting warmer," and that was all, so Peter had no opinion about him, except that he looked like the principal of a school.

But now Mrs. Chalmers was on her knees in the vestibule and her dress was torn and she was crying and there were black streaks on her cheeks and she didn't look as though she'd just come from the beauty parlor. And Mr. Chalmers wasn't wearing a jacket and he didn't have his glasses on and what hair he had was mussed all over his head and he was leaning against the Early American wallpaper making this animal noise, and he had a big, heavy pistol in his hand and he was pointing it right at Mrs. Chalmers.

"Let me in!" Mrs. Chalmers yelled, still on her knees. "You've got to let me in. He's going to kill me. Please!"

"Mrs. Chalmers ." Peter began. His voice sounded as though he were trying to talk under water, and it was very hard to say the "s" at the end of her name. He put out his hands uncertainly in front of him, as though he expected somebody to throw him something.

"Get inside, you," Mr. Chalmers said.

Peter looked at Mr. Chalmers. He was only five feet away and without his glasses he was squinting. Peter feinted with his eyes, or at least later in his life he thought he had feinted with his eyes. Mr. Chalmers didn't do anything. He just stood there, with the pistol pointed, somehow, it seemed to Peter, at both Mrs. Chalmers and himself at the same time. Five feet was a long distance, a long, long distance.

"Good night," Peter said, and he closed the door.

There was a single sob on the other side of the door and that was all.

Peter went in and put the uneaten grapes back in the refrigerator, flicking on the light as he went into the kitchen and leaving it on when he went out. Then he went back to the living room and got the stems from the first bunch of grapes and threw them into the fireplace, because otherwise his mother would notice and look for the seeds and not see them and give him four tablespoons of milk of magnesia the next day.

Then, leaving the lights on in the living room, although he knew what his mother would say about that when she got home, he went into his room and quickly got into bed. He waited for the sound of shots. There were two or three noises that might have been shots, but in the city it was hard to tell.

He was still awake when his parents came home. He heard his mother's voice, and he knew from the sound she was complaining about the lights in the living room and kitchen, but he pretended to be sleeping when she came into his room to look at him. He didn't want to start in with his mother about the Chalmers, because then she'd ask when it had happened and she'd want to know what he was doing up at twelve o'clock.

He kept listening for shots for a long time, and he got hot and damp under the covers and then freezing cold. He heard several sharp, ambiguous noises in the quiet night, but nothing that you could be sure about, and after a while he fell asleep.

In the morning, Peter got out of bed early, dressed quickly, and went silently out of the apartment without waking his parents. The vestibule looked just the way it always did, with the brass lamp and the flowered wallpaper and the Chalmers' doormat with "Welcome" on it. There were no bodies and no blood. Sometimes when Mrs. Chalmers had been standing there waiting for the elevator, you could smell her perfume for a long time after. But now there was no smell of perfume, just the dusty, apartment-house usual smell. Peter stared at the Chalmers' door nervously while waiting for the elevator to come up, but it didn't open and no sound came from within.

Sam, the man who ran the elevator and who didn't like him, anyway, only grunted when Peter got into the elevator, and Peter decided not to ask him any questions. He went out into the chilly, bright Sunday-morning street, half expecting to see the morgue wagon in front of the door, or at least two or three prowl cars. But there was only a sleepy woman in slacks airing a boxer and a man with his collar turned up hurrying up from the corner with the newspapers under his arm.

Peter went across the street and looked up to the sixth floor, at the windows of the Chalmers' apartment. The Venetian blinds were pulled shut in every room and all the windows were closed.

A policeman walked down the other side of the street, heavy, blue and purposeful, and for a moment Peter felt close to arrest. But the policeman continued on toward the avenue and turned the corner and disappeared and Peter said to himself, "They never know anything."

He walked up and down the street, first on one side, then on the other, waiting, although it was hard to know what he was waiting for. He saw a hand come out through the blinds in his parents' room and slam the window shut, and he knew he ought to get upstairs quickly with a good excuse for being out, but he couldn't face them this morning, and he would invent an excuse later. Maybe he would even say he had gone to the museum, although he doubted that his mother would swallow that.

Then, after he had been patrolling the street for almost two hours, and just as he was coming up to the entrance of his building, the door opened and Mr. and Mrs. Chalmers came out. He had on his pince-nez and a dark-gray hat, and Mrs. Chalmers had on her fur coat and a red hat with feathers on it. Mr. Chalmers was holding the door open politely for his wife, and she looked, as she came out the door, as though she had just come from the beauty parlor.

It was too late to turn back or avoid them, and Peter just stood still, five feet from the entrance.

"Good morning," Mr. Chalmers said as he took his wife's arm and they started walking past Peter.

"Good morning, Peter," said Mrs. Chalmers in her soft voice, smiling at him. "Isn't it a nice day today?"

"Good morning," Peter said, and he was surprised that it came out and sounded like good morning.

The Chalmers walked down the street toward Madison Avenue, two married people, arm in arm, going to church or to a big hotel for Sunday breakfast. Peter watched them, ashamed. He was ashamed of Mrs. Chalmers for looking the way she did the night before, down on her knees, and yelling like that and being so afraid. He was ashamed of Mr. Chalmers for making the noise that was not like the noise of a human being, and for threatening to shoot Mrs. Chalmers and not doing it. And he was ashamed of himself because he had been fearless when he opened the door, but had not been fearless ten seconds later, with Mr. Chalmers five feet away with the gun. He was ashamed of himself for not taking Mrs. Chalmers into the apartment, ashamed because he was not lying now with a bullet in his heart. But most of all he was ashamed because they had all said good morning to each other and the Chalmers were walking quietly together, arm in arm, in the windy sunlight, toward Madison Avenue.

It was nearly eleven o'clock when Peter got back to the apartment, but his parents had gone back to sleep. There was a pretty good program on at eleven, about counterspies in Asia, and he turned it on automatically, while eating an orange. It was pretty exciting, but then there was a part in which an Oriental held a ticking bomb in his hand in a roomful of Americans, and Peter could tell what was coming. The hero, who was fearless and who came from California, was beginning to feint with his eyes, and Peter reached over and turned the set off. It closed down with a shivering, collapsing pattern. Blinking a little, Peter watched the blind screen for a moment.

Ah, he thought in sudden, permanent disbelief, after the night in which he had faced the incomprehensible, shameless, weaponed grownup world and had failed to disarm it, ah, they can have that, that's for kids.

📖 Text 2 The Catcher in the Rye (Chapters 22, 24 and 25)

By J. D. Salinger

Chapter 22

When I came back, she had the pillow off her head all right—I knew she would— but she still wouldn't look at me, even though she was laying on her back and all. When I came around the side of the bed and sat down again, she turned her crazy face the other way. She was ostracizing the hell out of me. Just like the fencing team at Pencey when I left all the goddam foils on the subway.

"How's old Hazel Weatherfield?" I said. "You write any new stories about her? I got that one you sent me right in my suitcase. It's down at the station. It's very good."

"Daddy'll kill you."

Boy, she really gets something on her mind when she gets something on her mind.

"No, he won't. The worst he'll do, he'll give me hell again, and then he'll send me to that goddam military school. That's all he'll do to me. And in the first place, I won't even be around. I'll be away. I'll be—I'll probably be in Colorado on this ranch."

"Don't make me laugh. You can't even ride a horse."

"Who can't? Sure I can. Certainly I can. They can teach you in about two minutes," I said. "Stop picking at that." She was picking at that adhesive tape on her arm. "Who gave you that haircut?" I asked her. I just noticed what a stupid haircut somebody gave her. It was way too short.

"None of your business," she said. She can be very snotty sometimes. She can be quite snotty. "I suppose you failed in every single subject again," she said—very snotty. It was sort of funny, too, in a way. She sounds like a goddam schoolteacher sometimes, and she's only a little child.

"No, I didn't," I said. "I passed English." Then, just for the hell of it, I gave her a pinch on the behind. It was sticking way out in the breeze, the way she was laying on her side. She has hardly any behind. I didn't do it hard, but she tried to hit my hand anyway, but she missed.

Then all of a sudden, she said, "Oh, why did you do it?" She meant why did I get the ax again. It made me sort of sad, the way she said it.

"Oh, God, Phoebe, don't ask me. I'm sick of everybody asking me that," I said. "A million reasons why. It was one of the worst schools I ever went to. It was full of phonies. And mean guys. You never saw so many mean guys in your life. For instance, if you were having a bull session in somebody's room, and somebody wanted to come in, nobody'd let them in if they were some dopey, pimply guy. Everybody was always locking their door when somebody wanted to come in. And they had this goddam secret fraternity that I was too yellow not to join. There was this one pimply, boring guy, Robert Ackley, that wanted to get in. He kept trying to join, and they wouldn't let him. Just because he was boring and pimply. I don't even feel like talking about it. It was a stinking school. Take my word."

Old Phoebe didn't say anything, but she was listening. I could tell by the back of her neck that she was listening. She always listens when you tell her something. And the funny part is she knows, half the time, what the hell you're talking about. She really does.

I kept talking about old Pencey. I sort of felt like it.

"Even the couple of nice teachers on the faculty, they were phonies, too," I said. "There was this one old guy, Mr. Spencer. His wife was always giving you hot chocolate and all that stuff, and they were really pretty nice. But you should've seen him when the headmaster, old Thurmer, came in the history class and sat down in the back of the room. He was always coming in and sitting down in the back of the room for about a half an hour. He was supposed to be incognito or something. After a while, he'd be sitting back there and then he'd start interrupting what old Spencer was saying to crack a lot of corny jokes. Old Spencer'd practically kill himself chuckling and smiling and all, like as if Thurmer was a goddam prince or something."

"Don't swear so much."

"It would've made you puke, I swear it would," I said. "Then, on Veterans' Day. They have this day, Veterans' Day, that all the jerks that graduated from Pencey around 1776 come back and walk all over the place, with their wives and children and everybody. You should've seen this one old guy that was about fifty. What he did was, he came in our room and knocked on the door and asked us if we'd mind if he used the bathroom. The bathroom was at the end of the corridor— I don't know why the hell he asked us. You know what he said? He said he wanted to see if his initials were still in one of the can doors. What he did, he carved his goddam stupid sad old initials in one of the can doors about ninety years ago, and he wanted to see if they were still there. So my roommate and I walked him down to the bathroom and all, and we had to stand there while he looked for his initials in all the can doors. He kept talking to us the whole time, telling us how when he was at Pencey they were the happiest days of his life, and giving us a lot of advice for the future and all. Boy, did he depress me! I don't mean he was a bad guy—he wasn't. But you don't have to be a bad guy to depress somebody—you can be a good guy and do it. All you have to do to depress somebody is give them a lot of phony advice while you're looking for your initials in some can door—that's all you have to do. I don't know. Maybe it wouldn't have been so bad if he hadn't been all out of breath. He was all out of breath from just climbing up the stairs, and the whole time he was looking for his initials he kept breathing hard, with his nostrils all funny and sad, while he kept telling Stradlater and I to get all we could out of Pencey. God, Phoebe! I can't explain. I just didn't like anything that was happening at Pencey. I can't explain."

Old Phoebe said something then, but I couldn't hear her. She had the side of her mouth right smack on the pillow, and I couldn't hear her.

"What?" I said. "Take your mouth away. I can't hear you with your mouth that way."

"You don't like anything that's happening."

It made me even more depressed when she said that.

"Yes, I do. Yes, I do. Sure I do. Don't say that. Why the hell do you say that?"

"Because you don't. You don't like any schools. You don't like a million things. You don't."

"I do! That's where you're wrong—that's exactly where you're wrong! Why the hell do you have to say that?" I said. Boy, was she depressing me.

"Because you don't," she said. "Name one thing."

"One thing? One thing I like?" I said. "Okay."

The trouble was, I couldn't concentrate too hot. Sometimes it's hard to concentrate.

"One thing I like a lot you mean?" I asked her.

She didn't answer me, though. She was in a cockeyed position way the hell over the other side of the bed. She was about a thousand miles away. "C'mon answer me," I said. "One thing I like a lot, or one thing I just like?"

"You like a lot."

"All right," I said. But the trouble was, I couldn't concentrate. About all I could think of were those two nuns that went around collecting dough in those beatup old straw baskets. Especially the one with the glasses with those iron rims. And this boy I knew at Elkton Hills. There was this one boy at Elkton Hills, named James Castle, that wouldn't take back something he said about this very conceited boy, Phil Stabile. James Castle called him a very conceited guy, and one of Stabile's lousy friends went and squealed on him to Stabile. So Stabile, with about six other dirty bastards, went down to James Castle's room and went in and locked the goddam door and tried to make him take back what he said, but he wouldn't do it. So they started in on him. I won't even tell you what they did to him—it's too repulsive—but he still wouldn't take it back, old James Castle. And you should've seen him. He was a skinny little weak-looking guy, with wrists about as big as pencils. Finally, what he did, instead of taking back what he said, he jumped out the window. I was in the shower and all, and even I could hear him land outside. But I just thought something fell out the window, a radio or a desk or something, not a boy or anything. Then I heard everybody running through the corridor and down the stairs, so I put on my bathrobe and I ran downstairs too, and there was old James Castle laying right on the stone steps and all. He was dead, and his teeth, and blood, were all over the place, and nobody would even go near him. He had on this turtleneck sweater I'd lent him. All they did with the guys that were in the room with him was expel them. They didn't even go to jail.

That was about all I could think of, though. Those two nuns I saw at breakfast and this boy James

Castle I knew at Elkton Hills. The funny part is, I hardly even know James Castle, if you want to know the truth. He was one of these very quiet guys. He was in my math class, but he was way over on the other side of the room, and he hardly ever got up to recite or go to the blackboard or anything. Some guys in school hardly ever get up to recite or go to the blackboard. I think the only time I ever even had a conversation with him was that time he asked me if he could borrow this turtleneck sweater I had. I damn near dropped dead when he asked me, I was so surprised and all. I remember I was brushing my teeth, in the can, when he asked me. He said his cousin was coming in to take him for a drive and all. I didn't even know he knew I had a turtleneck sweater. All I knew about him was that his name was always right ahead of me at roll call. Cabel, R., Cabel, W., Castle, Caulfield—I can still remember it. If you want to know the truth, I almost didn't lend him my sweater. Just because I didn't know him too well.

"What?" I said to old Phoebe. She said something to me, but I didn't hear her.

"You can't even think of one thing."

"Yes, I can. Yes, I can."

"Well, do it, then."

"I like Allie," I said. "And I like doing what I'm doing right now. Sitting here with you, and talking, and thinking about stuff, and—"

"Allie's dead—You always say that! If somebody's dead and everything, and in Heaven, then it isn't really—"

"I know he's dead! Don't you think I know that? I can still like him, though, can't I? Just because somebody's dead, you don't just stop liking them, for God's sake—especially if they were about a thousand times nicer than the people you know that're alive and all."

Old Phoebe didn't say anything. When she can't think of anything to say, she doesn't say a goddam word.

"Anyway, I like it now," I said. "I mean right now. Sitting here with you and just chewing the fat and horsing—"

"That isn't anything really!"

"It is so something really! Certainly it is! Why the hell isn't it? People never think anything is anything really. I'm getting goddam sick of it,"

"Stop swearing. All right, name something else. Name something you'd like to be. Like a scientist. Or a lawyer or something."

"I couldn't be a scientist. I'm no good in science."

"Well, a lawyer—like Daddy and all."

"Lawyers are all right, I guess—but it doesn't appeal to me," I said. "I mean they're all right if they go around saving innocent guys' lives all the time, and like that, but you don't do that kind of stuff if you're a lawyer. All you do is make a lot of dough and play golf and play bridge and buy cars and drink Martinis and look like a hot-shot. And besides. Even if you did go around saving guys' lives and all, how would you know if you did it because you really wanted to save guys' lives, or because you did it because what you really wanted to do was be a terrific lawyer, with everybody slapping you on the back and congratulating you in court when the goddam trial was over, the reporters and everybody, the way it is in the dirty movies? How would you know you weren't being a phony? The trouble is, you wouldn't."

I'm not too sure old Phoebe knew what the hell I was talking about. I mean she's only a little child and all. But she was listening, at least. If somebody at least listens, it's not too bad.

"Daddy's going to kill you. He's going to kill you," she said.

I wasn't listening, though. I was thinking about something else—something crazy. "You know what I'd like to be?" I said. "You know what I'd like to be? I mean if I had my goddam choice?"

"What? Stop swearing."

"You know that song 'If a body catch a body comin' through the rye'? I'd like—"

"It's 'If a body meet a body coming through the rye'!" old Phoebe said. "It's a poem. By Robert Burns."

"I know it's a poem by Robert Burns."

She was right, though. It is "If a body meet a body coming through the rye." I didn't know it then, though.

"I thought it was 'If a body catch a body,'" I said. "Anyway, I keep picturing all these little kids playing some game in this big field of rye and all. Thousands of little kids, and nobody's around—nobody big, I mean—except me. And I'm standing on the edge of some crazy cliff. What I have to do, I have to catch everybody if they start to go over the cliff—I mean if they're running and they don't look where they're going I have to come out from somewhere and catch them. That's all I'd do all day. I'd just be the catcher in the rye and all. I know it's crazy, but that's the only thing I'd really like to be. I know it's crazy."

Old Phoebe didn't say anything for a long time. Then, when she said something, all she said was, "Daddy's going to kill you."

"I don't give a damn if he does," I said. I got up from the bed then, because what I wanted to do, I wanted to phone up this guy that was my English teacher at Elkton Hills, Mr. Antolini. He lived in New York now. He quit Elkton Hills. He took this job teaching English at N.Y.U. "I have to make a phone call," I told Phoebe. "I'll be right back. Don't go to sleep." I didn't want her to go to sleep while I was in the living room. I knew she wouldn't but I said it anyway, just to make sure.

While I was walking toward the door, old Phoebe said, "Holden!" and I turned around.

She was sitting way up in bed. She looked so pretty. "I'm taking belching lessons from this girl, Phyllis Margulies," she said. "Listen."

I listened, and I heard something, but it wasn't much. "Good," I said. Then I went out in the living room and called up this teacher I had, Mr. Antolini.

Chapter 24

Mr. and Mrs. Antolini had this very swanky apartment over on Sutton Place, with two steps that you go down to get in the living room, and a bar and all. I'd been there quite a few times, because after I left Elkton Hills Mr. Antoilni came up to our house for dinner quite frequently to find out how I was getting along. He wasn't married then. Then when he got married, I used to play tennis with he and Mrs. Antolini quite frequently, out at the West Side Tennis Club, in Forest Hills, Long Island. Mrs. Antolini, belonged there. She was lousy with dough. She was about sixty years older than Mr. Antolini, but they seemed to get along quite well. For one thing, they were both very intellectual, especially Mr. Antolini except that he was more witty than intellectual when you were with him, sort of like D.B. Mrs. Antolini was mostly serious. She had asthma pretty bad. They both read all D.B.'s stories—Mrs. Antolini, too—and when D.B. went to Hollywood, Mr. Antolini phoned him up and told him not to go. He went anyway, though. Mr. Antolini said that anybody that could write like D.B. had no business going out to Hollywood. That's exactly what I said, practically.

I would have walked down to their house, because I didn't want to spend any of Phoebe's Christmas dough that I didn't have to, but I felt funny when I got outside. Sort of dizzy. So I took a cab. I didn't want to, but I did. I had a helluva time even finding a cab.

Old Mr. Antolini answered the door when I rang the bell—after the elevator boy finally let me up, the bastard. He had on his bathrobe and slippers, and he had a highball in one hand. He was a pretty sophisticated guy, and he was a pretty heavy drinker. "Holden, m'boy!" he said. "My God, he's grown another twenty inches. Fine to see you."

"How are you, Mr. Antolini? How's Mrs. Antolini?"

"We're both just dandy. Let's have that coat." He took my coat off me and hung it up. "I expected to see a day-old infant in your arms. Nowhere to turn. Snowflakes in your eyelashes." He's a very witty guy sometimes. He turned around and yelled out to the kitchen, "Lillian! How's the coffee coming?" Lillian was Mrs. Antolini's first name.

"It's all ready," she yelled back. "Is that Holden? Hello, Holden!"

"Hello, Mrs. Antolini!"

You were always yelling when you were there. That's because the both of them were never in the same room at the same time. It was sort of funny.

"Sit down, Holden," Mr. Antolini said. You could tell he was a little oiled up. The room looked like they'd just had a party. Glasses were all over the place, and dishes with peanuts in them. "Excuse the appearance of the place," he said. "We've been entertaining some Buffalo friends of Mrs. Antolini's . . . Some buffaloes, as a matter of fact."

I laughed, and Mrs. Antolini yelled something in to me from the kitchen, but I couldn't hear her. "What'd she say?" I asked Mr. Antolini.

"She said not to look at her when she comes in. She just arose from the sack. Have a cigarette. Are you smoking now?"

"Thanks," I said. I took a cigarette from the box he offered me. "Just once in a while. I'm a moderate smoker."

"I'll bet you are," he said. He gave me a light from this big lighter off the table. "So. You and Pencey are no longer one," he said. He always said things that way. Sometimes it amused me a lot and sometimes it didn't. He sort of did it a little bit too much. I don't mean he wasn't witty or anything—he was—but sometimes it gets on your nerves when somebody's always saying things like "So you and Pencey are no longer one." D.B. does it too much sometimes, too.

"What was the trouble?" Mr. Antolini asked me. "How'd you do in English? I'll show you the door in short order if you flunked English, you little ace composition writer."

"Oh, I passed English all right. It was mostly literature, though. I only wrote about two compositions the whole term," I said. "I flunked Oral Expression, though. They had this course you had to take, Oral Expression. That I flunked."

"Why?"

"Oh, I don't know." I didn't feel much like going into It. I was still feeling sort of dizzy or something, and I had a helluva headache all of a sudden. I really did. But you could tell he was interested, so I told him a little bit about it. "It's this course where each boy in class has to get up in class and make a speech. You know. Spontaneous and all. And if the boy digresses at all, you're supposed to yell 'Digression!' at him as fast as you can. It just about drove me crazy. I got an F in it."

"Why?"

"Oh, I don't know. That digression business got on my nerves. I don't know. The trouble with me is, I like it when somebody digresses. It's more interesting and all."

"You don't care to have somebody stick to the point when he tells you something?"

"Oh, sure! I like somebody to stick to the point and all. But I don't like them to stick too much to the point. I don't know. I guess I don't like it when somebody sticks to the point all the time. The boys that got the best marks in Oral Expression were the ones that stuck to the point all the time—I admit it. But there was this one boy, Richard Kinsella. He didn't stick to the point too much, and they were always yelling 'Digression!' at him. It was terrible, because in the first place, he was a very nervous guy—I mean he was a very nervous guy—and his lips were always shaking whenever it was his time to make a speech, and you could hardly hear him if you were sitting way in the back of the room. When his lips sort of quit shaking a little bit, though, I liked his speeches better than anybody else's. He practically flunked the course, though, too. He got a D plus because they kept yelling 'Digression!' at him all the time. For instance, he made this speech about this farm his father bought in Vermont. They kept yelling 'Digression!' at him the whole time he was making it, and this teacher, Mr. Vinson, gave him an F on it because he hadn't told what kind of animals and vegetables and stuff grew on the farm and all. What he did was, Richard Kinsella, he'd start telling you all about that stuff—then all of a sudden he'd start telling you about this letter his mother got from his uncle, and how his uncle got polio and all when he was forty-two years old, and how he wouldn't let anybody come to see him in the hospital because he didn't want anybody to see him with a brace on. It didn't have much to do with the farm—I admit it—but it was nice. It's nice when somebody tells you about their uncle. Especially when they start out telling you about their father's farm and then all of a sudden get more interested in their uncle. I mean it's dirty to keep yelling 'Digression!' at him when he's all nice and excited. I don't know. It's hard to explain." I didn't feel too much like trying, either. For one thing, I had this terrific headache all of a sudden. I wished to God old Mrs. Antolini would come in with the coffee. That's something that annoys hell out of me—I mean if somebody says the coffee's all ready and it isn't.

"Holden... One short, faintly stuffy, pedagogical question. Don't you think there's a time and place for everything? Don't you think if someone starts out to tell you about his father's farm, he should stick to his guns, then get around to telling you about his uncle's brace? Or, if his uncle's brace is such a provocative subject, shouldn't he have selected it in the first place as his subject—not the farm?"

I didn't feel much like thinking and answering and all. I had a headache and I felt lousy. I even had sort of a stomach-ache, if you want to know the truth.

"Yes—I don't know. I guess he should. I mean I guess he should've picked his uncle as a subject, instead of the farm, if that interested him most. But what I mean is, lots of time you don't know what interests you most till you start talking about something that doesn't interest you most. I mean you can't help it sometimes. What I think is, you're supposed to leave somebody alone if he's at least being interesting and he's getting all excited about something. I like it when somebody gets excited about something. It's nice. You just didn't know this teacher, Mr. Vinson. He could drive you crazy sometimes, him and the goddam class. I mean he'd keep telling you to unify and simplify all the time.

Some things you just can't do that to. I mean you can't hardly ever simplify and unify something just because somebody wants you to. You didn't know this guy, Mr. Vinson. I mean he was very intelligent and all, but you could tell he didn't have too much brains."

"Coffee, gentlemen, finally," Mrs. Antolini said. She came in carrying this tray with coffee and cakes and stuff on it. "Holden, don't you even peek at me. I'm a mess."

"Hello, Mrs. Antolini," I said. I started to get up and all, but Mr. Antolini got hold of my jacket and pulled me back down. Old Mrs. Antolini's hair was full of those iron curler jobs, and she didn't have any lipstick or anything on. She didn't look too gorgeous. She looked pretty old and all.

"I'll leave this right here. Just dive in, you two," she said. She put the tray down on the cigarette table, pushing all these glasses out of the way. "How's your mother, Holden?"

"She's fine, thanks. I haven't seen her too recently, but the last I—"

"Darling, if Holden needs anything, everything's in the linen closet. The top shelf. I'm going to bed. I'm exhausted," Mrs. Antolini said. She looked it, too. "Can you boys make up the couch by yourselves?"

"We'll take care of everything. You run along to bed," Mr. Antolini said. He gave Mrs. Antolini a kiss and she said good-by to me and went in the bedroom. They were always kissing each other a lot in public.

I had part of a cup of coffee and about half of some cake that was as hard as a rock. All old Mr. Antolini had was another highball, though. He makes them strong, too, you could tell. He may get to be an alcoholic if he doesn't watch his step.

"I had lunch with your dad a couple of weeks ago," he said all of a sudden. "Did you know that?"

"No, I didn't."

"You're aware, of course, that he's terribly concerned about you."

"I know it. I know he is," I said.

"Apparently before he phoned me he'd just had a long, rather harrowing letter from your latest headmaster, to the effect that you were making absolutely no effort at all. Cutting classes. Coming unprepared to all your classes. In general, being an all-around—"

"I didn't cut any classes. You weren't allowed to cut any. There were a couple of them I didn't attend once in a while, like that Oral Expression I told you about, but I didn't cut any."

I didn't feel at all like discussing it. The coffee made my stomach feel a little better, but I still had this awful headache.

Mr. Antolini lit another cigarette. He smoked like a fiend. Then he said, "Frankly, I don't know what the hell to say to you, Holden."

"I know. I'm very hard to talk to. I realize that."

"I have a feeling that you're riding for some kind of a terrible, terrible fall. But I don't honestly know what kind. . . Are you listening to me?"

"Yes."

You could tell he was trying to concentrate and all.

"It may be the kind where, at the age of thirty, you sit in some bar hating everybody who comes in looking as if he might have played football in college. Then again, you may pick up just enough education to hate people who say, 'It's a secret between he and I.' Or you may end up in some business office, throwing paper clips at the nearest stenographer. I just don't know. But do you know what I'm driving at, at all?"

"Yes. Sure," I said. I did, too. "But you're wrong about that hating business. I mean about hating football players and all. You really are. I don't hate too many guys. What I may do, I may hate them for a little while, like this guy Stradlater I knew at Pencey, and this other boy, Robert Ackley. I hated them once in a while—I admit it—but it doesn't last too long, is what I mean. After a while, if I didn't see them, if they didn't come in the room, or if I didn't see them in the dining room for a couple of meals, I sort of missed them. I mean I sort of missed them."

Mr. Antolini didn't say anything for a while. He got up and got another hunk of ice and put it in his drink, then he sat down again. You could tell he was thinking. I kept wishing, though, that he'd continue the conversation in the morning, instead of now, but he was hot. People are mostly hot to have a discussion when you're not.

"All right. Listen to me a minute now... I may not word this as memorably as I'd like to, but I'll write you a letter about it in a day or two. Then you can get it all straight. But listen now, anyway." He started concentrating again. Then he said, "This fall I think you're riding for—it's a special kind of fall, a horrible kind. The man falling isn't permitted to feel or hear himself hit bottom. He just keeps falling and falling. The whole arrangement's designed for men who, at some time or other in their lives, were looking for something their own environment couldn't supply them with. Or they thought their own environment couldn't supply them with. So they gave up looking. They gave it up before they ever really even got started. You follow me?"

"Yes, sir."

"Sure?"

"Yes."

He got up and poured some more booze in his glass. Then he sat down again. He didn't say anything for a long time.

"I don't want to scare you," he said, "but I can very clearly see you dying nobly, one way or another, for some highly unworthy cause." He gave me a funny look. "If I write something down for you, will you read it carefully? And keep it?"

"Yes. Sure," I said. I did, too. I still have the paper he gave me.

He went over to this desk on the other side of the room, and without sitting down wrote something on a piece of paper. Then he came back and sat down with the paper in his hand. "Oddly enough, this wasn't written by a practicing poet. It was written by a psychoanalyst named Wilhelm Stekel. Here's what he—Are you still with me?"

"Yes, sure I am."

"Here's what he said: 'The mark of the immature man is that he wants to die nobly for a cause, while the mark of the mature man is that he wants to live humbly for one.'"

He leaned over and handed it to me. I read it right when he gave it to me, and then I thanked him and all and put it in my pocket. It was nice of him to go to all that trouble. It really was. The thing was, though, I didn't feel much like concentrating. Boy, I felt so damn tired all of a sudden.

You could tell he wasn't tired at all, though. He was pretty oiled up, for one thing. "I think that one of these days," he said, "you're going to have to find out where you want to go. And then you've got to start going there. But immediately. You can't afford to lose a minute. Not you."

I nodded, because he was looking right at me and all, but I wasn't too sure what he was talking about. I was pretty sure I knew, but I wasn't too positive at the time. I was too damn tired.

"And I hate to tell you," he said, "but I think that once you have a fair idea where you want to go, your first move will be to apply yourself in school. You'll have to. You're a student—whether the idea appeals to you or not. You're in love with knowledge. And I think you'll find, once you get past all the Mr. Vineses and their Oral Comp—"

"Mr. Vinsons," I said. He meant all the Mr. Vinsons, not all the Mr. Vineses. I shouldn't have interrupted him, though.

"All right—the Mr. Vinsons. Once you get past all the Mr. Vinsons, you're going to start getting closer and closer—that is, if you want to, and if you look for it and wait for it—to the kind of information that will be very, very dear to your heart. Among other things, you'll find that you're not the first person who was ever confused and frightened and even sickened by human behavior. You're by no means alone on that score, you'll be excited and stimulated to know. Many, many men have been just as troubled morally and spiritually as you are right now. Happily, some of them kept records of their troubles. You'll learn from them—if you want to. Just as someday, if you have something to offer, someone will learn something from you. It's a beautiful reciprocal arrangement. And it isn't education. It's history. It's poetry." He stopped and took a big drink out of his highball. Then he started again. Boy, he was really hot. I was glad I didn't try to stop him or anything. "I'm not trying to tell you," he said, "that only educated and scholarly men are able to contribute something valuable to the world. It's not so. But I do say that educated and scholarly men, if they're brilliant and creative to begin with—which, unfortunately, is rarely the case—tend to leave infinitely more valuable records behind them than men do who are merely brilliant and creative. They tend to express themselves more clearly, and they usually have a passion for following their thoughts through to the end. And—most important—nine times out of ten they have more humility than the unscholarly thinker. Do you follow me at all?"

"Yes, sir."

He didn't say anything again for quite a while. I don't know if you've ever done it, but it's sort of hard to sit around waiting for somebody to say something when they're thinking and all. It really is. I kept trying not to yawn. It wasn't that I was bored or anything—I wasn't—but I was so damn sleepy all of a sudden.

"Something else an academic education will do for you. If you go along with it any considerable distance, it'll begin to give you an idea what size mind you have. What it'll fit and, maybe, what it won't. After a while, you'll have an idea what kind of thoughts your particular size mind should be wearing. For one thing, it may save you an extraordinary amount of time trying on ideas that don't suit you, aren't becoming to you. You'll begin to know your true measurements and dress your mind accordingly."

Then, all of a sudden, I yawned. What a rude bastard, but I couldn't help it!

Mr. Antolini just laughed, though. "C'mon," he said, and got up. "We'll fix up the couch for you."

I followed him and he went over to this closet and tried to take down some sheets and blankets and stuff that was on the top shelf, but he couldn't do it with this highball glass in his hand. So he drank it and then put the glass down on the floor and then he took the stuff down. I helped him bring it over to the couch. We both made the bed together. He wasn't too hot at it. He didn't tuck anything in very tight. I didn't care, though. I could've slept standing up I was so tired.

"How're all your women?"

"They're okay." I was being a lousy conversationalist, but I didn't feel like it.

"How's Sally?" He knew old Sally Hayes. I introduced him once.

"She's all right. I had a date with her this afternoon." Boy, it seemed like twenty years ago! "We don't have too much in common anymore."

"Helluva pretty girl. What about that other girl? The one you told me about, in Maine?"

"Oh—Jane Gallagher. She's all right. I'm probably gonna give her a buzz tomorrow."

We were all done making up the couch then. "It's all yours," Mr. Antolini said. "I don't know what the hell you're going to do with those legs of yours."

"That's all right. I'm used to short beds," I said. "Thanks a lot, sir. You and Mrs. Antolini really saved my life tonight."

"You know where the bathroom is. If there's anything you want, just holler. I'll be in the kitchen for a while—will the light bother you?"

"No—heck, no. Thanks a lot."

"All right. Good night, handsome."

"G'night, sir. Thanks a lot."

He went out in the kitchen and I went in the bathroom and got undressed and all. I couldn't brush my teeth because I didn't have any toothbrush with me. I didn't have any pajamas either and Mr. Antolini forgot to lend me some. So I just went back in the living room and turned off this little lamp next to the couch, and then I got in bed with just my shorts on. It was way too short for me, the couch, but I really could've slept standing up without batting an eyelash. I laid awake for just a couple of seconds thinking about all that stuff Mr. Antolini'd told me. About finding out the size of your mind and all. He was really a pretty smart guy. But I couldn't keep my goddam eyes open, and I fell asleep.

Then something happened. I don't even like to talk about it.

I woke up all of a sudden. I don't know what time it was or anything, but I woke up. I felt something on my head, some guy's hand. Boy, it really scared hell out of me. What it was, it was Mr. Antolini's hand. What he was doing was, he was sitting on the floor right next to the couch, in the dark and all, and he was sort of petting me or patting me on the goddam head. Boy, I'll bet I jumped about a thousand feet.

"What the hellya doing?" I said.

"Nothing! I'm simply sitting here, admiring—"

"What're ya doing, anyway?" I said over again. I didn't know what the hell to say—I mean I was embarrassed as hell.

"How 'bout keeping your voice down? I'm simply sitting here—"

"I have to go, anyway," I said—boy, was I nervous! I started putting on my damn pants in the dark. I could hardly get them on I was so damn nervous. I know more damn perverts, at schools and all, than anybody you ever met, and they're always being perverty when I'm around.

"You have to go where?" Mr. Antolini said. He was trying to act very goddam casual and cool and all, but he wasn't any too goddam cool. Take my word.

"I left my bags and all at the station. I think maybe I'd better go down and get them. I have all my stuff in them."

"They'll be there in the morning. Now, go back to bed. I'm going to bed myself. What's the matter with you?"

"Nothing's the matter, it's just that all my money and stuff's in one of my bags. I'll be right back. I'll get a cab and be right back," I said. Boy, I was falling all over myself in the dark. "The thing is, it isn't mine, the money. It's my mother's, and I—"

"Don't be ridiculous, Holden. Get back in that bed. I'm going to bed myself. The money will be there safe and sound in the morn—"

"No, no kidding. I gotta get going. I really do." I was damn near all dressed already, except that I couldn't find my tie. I couldn't remember where I'd put my tie. I put on my jacket and all without it. Old Mr. Antolini was sitting now in the big chair a little ways away from me, watching me. It was dark and all and I couldn't see him so hot, but I knew he was watching me, all right. He was still boozing, too. I could see his trusty highball glass in his hand.

"You're a very, very strange boy."

"I know it," I said. I didn't even look around much for my tie. So I went without it. "Good-by, sir," I said, "Thanks a lot. No kidding."

He kept walking right behind me when I went to the front door, and when I rang the elevator bell he stayed in the damn doorway. All he said was that business about my being a "very, very strange boy" again. Strange, my ass. Then he waited in the doorway and all till the goddam elevator came. I never waited so long for an elevator in my whole goddam life. I swear.

I didn't know what the hell to talk about while I was waiting for the elevator, and he kept standing there, so I said, "I'm gonna start reading some good books. I really am." I mean you had to say something. It was very embarrassing.

"You grab your bags and scoot right on back here again. I'll leave the door unlatched."

"Thanks a lot," I said. "G'by!" The elevator was finally there. I got in and went down. Boy, I was shaking like a madman. I was sweating, too. When something perverty like that happens, I start sweating like a bastard. That kind of stuff's happened to me about twenty times since I was a kid. I can't stand it.

Chapter 25

When I got outside, it was just getting light out. It was pretty cold, too, but it felt good because I was sweating so much.

I didn't know where the hell to go. I didn't want to go to another hotel and spend all Phoebe's dough. So finally all I did was I walked over to Lexington and took the subway down to Grand Central. My bags were there and all, and I figured I'd sleep in that crazy waiting room where all the benches are. So that's what I did. It wasn't too bad for a while because there weren't many people around and I could stick my feet up. But I don't feel much like discussing it. It wasn't too nice. Don't ever try it. I mean it. It'll depress you.

I only slept till around nine o'clock because a million people started coming in the waiting room and I had to take my feet down. I can't sleep so hot if I have to keep my feet on the floor. So I sat up. I still had that headache. It was even worse. And I think I was more depressed than I ever was in my whole life.

I didn't want to, but I started thinking about old Mr. Antolini and I wondered what he'd tell Mrs. Antolini when she saw I hadn't slept there or anything. That part didn't worry me too much, though, because I knew Mr. Antolini was very smart and that he could make up something to tell her. He could tell her I'd gone home or something. That part didn't worry me much. But what did worry me was the part about how I'd woke up and found him patting me on the head and all.

I mean I wondered if just maybe I was wrong about thinking he was making a flitty pass at me. I wondered if maybe he just liked to pat guys on the head when they're asleep. I mean how can you tell about that stuff for sure? You can't. I even started wondering if maybe I should've got my bags and gone back to his house, the way I'd said I would. I mean I started thinking that even if he was a flit he certainly'd been very nice to me. I thought how he hadn't minded it when I'd called him up so late, and how he'd told me to come right over if I felt like it. And how he went to all that trouble giving me that advice about finding out the size of your mind and all, and how he was the only guy that'd even gone near that boy James Castle I told you about when he was dead. I thought about all that stuff. And the more I thought about it, the more depressed I got. I mean I started thinking maybe I should've gone back to his house. Maybe he was only patting my head just for the hell of it. The more I thought about it, though, the more depressed and screwed up about it I got. What made it even worse, my eyes were sore as hell. They felt sore and burny from not getting too much sleep. Besides that, I was getting sort of a cold, and I didn't even have a goddam handkerchief with me. I had some in my suitcase, but I didn't feel like taking it out of that strong box and opening it up right in public and all.

There was this magazine that somebody'd left on the bench next to me, so I started reading it, thinking it'd make me stop thinking about Mr. Antolini and a million other things for at least a little while. But this damn article I started reading made me feel almost worse. It was all about hormones. It described how you should look, your face and eyes and all, if your hormones were in good shape, and I didn't look that way at all. I looked exactly like the guy in the article with lousy hormones. So I started getting worried about my hormones. Then I read this other article about how you can tell if you have cancer or not. It said if you had any sores in your mouth that didn't heal pretty quickly, it was a sign that you probably had cancer. I'd had this sore on the inside of my lip for about two weeks. So figured I was getting cancer. That magazine was some little cheerer upper. I finally quit reading it and went outside for a walk. I figured I'd be dead in a couple of months because I had cancer. I really did. I was even positive I would be. It certainly didn't make me feel too gorgeous. It'sort of looked like it was going to rain, but I went for this walk anyway. For one thing, I figured I ought to get some breakfast. I wasn't at all hungry, but I figured I ought to at least eat something. I mean at least get something with some vitamins in it. So I started walking way over east, where the pretty cheap restaurants are, because I didn't want to spend a lot of dough.

While I was walking, I passed these two guys that were unloading this big Christmas tree off a truck. One guy kept saying to the other guy, "Hold the sonuvabitch up! Hold it up, for Chris sake!" It certainly was a gorgeous way to talk about a Christmas tree. It was sort of funny, though, in an awful way, and I started to sort of laugh. It was about the worst thing I could've done, because the minute I started to laugh I thought I was going to vomit. I really did. I even started to, but it went away. I don't know why. I mean I hadn't eaten anything unsanitary or like that and usually I have quite a strong stomach. Anyway, I got over it, and I figured I'd feel better if I had something to eat. So I went in this very cheap-looking restaurant and had doughnuts and coffee. Only, I didn't eat the doughnuts. I couldn't swallow them too well. The thing is, if you get very depressed about something, it's hard as hell to swallow. The waiter was very nice, though. He took them back without charging me. I just drank the coffee. Then I left and started walking over toward Fifth Avenue.

It was Monday and all, and pretty near Christmas, and all the stores were open. So it wasn't too bad walking on Fifth Avenue. It was fairly Christmasy. All those scraggy- looking Santa Clauses were standing on corners ringing those bells, and the Salvation Army girls, the ones that don't wear any lipstick or anything, were tinging bells too. I sort of kept looking around for those two nuns I'd met at breakfast the day before, but I didn't see them. I knew I wouldn't, because they'd told me they'd come to New York to be schoolteachers, but I kept looking for them anyway. Anyway, it was pretty Christmasy all of a sudden. A million little kids were downtown with their mothers, getting on and off buses and coming in and out of stores. I wished old Phoebe was around. She's not little enough any more to go stark staring mad in the toy department, but she enjoys horsing around and looking at the people. The Christmas before last I took her downtown shopping with me. We had a helluva time. I think it was in Bloomingdale's. We went in the shoe department and we pretended she—old Phoebe—wanted to get a pair of those very high storm shoes, the kind that have about a million holes to lace up. We had the poor salesman guy going crazy. Old Phoebe tried on about twenty pairs, and each time the poor guy had to lace one shoe all the way up. It was a dirty trick, but it killed old Phoebe. We finally bought a pair of moccasins and charged them. The salesman was very nice about it. I think he knew we were horsing around, because old Phoebe always starts giggling.

Anyway, I kept walking and walking up Fifth Avenue, without any tie on or anything. Then all of a sudden, something very spooky started happening. Every time I came to the end of a block and stepped off the goddam curb, I had this feeling that I'd never get to the other side of the street. I thought I'd just go down, down, down, and nobody'd ever see me again. Boy, did it scare me. You can't imagine. I started sweating like a bastard—my whole shirt and underwear and everything. Then I started doing something else. Every time I'd get to the end of a block I'd make believe I was talking to my brother Allie. I'd say to him, "Allie, don't let me disappear. Allie, don't let me disappear. Allie, don't let me disappear. Please, Allie." And then when I'd reach the other side of the street without disappearing, I'd thank him. Then it would start all over again as soon as I got to the next corner. But I kept going and all. I was sort of afraid to stop, I think—I don't remember, to tell you the truth. I know I didn't stop till I was way up in the Sixties, past the zoo and all. Then I sat down on this bench. I could hardly get my breath, and I was still sweating like a bastard. I sat there, I guess, for about an hour. Finally, what I decided I'd do, I decided I'd go away. I decided I'd never go home again and I'd never go away to another school again. I decided I'd just see old Phoebe and sort of say good- by to her and all, and give her back her Christmas dough, and then I'd start hitchhiking my way out West. What I'd do, I figured, I'd go down to the Holland Tunnel and bum a ride, and then I'd bum another one, and another one, and another one, and in a few days I'd be somewhere out West where it was very pretty and sunny and where nobody'd know me and I'd get a job. I figured I could get a job at a filling station somewhere, putting gas and oil in people's cars. I didn't care what kind of job it was, though. Just so people didn't know me and I didn't know anybody. I thought what I'd do was, I'd pretend I was one of those deaf-mutes. That way I wouldn't have to have any goddam stupid useless conversations with anybody. If anybody wanted to tell me something, they'd have to write it on a piece of paper and shove it over to me. They'd get bored as hell doing that after a while, and then I'd be through with having conversations for the rest of my life. Everybody'd think I was just a poor deaf-mute bastard and they'd leave me alone. They'd let me put gas and oil in their stupid cars, and they'd pay me a salary and all for it, and I'd build me a little cabin somewhere with the dough I made and live there for the rest of my life. I'd build it right near the woods, but not right in them, because I'd want it to be sunny as hell all the time. I'd cook all my own food, and later on, if I wanted to get married or something, I'd meet this beautiful girl that was also a deaf-mute and we'd get married. She'd come and live in my cabin with me, and if she wanted to say anything to me, she'd have to write it on a goddam piece of paper, like everybody else. If we had any children, we'd hide them somewhere. We could buy them a lot of books and teach them how to read and write by ourselves.

I got excited as hell thinking about it. I really did. I knew the part about pretending I was a deaf-mute was crazy, but I liked thinking about it anyway. But I really decided to go out West and all. All I wanted to do first was say good-by to old Phoebe. So all of a sudden, I ran like a madman across the street—I damn near got killed doing it, if you want to know the truth—and went in this stationery store and bought a pad and pencil. I figured I'd write her a note telling her where to meet me so I could say good-by to her and give her back her Christmas dough, and then I'd take the note up to her school and get somebody in the principal's office to give it to her. But I just put the pad and pencil in my pocket and started walking fast as hell up to her school—I was too excited to write the note right in the stationery store. I walked fast because I wanted her to get the note before she went home for lunch, and I didn't have any too much time.

I knew where her school was, naturally, because I went there myself when I was a kid. When I got there, it felt funny. I wasn't sure I'd remember what it was like inside, but I did. It was exactly the same as it was when I went there. They had that same big yard inside, that was always sort of dark, with those cages around the light bulbs so they wouldn't break if they got hit with a ball. They had those same white circles painted all over the floor, for games and stuff. And those same old basketball rings without any nets—just the backboards and the rings.

Nobody was around at all, probably because it wasn't recess period, and it wasn't lunchtime yet. All I saw was one little kid, a colored kid, on his way to the bathroom. He had one of those wooden passes sticking out of his hip pocket, the same way we used to have, to show he had permission and all to go to the bathroom.

I was still sweating, but not so bad any more. I went over to the stairs and sat down on the first step and took out the pad and pencil I'd bought. The stairs had the same smell they used to have when I went there. Like somebody'd just taken a leak on them. School stairs always smell like that. Anyway, I sat there and wrote this note:

DEAR PHOEBE,

I can't wait around till Wednesday any more so I will probably hitch hike out west this afternoon. Meet me at the Museum of art near the door at quarter past 12 if you can and I will give you your Christmas dough back. I didn't spend much.

Love,

HOLDEN

Her school was practically right near the museum, and she had to pass it on her way home for lunch anyway, so I knew she could meet me all right.

Then I started walking up the stairs to the principal's office so I could give the note to somebody that would bring it to her in her classroom. I folded it about ten times so nobody'd open it. You can't trust anybody in a goddam school. But I knew they'd give it to her if I was her brother and all.

While I was walking up the stairs, though, all of a sudden I thought I was going to puke again. Only, I didn't. I sat down for a second, and then I felt better. But while I was sitting down, I saw something that drove me crazy. Somebody'd written "Fuck you" on the wall. It drove me damn near crazy. I thought how Phoebe and all the other little kids would see it, and how they'd wonder what the hell it meant, and then finally some dirty kid would tell them—all cockeyed, naturally—what it meant, and how they'd all think about it and maybe even worry about it for a couple of days. I kept wanting to kill whoever'd written it. I figured it was some perverty bum that'd sneaked in the school late at night to take a leak or something and then wrote it on the wall. I kept picturing myself catching him at it, and how I'd smash his head on the stone steps till he was good and goddam dead and bloody. But I knew, too, I wouldn't have the guts to do it. I knew that. That made me even more depressed. I hardly even had the guts to rub it off the wall with my hand, if you want to know the truth. I was afraid some teacher would catch me rubbing it off and would think I'd written it. But I rubbed it out anyway, finally. Then I went on up to the principal's office.

The principal didn't seem to be around, but some old lady around a hundred years old was sitting at a typewriter. I told her I was Phoebe Caulfield's brother, in 4B-1, and I asked her to please give Phoebe the note. I said it was very important because my mother was sick and wouldn't have lunch ready for Phoebe and that she'd have to meet me and have lunch in a drugstore. She was very nice about it, the old lady. She took the note off me and called some other lady, from the next office, and the other lady went to give it to Phoebe. Then the old lady that was around a hundred years old and I shot the breeze for a while. She was pretty nice, and I told her how I'd gone there to school, too, and my brothers. She asked me where I went to school now, and I told her Pencey, and she said Pencey was a very good school. Even if I'd wanted to, I wouldn't have had the strength to straighten her out. Besides, if she thought Pencey was a very good school, let her think it. You hate to tell new stuff to somebody around a hundred years old. They don't like to hear it. Then, after a while, I left. It was funny. She yelled "Good luck!" at me the same way old Spencer did when I left Pencey. God, how I hate it when somebody yells "Good luck!" at me when I'm leaving somewhere. It's depressing.

I went down by a different staircase, and I saw another "Fuck you" on the wall. I tried to rub it off with my hand again, but this one was scratched on, with a knife or something. It wouldn't come off. It's hopeless, anyway. If you had a million years to do it in, you couldn't rub out even half the "Fuck you" signs in the world. It's impossible.

I looked at the clock in the recess yard, and it was only twenty to twelve, so I had quite a lot of time to kill before I met old Phoebe. But I just walked over to the museum anyway. There wasn't any place else to go. I thought maybe I might stop in a phone booth and give old Jane Gallagher a buzz before I started bumming my way west, but I wasn't in the mood. For one thing, I wasn't even sure she was home for vacation yet. So I just went over to the museum, and hung around.

While I was waiting around for Phoebe in the museum, right inside the doors and all, these two little kids came up to me and asked me if I knew where the mummies were. The one little kid, the one that asked me, had his pants open. I told him about it. So he buttoned them up right where he was standing talking to me—he didn't even bother to go behind a post or anything. He killed me. I would've laughed, but I was afraid I'd feel like vomiting again, so I didn't. "Where're the mummies, fella?" the kid said again. "Ya know?"

I horsed around with the two of them a little bit. "The mummies? What're they?" I asked the one kid.

"You know. The mummies—them dead guys. That get buried in them toons and all."

Toons. That killed me. He meant tombs.

"How come you two guys aren't in school?" I said.

"No school t'day," the kid that did all the talking said. He was lying, sure as I'm alive, the little bastard. I didn't have anything to do, though, till old Phoebe showed up, so I helped them find the place where the mummies were. Boy, I used to know exactly where they were, but I hadn't been in that museum in years.

"You two guys so interested in mummies?" I said.

"Yeah."

"Can't your friend talk?" I said.

"He ain't my friend. He's my brudda."

"Can't he talk?" I looked at the one that wasn't doing any talking. "Can't you talk at all?" I asked him.

"Yeah," he said. "I don't feel like it."

Finally we found the place where the mummies were, and we went in.

"You know how the Egyptians buried their dead?" I asked the one kid.

"Naa."

"Well, you should. It's very interesting. They wrapped their faces up in these cloths that were treated with some secret chemical. That way they could be buried in their tombs for thousands of years and their faces wouldn't rot or anything. Nobody knows how to do it except the Egyptians. Even modern science."

To get to where the mummies were, you had to go down this very narrow sort of hall with stones on the side that they'd taken right out of this Pharaoh's tomb and all. It was pretty spooky, and you could tell the two hot-shots I was with weren't enjoying it too much. They stuck close as hell to me, and the one that didn't talk at all practically was holding onto my sleeve. "Let's go," he said to his brother. "I seen 'em awreddy. C'mon, hey." He turned around and beat it.

"He's got a yella streak a mile wide," the other one said. "So long!" He beat it too.

I was the only one left in the tomb then. I sort of liked it, in a way. It was so nice and peaceful. Then, all of a sudden, you'd never guess what I saw on the wall. Another "Fuck you." It was written with a red crayon or something, right under the glass part of the wall, under the stones.

That's the whole trouble. You can't ever find a place that's nice and peaceful, because there isn't any. You may think there is, but once you get there, when you're not looking, somebody'll sneak up and write "Fuck you" right under your nose. Try it sometime. I think, even, if I ever die, and they stick me in a cemetery, and I have a tombstone and all, it'll say "Holden Caulfield" on it, and then what year I was born and what year I died, and then right under that it'll say "Fuck you." I'm positive, in fact.

After I came out of the place where the mummies were, I had to go to the bathroom. I sort of had diarrhea, if you want to know the truth. I didn't mind the diarrhea part too much, but something else happened. When I was coming out of the can, right before I got to the door, I sort of passed out. I was lucky, though. I mean I could've killed myself when I hit the floor, but all I did was sort of land on my side. it was a funny thing, though. I felt better after I passed out. I really did. My arm sort of hurt, from where I fell, but I didn't feel so damn dizzy any more.

It was about ten after twelve or so then, and so I went back and stood by the door and waited for old Phoebe. I thought how it might be the last time I'd ever see her again. Any of my relatives, I mean. I figured I'd probably see them again, but not for years. I might come home when I was about thirty-five. I figured, in case somebody got sick and wanted to see me before they died, but that would be the only reason I'd leave my cabin and come back. I even started picturing how it would be when I came back. I knew my mother'd get nervous as hell and start to cry and beg me to stay home and not go back to my cabin, but I'd go anyway. I'd be casual as hell. I'd make her calm down, and then I'd go over to the other side of the living room and take out this cigarette case and light a cigarette, cool as all hell. I'd ask them all to visit me sometime if they wanted to, but I wouldn't insist or anything. What I'd do, I'd let old Phoebe come out and visit me in the summertime and on Christmas vacation and Easter vacation. And I'd let D.B. come out and visit me for a while if he wanted a nice, quiet place for his writing, but he couldn't write any movies in my cabin, only stories and books. I'd have this rule that nobody could do anything phony when they visited me. If anybody tried to do anything phony, they couldn't stay.

All of a sudden I looked at the clock in the checkroom and it was twenty-five of one. I began to get scared that maybe that old lady in the school had told that other lady not to give old Phoebe my message. I began to get scared that maybe she'd told her to burn it or something. It really scared hell out of me. I really wanted to see old Phoebe before I hit the road. I mean I had her Christmas dough and all.

Finally, I saw her. I saw her through the glass part of the door. The reason I saw her, she had my crazy hunting hat on—you could see that hat about ten miles away.

I went out the doors and started down these stone stairs to meet her. The thing I couldn't understand, she had this big suitcase with her. She was just coming across Fifth Avenue, and she was dragging this goddam big suitcase with her. She could hardly drag it. When I got up closer, I saw it was my old suitcase, the one I used to use when I was at Whooton. I couldn't figure out what the hell she was doing with it. "Hi," she said when she got up close. She was all out of breath from that crazy suitcase.

"I thought maybe you weren't coming," I said. "What the hell's in that bag? I don't need anything. I'm just going the way I am. I'm not even taking the bags I got at the station. What the hellya got in there?"

She put the suitcase down. "My clothes," she said. "I'm going with you. Can I? Okay?"

"What?" I said. I almost fell over when she said that. I swear to God I did. I got sort of dizzy and I thought I was going to pass out or something again.

"I took them down the back elevator so Charlene wouldn't see me. It isn't heavy. All I have in it is two dresses and my moccasins and my underwear and socks and some other things. Feel it. It isn't heavy. Feel it once. . . Can't I go with you? Holden? Can't I? Please."

"No. Shut up."

I thought I was going to pass out cold. I mean I didn't mean to tell her to shut up and all, but I thought I was going to pass out again.

"Why can't I? Please, Holden! I won't do anything— I'll just go with you, that's all! I won't even take my clothes with me if you don't want me to—I'll just take my—"

"You can't take anything. Because you're not going. I'm going alone. So shut up."

"Please, Holden. Please let me go. I'll be very, very, very—You won't even—"

"You're not going. Now, shut up! Gimme that bag," I said. I took the bag off her. I was almost all set to hit her, I thought I was going to smack her for a second. I really did.

She started to cry.

"I thought you were supposed to be in a play at school and all I thought you were supposed to be Benedict Arnold in that play and all," I said. I said it very nasty. "Whuddaya want to do? Not be in the play, for God's sake?" That made her cry even harder. I was glad. All of a sudden I wanted her to cry till her eyes practically dropped out. I almost hated her. I think I hated her most because she wouldn't be in that play any more if she went away with me.

"Come on," I said. I started up the steps to the museum again. I figured what I'd do was, I'd check the crazy suitcase she'd brought in the checkroom, and then she could get it again at three o'clock, after school. I knew she couldn't take it back to school with her. "Come on, now," I said.

She didn't go up the steps with me, though. She wouldn't come with me. I went up anyway, though, and brought the bag in the checkroom and checked it, and then I came down again. She was still standing there on the sidewalk, but she turned her back on me when I came up to her. She can do that. She can turn her back on you when she feels like it. "I'm not going away anywhere. I changed my mind. So stop crying, and shut up," I said. The funny part was, she wasn't even crying when I said that. I said it anyway, though, "C'mon, now. I'll walk you back to school. C'mon, now. You'll be late."

She wouldn't answer me or anything. I sort of tried to get hold of her old hand, but she wouldn't let me. She kept turning around on me.

"Didja have your lunch? Ya had your lunch yet?" I asked her.

She wouldn't answer me. All she did was, she took off my red hunting hat—the one I gave her—and practically chucked it right in my face. Then she turned her back on me again. It nearly killed me, but I didn't say anything. I just picked it up and stuck it in my coat pocket.

"Come on, hey. I'll walk you back to school," I said.

"I'm not going back to school."

I didn't know what to say when she said that. I just stood there for a couple of minutes.

"You have to go back to school. You want to be in that play, don't you? You want to be Benedict Arnold, don't you?"

"No."

"Sure you do. Certainly you do. C'mon, now, let's go," I said. "In the first place, I'm not going away anywhere, I told you. I'm going home. I'm going home as soon as you go back to school. First I'm gonna go down to the station and get my bags, and then I'm gonna go straight—"

"I said I'm not going back to school. You can do what you want to do, but I'm not going back to school," she said. "So shut up." It was the first time she ever told me to shut up. It sounded terrible. God, it sounded terrible. It sounded worse than swearing. She still wouldn't look at me either, and every time I sort of put my hand on her shoulder or something, she wouldn't let me.

"Listen, do you want to go for a walk?" I asked her. "Do you want to take a walk down to the zoo? If I let you not go back to school this afternoon and go for walk, will you cut out this crazy stuff?"

She wouldn't answer me, so I said it over again. "If I let you skip school this afternoon and go for a little walk, will you cut out the crazy stuff? Will you go back to school tomorrow like a good girl?"

"I may and I may not," she said. Then she ran right the hell across the street, without even looking to see if any cars were coming. She's a madman sometimes.

I didn't follow her, though. I knew she'd follow me, so I started walking downtown toward the zoo, on the park side of the street, and she started walking downtown on the other goddam side of the street, She wouldn't look over at me at all, but I could tell she was probably watching me out of the corner of her crazy eye to see where I was going and all. Anyway, we kept walking that way all the way to the zoo. The only thing that bothered me was when a double-decker bus came along because then I couldn't see across the street and I couldn't see where the hell she was. But when we got to the zoo, I yelled over to her, "Phoebe! I'm going in the zoo! C'mon, now!" She wouldn't look at me, but I could tell she heard me, and when I started down the steps to the zoo I turned around and saw she was crossing the street and following me and all.

There weren't too many people in the zoo because it was sort of a lousy day, but there were a few around the sea lions' swimming pool and all. I started to go by but old Phoebe stopped and made out she was watching the sea lions getting fed—a guy was throwing fish at them—so I went back. I figured it was a good chance to catch up with her and all. I went up and sort of stood behind her and sort of put my hands on her shoulders, but she bent her knees and slid out from me—she can certainly be very snotty when she wants to. She kept standing there while the sea lions were getting fed and I stood right behind her. I didn't put my hands on her shoulders again or anything because if I had she really would've beat it on me. Kids are funny. You have to watch what you're doing.

She wouldn't walk right next to me when we left the sea lions, but she didn't walk too far away. She sort of walked on one side of the sidewalk and I walked on the other side. It wasn't too gorgeous, but it was better than having her walk about a mile away from me, like before. We went up and watched the bears, on that little hill, for a while, but there wasn't much to watch. Only one of the bears was out, the polar bear. The other one, the brown one, was in his goddam cave and wouldn't come out. All you could see was his rear end. There was a little kid standing next to me, with a cowboy hat on practically over his ears, and he kept telling his father, "Make him come out, Daddy. Make him come out." I looked at old Phoebe, but she wouldn't laugh. You know kids when they're sore at you. They won't laugh or anything.

After we left the bears, we left the zoo and crossed over this little street in the park, and then we went through one of those little tunnels that always smell from somebody's taking a leak. It was on the way to the carrousel. Old Phoebe still wouldn't talk to me or anything, but she was sort of walking next to me now. I took a hold of the belt at the back of her coat, just for the hell of it, but she wouldn't let me. She said, "Keep your hands to yourself, if you don't mind." She was still sore at me. But not as sore as she was before. Anyway, we kept getting closer and closer to the carrousel and you could start to hear that nutty music it always plays. It was playing "Oh, Marie!" It played that same song about fifty years ago when I was a little kid. That's one nice thing about carrousels, they always play the same songs.

"I thought the carrousel was closed in the wintertime," old Phoebe said. It was the first time she practically said anything. She probably forgot she was supposed to be sore at me.

"Maybe because it's around Christmas," I said.

She didn't say anything when I said that. She probably remembered she was supposed to be sore at me.

"Do you want to go for a ride on it?" I said. I knew she probably did. When she was a tiny little kid, and Allie and D.B. and I used to go to the park with her, she was mad about the carrousel. You couldn't get her off the goddam thing.

"I'm too big." she said. I thought she wasn't going to answer me, but she did.

"No, you're not. Go on. I'll wait for ya. Go on," I said. We were right there then. There were a few kids riding on it, mostly very little kids, and a few parents were waiting around outside, sitting on the benches and all. What I did was, I went up to the window where they sell the tickets and bought old Phoebe a ticket. Then I gave it to her. She was standing right next to me. "Here," I said. "Wait a second—take the rest of your dough, too." I started giving her the rest of the dough she'd lent me.

"You keep it. Keep it for me," she said. Then she said right afterward—"Please."

That's depressing, when somebody says "please" to you. I mean if it's Phoebe or somebody. That depressed the hell out of me. But I put the dough back in my pocket.

"Aren't you gonna ride, too?" she asked me. She was looking at me sort of funny. You could tell she wasn't too sore at me anymore.

"Maybe I will the next time. I'll watch ya," I said. "Got your ticket?"

"Yes."

"Go ahead, then—I'll be on this bench right over here. I'll watch ya." I went over and sat down on this bench, and she went and got on the carrousel. She walked all around it. I mean she walked once all the way around it. Then she sat down on this big, brown, beat-up-looking old horse. Then the carrousel started, and I watched her go around and around. There were only about five or six other kids on the ride, and the song the carrousel was playing was "Smoke Gets in Your Eyes." It was playing it very jazzy and funny. All the kids kept trying to grab for the gold ring, and so was old Phoebe, and I was sort of afraid she'd fall off the goddam horse, but I didn't say anything or do anything. The thing with kids is, if they want to grab the gold ring, you have to let them do it, and not say anything. If they fall off they fall off, but it's bad if you say anything to them.

When the ride was over she got off her horse and came over to me. "You ride once, too, this time," she said.

"No, I'll just watch ya. I think I'll just watch," I said. I gave her some more of her dough. "Here. Get some more tickets."

She took the dough off me. "I'm not mad at you anymore," she said.

"I know. Hurry up—the thing's gonna start again."

Then all of a sudden she gave me a kiss. Then she held her hand out, and said, "It's raining. It's starting to rain."

"I know."

Then what she did—it damn near killed me—she reached in my coat pocket and took out my red hunting hat and put it on my head.

"Don't you want it?" I said.

"You can wear it a while."

"Okay. Hurry up, though, now. You're gonna miss your ride. You won't get your own horse or anything."

She kept hanging around, though.

"Did you mean it what you said? You really aren't going away anywhere? Are you really going home afterwards?" she asked me.

"Yeah," I said. I meant it, too. I wasn't lying to her. I really did go home afterwards. "Hurry up, now," I said. "The thing's starting."

She ran and bought her ticket and got back on the goddam carrousel just in time. Then she walked all the way around it till she got her own horse back. Then she got on it. She waved to me and I waved back.

Boy, it began to rain like a bastard. In buckets, I swear to God. All the parents and mothers and everybody went over and stood right under the roof of the carrousel, so they wouldn't get soaked to the skin or anything, but I stuck around on the bench for quite a while. I got pretty soaking wet, especially my neck and my pants. My hunting hat really gave me quite a lot of protection, in a way; but I got soaked anyway. I didn't care, though. I felt so damn happy all of sudden, the way old Phoebe kept going around and around. I was damn near bawling, I felt so damn happy, if you want to know the truth. I don't know why. It was just that she looked so damn nice, the way she kept going around and around, in her blue coat and all. God, I wish you could've been there.

Classroom activities

Text analysis

Text 1:

1. What would Peter Two's mother forbid him to do if she were at home? Is Peter Two an obedient boy?

2. What leads Peter Two to help Peter the Great? How does this incident influence Peter Two?

3. What makes Peter Two feel ashamed after encountering the couple the next morning? What is he ashamed of most? How does this incident influence him?

4. Is there a change in the way Peter treats the "rules" set by his mother as the story develops? Why does he behave in this/these way(s)?

5. When Peter Two opens the door for Mrs. Chalmers, it is said that "he was only five feet way," and then in the same paragraph "five feet" is described as "a long distance, a long, long distance." The two expressions are literally contradictory. Since this incongruity is too obvious to escape anyone's attention, there must be an implication behind this arrangement. Can you explain it?

6. When does the story reach its climax? Is it the moment when Mr. Chalmers points a gun at both Peter and Mrs. Chalmers, or when Peter turns his back on Mrs. Chalmers by closing the door and going to bed, or any other time?

7. The ending paragraph of Peter Two is a one-sentence paragraph, which explains the

psychological change experienced by the boy. What is the change? And there are two puns in this sentence. Please identify and explain them.

8. The title of the story *Peter Two* may also be viewed as a pun. Can you find its two interpretations?

    Text 2:

1. What is the word that Holden uses most to comment on other people or things? What does the word reveal about the theme of the story?

2. What can be learned about Holden's mental state from the conversation he holds with his younger sister in chapter 22?

3. Why is the story entitled *The Catcher in the Rye*?

4. In what ways does Mr. Antolini differ from stereotypical teachers?

5. Do you think Mr. Antolini is making a homosexual overture when touching Holden's forehead?

6. Why does Holden finally decide to stay in chapter 25? What does this suggest about Holden's change of heart?

7. Is Holden qualified as a catcher in the rye? Or who are the real catchers in the rye in his case?

Class discussion

1. There is a dash of black humor in the story *Peter Two*. Can you sense it? Please state your understanding of this.

2. Can you sympathize with Holden's feelings about the adult world? What do you think of Holden, a great hero or a pitiful boy suffering from mental disorder?

3. What is the theme shared by the two stories in this unit? Is there a difference in the authors' implicit attitudes towards the theme? Which author do you side with?

Story-telling

Retell *Peter Two* with no more than ten sentences. Make sure that no key information is missing and no trivial details are included. To put it another way, no digression from the theme of the story should be made. You may volunteer to present your version if you think yours is better than the chosen group's.

Group discussion and presentation

Have a discussion with group members, and then present the group view on the common theme of the two stories. What do you think of this growing pains that no adolescent can be spared? How are you going to face up to it?

Sources of Texts

Newspapers and Magazines:

The Atlantic

BBC News

Business Week

The Daily Mail

The Economist

The Huffington Post

National Geographic

The New York Times

The New Yorker

Vanity Fair

The Washington Post

Books:

75 Readings: An Anthology

Bulfinch's Mythology: The Age of Fable or Stories of Gods and Heroes

The Catcher in the Rye

The Oxford Book of American Detective Stories

The Return of Sherlock Holmes: A Collection of Holmes Adventures

《典藏书屋——午后咖啡（MP3 有声英文读物）》

Websites:

www.all-creatures.org

www.chinadailyasia.com

www.iteslj.org

www.tushuo.com

www.wikipedia.org